THE MENOMINI INDIANS OF WISCONSIN

THE MENOMINI INDIANS OF WISCONSIN

A Study of Three Centuries
of Cultural Contact and Change

FELIX M. KEESING

The University of Wisconsin Press

Published 1987

The University of Wisconsin Press
114 North Murray Street
Madison, Wisconsin 53715

The University of Wisconsin Press, Ltd.
1 Gower Street
London WC1E 6HA, England

First Wisconsin printing

Printed in the United States of America

Library of Congress Cataloging-in-Publication Data
Keesing, Felix Maxwell, 1902–1961.
  The Menomini Indians of Wisconsin.
  Reprint. Originally published: Philadelphia, Pa.:
American Philosophical Society, 1939.
  Bibliography: pp. 249–253.
  Includes index.
  1. Menominee Indians. I. Title.
[E99.M44K4 1987   977.5′00497   86-24650
ISBN 0-299-10970-4
ISBN 0-299-10974-7 (pbk.)

CONTENTS

LIST OF ILLUSTRATIONS

PLATES

FOREWORD

As long as the Menomini can remember, they have lived in the vicinity of Green Bay, Wisconsin. Their legends speak of emerging from the underground near the mouth of the Menominee River and it was here along this river and at Green Bay that they first encountered Europeans. Yet, despite accounts by the Jesuits, by French, British, and American traders and travelers, the Menomini Indians, an Algonquian-speaking people, remained little known until Walter James Hoffman prepared his detailed ethnographic account of them in 1892.[1]

Today the Menomini still reside in the same region where they were first encountered by Sieur Jean Nicolet, who was sent in 1634 by Samuel de Champlain, Governor of New France, to negotiate a peace with the Winnebago Indians living near Green Bay. Thirty years after Nicolet's brief visit, other Frenchmen entered the region. By then the Menomini were surrounded by other Algonquins, who, after suffering threats and attacks from Iroquoian-speaking peoples, had fled westward from Lake Huron and southern Michigan to the Menomini homeland near Green Bay. Because the Menomini were far less warlike than their Winnebago, Sauk, and Fox neighbors in their dealings with the French, English, and Americans, their name is not generally encountered in the military annals of Indian-white history.

Thus, when Hoffman visited the Menomini between 1887 and 1890, he discovered a people who had "not hitherto received careful attention by students, the fugitive papers relating to this tribe being exceedingly brief, and often difficult of access to the general reader." Intending only to study the Menomini version of Mitawin, or the "Grand Medicine So-

---

[1] Walter James Hoffman, "The Menomini Indians," *14th Annual Report of the Bureau of Ethnology for the Years 1892–1893*. Pt. 1. (Washington: GPO, 1896).

ciety," Hoffman remained long enough to gather material for
the first full ethnographic study of the Menomini. He published this highly discriptive account in the *14th Annual Report of the Bureau of Ethnology.*[2]

In the early twentieth century, two other writers interested in Algonquian-speaking peoples—Alanson Skinner and
Leonard Bloomfield—also wrote on the Menomini. Skinner,
taking his lead from Hoffman, gathered more material on
Menomini culture, focusing primarily on social structure, religion, and folklore.[3] The linguist Bloomfield directed his attention to collecting Menomini legends and publishing them in
both Menomini and English.[4] The belief that the old ways of
the Menomini would soon be lost added a sense of urgency to
the work of both Skinner and Bloomfield.

This same sense of urgency infused the work of Felix Maxwell Keesing. In a paper entitled "Leaders of the Menomini
Tribe" (1930), which he sent to his friend Charles E. Brown of
the Wisconsin Historical Society, Keesing noted that there
was an "urgent need for a student or students to explore the
minds of these old people for the sake of a fuller and more
accurate rendering of the earlier backgrounds of Indian and
white interaction in Wisconsin."[5] In a cover letter to Brown
that mentioned completion of his manuscript on the Menomini, Keesing stressed that a more detailed investigation of
Menomini chiefs and families "would serve as the basis of a
fuller and more detailed study of the tribe, [and] also of the
exploration of the minds of the old people."[6] Here among the

[2] Ibid., pp. 11–12.

[3] See Alanson B. Skinner, "Social Life and Ceremonial Bundles of the Menomini Indians," *Anthropological Papers of the American Museum of Natural History* 13 (1913):
1–165; "Associations and Ceremonies of the Menomini Indians," *Anthropological Papers of
the American Museum of Natural History* 13 (1915): 167–215; "Material Culture of the
Menomini," *Museum of the American Indian, Heye Foundation. Indian Notes and Monographs, Misc. ser.* 20 (1921); and with John V. Satterlee, "Folklore of the Menomini Indians," *Anthropological Papers of the American Museum of Natural History* 13 (1915):
217–546.

[4] Leonard Bloomfield, *Menomini Texts*. Publications of the American Ethnological Society 12 (New York: American Ethnological Society, 1928).

[5] Felix M. Keesing, "Leaders of the Menomini Tribe," [1930] MS, Charles E. Brown
Papers, State Historical Society of Wisconsin, p. 23.

[6] Felix Maxwell Keesing to Charles E. Brown, January 19, 1930, Charles E. Brown
Papers, State Historical Society of Wisconsin, p. 1.

old people, Keesing believed, was information more rich than that existing in books and documents. The mere mention of old names such as Tomah, Oshkosh, and Shawano to the elders would "call up intimate associations with the past."[7]

> Mention a name to them, and they will give a flood of reminiscence concerning men of the past and events of the past, Indian and white, far exceeding in quantity and vividness that recorded in even the best documents. But mostly such people are very old, and every year takes its toll of their ranks. Facts that could have been gotten two years ago are now inaccessible, and those available today may be gone within two months. Yet so far little or no attempt has been made by any student of history to set them down systematically—this all the more strange seeing that these folk will be found not only willing but in some cases keen to give them to a sympathetic listener. Most are well used to drawing on their stock of knowledge for white students, but so far these latter have had almost exclusively ethnological interests. The young Indians of today 'take little stock of this old stuff,' and so all this very accessible source material is passing unrecorded.[8]

Despite Keesing's plea for what some have called "salvage anthropology,"[9] and his expression of such concerns in his Menomini study, the writing of *Menomini Indians* in 1939 proceeded from other objectives. In order to understand those objectives, it is useful to examine briefly the career of Felix Keesing and his Menomini study in the larger context of his research interests.

Born on the island of Penang, in Malaysia in 1902 and educated in Auckland, New Zealand, Keesing won first-class honors at the University of Auckland in education and a diploma in journalism. From 1929 to 1930 he studied at Yale University and at the University of Chicago on a Rockefeller fellowship and later pursued research at the London School of

---

[7] Ibid.

[8] Keesing, "Leaders of the Menomini Tribe," p. 1.

[9] For a discussion of "salvage anthropology," see Jacob W. Gruber, "Ethnographic Salvage and the Shaping of Anthropology," *American Anthropologist* 72 (1970): 1289–99; and Bruce G. Trigger, *Natives and Newcomers: Canada's 'Heroic Age' Reconsidered* (Kingston and Montreal: McGill-Queen's University Press, 1985), p. 114.

Economics. In 1933, he received a doctorate of literature from
the University of New Zealand. Except for his book on the
Menomini Indians, Keesing's anthropological career is associated primarily with the South Pacific and southeast Asia.[10]
The questions then remain, what influences motivated Keesing to write on the Menomini Indians and does a link exist
between that work and his studies of Pacific cultures? A clue
is found in Keesing's subsequent writings.

In the 1950s, Keesing noted that the years he spent at Yale
and Chicago researching and writing *Menomini Indians* were
transitional years in anthropology.[11] The descriptive evolu-
tionary tradition in anthropological writing that marked the
work of Hoffman had nearly disappeared. The period from
1920 to 1929, Keesing claimed, was the decade of "historicalism" and of an ethnology that stressed the "study of
cultural differences, with their historical relationships."[12]
Keesing places Skinner's and Bloomfield's work on the Menomini in this latter tradition since written records were used
solely to promote historical ethnography. By the end of the
decade historicalism that emphasized "the counting of cultural
traits in time and space" came under attack. Many thought
historicalism atomistic and mechanical. New directions in anthropology emphasized the organization and operation of
cultures and stressed "integration," "relativity," and "structure."[13] It was while Keesing was at Yale and Chicago that
American universities took up this more theoretical approach
to the study of cultures.[14]

Afloat in the exciting currents of changing theoretical concerns in anthropology, Keesing found himself attracted to the

---

[10] "Keesing, Felix Maxwell," *Who Was Who 1961–1970* 6 (London: Adam and Black,
1972), pp. 617–18; "Keesing, Felix Maxwell," *American Authors and Books: 1640 to the
Present Day*, 3d ed. (New York: Crown Publisher, 1972), p. 342.

[11] Felix M. Keesing, *Culture Change: An Analysis and Bibliography of Anthropological Sources to 1952* (Stanford: Stanford University Press, 1953), pp. 20–38.

[12] Ibid., p. 20.

[13] Ibid., pp. 22–23.

[14] For a discussion of this change at the University of Chicago, see George W. Stocking,
Jr., *Anthropology at Chicago: Tradition, Discipline, Department* (Chicago: The University of Chicago Library, 1979), p. 29.

study of "culture change, or as now often called, 'accultura-tion.'"[15] The newness of acculturation studies in 1930—a field now so significant in anthropology—is revealed in the fact that it was not until 1936 that a Social Science Research Council committee even defined acculturation as the "phenomena which result when groups of individuals having different cultures come into continuous first-hand contact, with subsequent changes in the original cultural patterns of either or both groups."[16]

Perhaps it was Keesing's awareness of the disruptive nature of rapid change in the indigenous cultures of the South Pacific and southeast Asia, change that followed in the wake of European colonialism and forced acculturation, that influenced his decision to pursue acculturation studies. Or perhaps colleagues at Yale or Chicago suggested this field, and in the context of Keesing's past, the suggestion struck a responsive chord. Whatever the reason, Keesing, far from the South Pacific, decided to test certain ideas regarding acculturation in a study of an American Indian tribe. *Menomini Indians* proved, in part, a theoretical exercise. It represented, according to Keesing, "an experiment in methods of studying the all too little known and documented processes of culture change."[17]

As Keesing's own introduction makes clear, the Menomini Indians were chosen over other Indians at the suggestion of Clark Wissler of the American Museum of Natural History.[18] The Menomini still resided in their original territory and, despite change, had maintained a sense of their own identity. Documentary records for reconstructing Menomini history for three centuries were also available and proved equally important for they enabled Keesing to study Menomini "contact and interaction" with various cultures.

[15] Felix M. Keesing, *The Menomini Indians of Wisconsin: A Study of Three Centuries of Cultural Contact and Change.* Memoirs of the American Philosophical Society 10 (Philadelphia: American Philosophical Society, 1939), p. 4.

[16] Robert Redfield, Ralph Linton, and Melville J. Herskovits, "Memorandum for the Study of Acculturation," *American Anthropologist*, n.s. 38 (1936): 149–52.

[17] Keesing, *Menomini Indians*, p. 4.

[18] Ibid., p. 2.

This objective is made explicit in the subtitle *A Study of Three Centuries of Cultural Contact and Change*, and in the structure of the book. After providing an ethnographic baseline in the early chapters, Keesing examines French, British, and American influences on Menomini culture. The titles of the chapters—"After Two Centuries of Change," "White Pressure and Passing Lands," "The First Reservation Experiments," and "Progress in Wardship"—demonstrate Keesing's theoretical focus. All underscore change and response.

As both Skinner and Bloomfield did, Keesing utilized information he acquired from the Menomini, including contributions by Reginald Oshkosh, Mitchell Beauprey, Abram and Paul Brunette, John V. Satterlee, Charles Dutchman, Louis Kashketopy, Peter Lamotte, and from Mrs. Dutchman and Mrs. Lamotte.[19] Keesing differed from Skinner and Bloomfield in that he integrated the oral data, acquired from the Menomini in a four-month stay on the reservation, with information drawn from his own field notes and historical sources. Keesing's critical use of historical documents and oral tradition enabled him to present an elegant diachronic interpretation of changing Menomini culture. Through his adroit use of historical documents to reconstruct the past, Keesing became one of the earliest exponents of what would in the 1950s constitute the field of ethnohistory. Only by understanding Keesing's ethnohistorical approach to Menomini acculturation is it possible to appreciate how much his work differed from what went before. Keesing went far beyond the works of Hoffman, Skinner, and Bloomfield, whose great contributions to Menomini studies he did not disregard although he was at times critical of their interpretations. There are, to be sure, errors of interpretation in Keesing's work that scholars today can point to, but such errors pale beside the larger significance of this pioneering ethnohistorical study.

In a final review, probably written several years after he completed the manuscript, Keesing underscored what he considered the main threads that emerged in his work: "first, the

[19] Keesing, "Leaders," p. 2.

progressive modification and in most recent times the disintegration of the old Menomini culture; second, the building up of a reservation life based on the dependence relation of wardship; and third, the manifestation of not a little social and personal disorganization, also of opposition to white control and penetration."[20] He had planned to visit the Menomini again, assess their situation under the Indian Reorganization Act of 1934 and incorporate this new material into the text. Unfortunately, a return proved impossible. Keesing decided to publish *Menomini Indians* in 1939.[21]

Keesing apparently never returned to the Menomini reservation or to Menomini studies, but others built on Keesing's contribution. In the 1950s, James S. Slotkin published two works, "Menomini Peyotism" and *The Menomini Powwow: A Study in Cultural Decay*, recording ceremonies, beliefs, and resistance to acculturation exhibited by the Zoar community, the most conservative community on the Menomini Reservation.[22] In 1971, George and Louise Spindler published *Dreamers Without Power: The Menomini Indians*.[23] The Spindlers, as graduate students in anthropology at the University of Wisconsin, began their field work on the Menomini Reservation in 1948. Whether the Spindlers were influenced by Keesing—George was a colleague and Louise worked as a graduate assistant to Keesing when he was at Stanford University—is not known, but the thrust of their argument in *Dreamers* regarding acculturation is similar to Keesing's earlier concerns.[24] According to the Spindlers, in order to survive as a people the Menomini were forced to devise "adaptive strategies." Such strategies were clearly evident in the Menomini struggle to regain their reservation

[20] Keesing, *Menomini Indians*, p. 244.

[21] Ibid., p. 4.

[22] James S. Slotkin, "Menomini Peyotism: A Study of Individual Variation in a Primary Group with a Homogeneous Culture," *Transactions of the American Philosophical Society* 42 (1952) and *The Menomini Powwow: A Study in Cultural Decay*, Milwaukee Public Museum Publications in Anthropology 42 (1957).

[23] George and Louise Spindler, *Dreamers Without Power: The Menomini Indians* (New York: Holt, Rinehart and Winston, 1971).

[24] Keesing, *Culture Change*, p. vii.

status after Congress terminated the reservation in 1961.[25]
Several works, such as *Freedom with Reservation: The Menominee Struggle to Save Their Land and People*[26] and Nicholas C. Peroff's *Menominee Drums: Tribal Termination and
Restoration, 1954–1974*[27] cover this story.

Ironically, Felix M. Keesing died in 1961, the very year
that the Menomini lost their reservation. Today the Menomini
have regained their reservation and a sense of control in shaping their destiny. Given this renewal of the Menomini Reservation community, the decision by the University of Wisconsin
Press to republish Felix Keesing's classic account of Menomini
cultural history must be applauded. It remains one of the best
ethnohistorical accounts of Menomini culture.

Robert E. Bieder
Indiana University

[25] Louise S. Spindler, "Menominee," *Handbook of North American Indians* 15, ed.
Bruce G. Trigger (Washington: Smithsonian Institution, 1978), p. 722.

[26] Deborah Shames, ed., *Freedom with Reservation: The Menominee Struggle to Save Their
Land and People* (Madison: National Committee to Save the Menominee People and Forests, 1972).

[27] Nicholas C. Peroff, *Menominee Drums: Tribal Termination and Restoration, 1954–
1974* (Norman: University of Oklahoma Press, 1982).

NOTE ON TERMINOLOGY

The student of Indian matters finds a considerable variation in the tribal names, and it seems necessary from the first to agree on certain forms of spelling. The word "Menomini" itself, though standardized in anthropological and other scientific writings, is customarily spelled "Menominee" in the historical and official records; again there are other forms such as "Malhominie", "Menomonee", and the name given by the early French, "Folles Avoines", that is people of the "false oat" or wild rice.

The name "Chippewa" will be used for the tribe immediately to the north of the Menomini rather than "Ojibwa", as the former appears in nearly all quotations cited; in the same way "Sioux" will be used instead of "Dakotah". Other tribal names such as Ottawa, Potawatomi, Sauk, Fox (called by the French "Renards" or "Outagami"), Kickapoo, and Illinois will be clear. Again "Algonquin", with the corresponding adjective "Algonquian" will be adopted, though "Algonkin" would also be correct. One difficulty of such a study is to get a suitable term for the incoming people: French, British, and later American. Since such terms as "Euro-American", "Anglo-Saxon" and the like are clumsy, the words "white man", "whites" will be used, with the adjective "white". The term "half breed" as referring to people of mixed Indian and white descent will be avoided as being inaccurate and having unfortunate emotional associations; "mixed blood" will be used in its place.

F. L. M.

INTRODUCTORY

The Menomini Indians live today on a tribal reservation close to the area occupied by them when the first whites arrived in the early part of the seventeenth century. They number about two thousand—approximately their strength throughout their known history. Though their ways of living are vastly changed from pre-white times they still retain their identity as a group. Documentary records are available to reconstruct in fair detail their history and ways of living throughout some three centuries of contact.

As such, this people offer an excellent opportunity for study of the processes of cultural contact and change. Their fortunes can be followed from aboriginal times through the eras of early bartering, missionizing and warfare, of the fur-trade, of lumbering, and finally of agricultural and industrial development. Once more or less sedentary village dwellers whose staple foods were the wild rice and fish of the Upper Lakes country, they became scattered in mobile bands to hunt the furbearing animals sought by the trader; later, with hunting grounds sold, and the bands settled on a reservation, still other economic and social readjustments were made. Today, with a minority of the tribe still "pagan", but the majority Christian, with an older generation counting much of the Indian past vital, but the youth turning from it, with the tribal members ranged from ultra-conservative to ultra-progressive, the historical process of change itself appears to be in large degree spread out in living personalities. Such a dynamic approach likewise throws new light on the problem of reconstructing the aboriginal culture of such a people; it will be seen that numbers of cultural elements which ethnologists, visiting the tribe in later days, have considered pre-Columbian in the life of the Menomini and near-by tribes have been partly or even wholly a product of post-Columbian times.

1

The main research work on which this monograph is based was carried out in 1928–30. The author was interested in the study of culture contacts, and while holding a two-year fellowship that enabled him to work at various universities in the East and Middle West took the opportunity to investigate the experience of the Menomini people from this viewpoint. In this he was assisted throughout by his wife, Marie Martin Keesing. The Menomini were chosen at the suggestion of Dr. Clark Wissler of the American Museum of Natural History and Yale University as being more or less in their original habitat and still retaining their identity while yet having changed vastly under new influences.

Various methods were used to approach the subject-matter. All the writings of ethnologists dealing with the Menomini and near-by tribes, with their accompanying photographs, were worked through (see the bibliography). To get at the early history the effort was made to locate every documentary reference mentioning the Menomini; not only were the published Wisconsin Historical Collections examined, but a visit was paid to the state archives in Madison, Wisconsin, in order to search through some of the material not accessible in standard libraries. The valuable *Jesuit Relations* were studied carefully in order to see the processes of contact among the various Indian tribes including the Menomini through the eyes of contemporary writers. All direct references to the Menomini in these early sources were copied out and placed in their time sequence to see what, subject to the qualifications of historical criticism, they might reveal.

In 1852 the tribe moved to their reservation. As a means of analyzing their subsequent experience some very profitable days were spent working through the official correspondence files of the Office of Indian Affairs in Washington, D. C., seeking in the old letters, reports and petitions material relevant to the study. On the Menomini reservation, too, the records at the government agency were courteously opened by the officials for similar examination. Besides these documents, mainly unpublished, the published reports of the Indian Office, also the publications of the Indian Rights Association and other sources listed in the bibliography were worked through.

A different approach to the earlier story of the tribe was offered by the various collections of Menomini artifacts to be found in museums and private collections. In certain aspects of life, especially the technological and artistic sides, these give important clues to cultural change. To experiment with this approach every collection containing Menomini materials which could be traced was visited, and the objects examined piece by piece in relation to this: the American Museum of Natural History and the Museum of the American Indian, Heye Foundation, both in New York; the Peabody Museum at Harvard; the National Museum, Washington, D. C.; the Field Museum, Chicago; and the Public Museums of Milwaukee and Oshkosh, the Wisconsin Historical Society, Madison (which also has important pictures of Menomini life and of individuals), and the Neville Museum at Green Bay, in which much of the oldest material is lodged, these four all in Wisconsin. A private collection in the possession of Mr. R. H. Robinson of Chicago was also examined, thanks to his courtesy.

With this material in hand, and after a tour of the territories formerly occupied by the Menomini in Wisconsin and Michigan, the author and his wife settled for somewhat over four months on the Menomini reservation to observe the process of change as represented by the contemporary Menomini life. From a "neutral" tent and later a small cabin they were able to establish contact with both Christians and "pagans", with government officials and with those of the people who were "agin the government", with the auto-equipped moderns living on the state highway through the reservation and the conservatives who dwelt in the deep forest recesses of the quarter million acre reserve. Several of the older Indians whom they came to count as friends have since that time passed on to the spirit-land, including the late "Chief" Reginald Oshkosh, Louis Kashketopy, and Abraham Brunette.

The study, apart from its human interest, represents primarily an experiment in methods of studying the all too little known and documented processes of culture change, or as now often called, "acculturation". Theory is minimized, and so too are the practical implications important for that newest phase of the science of anthropology usually called "applied anthropology". The first draft of the manuscript, worked upon in places as far apart as Samoa and China, Australia and England, had two sections, one covering the past and the other the contemporary scene. It has been held over during the intervening period in the expectation that a further visit could be paid to the Menomini reservation in order to bring fully up to date the material on present day conditions, especially in view of changed government policies in Washington—the "New Deal" for Indians as launched in the Indian Reorganization Act has been particularly important for the Menomini as they have chosen to accept the act and adopt a constitution for their tribal organization and self-government. But such a visit cannot seemingly be made short of a year or two; hence it has been decided to issue without further delay the material covering the past, *i.e.*, from about 1634 to 1929. This contains the main body of ethnological and historical data, and forms a rather different kind of study from the more sociological survey of present day life to be covered in due course.

While unable to make anything like complete acknowledgment of those contributing to the study, the writer must mention specifically his debt to the following: to Dr. Wissler whose initial encouragement caused it to be undertaken and who helped throughout; to officials of the Department of Indian Affairs at Washington and on the reservation, particularly Mr. W. R. Beyer, Superintendent of the Menomini agency at the time; and to Mr. Roy H. Robinson, of Chicago, who gave access to his private collection of Indian material. The author's wife, as noted already, assisted throughout, both as a trained historian giving help in handling critically the documentary sections of the study and as collaborator in the field investigations on the reservation. As regards the many members of the Menomini tribe who gave information and assistance, it is hoped that the preservation of this record of the history and experience of their people may serve as something of a return for their tolerance of, and friendship towards what must have appeared a pair of very inquisitive "palefaces". Finally, the writer expresses his deep appreciation to the American Philosophical Society for undertaking the publication of the study.

I. THE MENOMINI AND THEIR NEIGHBORS

The Menomini tribe claim, in their sacred lore, to have originated from a Great Bear and other spirit beings of animal form which emerged "at the mouth of the Menominee river", about where the twin cities of Marinette, Wisconsin, and Menominee, Michigan, now stand on the western shores of Green Bay. The first whites coming to Lake Michigan found their main village at that very spot.

A French furtrader, Nicholas Perrot, visited the Menomini here about 1667, the earliest record of actual contact. A previous traveller in the region, Jean Nicolet, passed by their country in 1634 and reported their existence. The first more permanent white residents, Jesuit missionaries, came in 1671.

It seems doubtful, however, that these represent the earliest contact of the Menomini and neighboring Indians with incoming European influences. For more than a century before this there had been intercourse between American Indian peoples and whites: the Spaniards had been penetrating from the south; the Atlantic shores of America had became a resort for European fishermen, and the British, French and Dutch had already formed settlements there. The French particularly had been exploring westward along the valley of the St. Lawrence towards the Upper Great Lakes. The Menomini must seemingly have heard something of the presence on the continent of this strange pale-faced people. Perhaps trade goods had been carried west into Menomini country as the result of intertribal barter or of war plunder.

This fact is disconcerting to the student who may seek precise dates. Actually it is impossible to know even within the margin of half a century just when the first white influences penetrated to the tribe. For the purpose of this study, however, it is sufficient to say that, in seeking to know the Menomini life as it was at the beginning of such contact, reference is being made to the early part of the seventeenth century—perhaps even some decades earlier.

6

A comprehensive picture of the Menomini at this time should show something of the physical environment in which they lived, their tribal strength and the extent of their territories, their customs, ideas and beliefs, and their relation to other tribes in the region. Anyone familiar with the extensive literature of American ethnology might at first consider it relatively easy to summarize these. Studies have been made by Hoffman, Jenks, Skinner, Michelson, Bloomfield, Huron Smith and Densmore on various phases of Menomini life (see the bibliography), while classifications of a more general nature have been worked out dealing with the wider cultural and linguistic affiliations of the Great Lakes peoples. But actually the evidence now available from early documents dealing with the region, together with that forthcoming from an analysis of post-Columbian changes, makes the task of reconstruction far more complicated than is usually thought.

The Menomini are rightly referred to as one of the Central Algonquian tribes, belonging to the "Woodland" culture area or type and the Algonquian language stock. This means that they represent one sub-group within a great common area of culture and language found throughout the forest lands of the eastern and central parts of the United States and Canada. Before the whites came, the main body of Algonquian peoples seem to have been split into two main groups by a northward thrusting wedge of the Iroquoian peoples. Those who came to occupy the region of the Great Lakes (Superior, Michigan and the west part of Huron), are now usually called the Central Algonquins, and comprise in addition to the Menomini, the Chippewa (or Ojibway), Ottawa, Potawatomi, Sauk, Fox, Kickapoo, Miami, Mascouten and Illinois. They are thus distinguished from other tribes found in the lower St. Lawrence and along the Atlantic seaboard, called the Eastern Algonquins, also from certain Algonquian-speaking tribes to the southeast, the north, and away west on the great plains. Directly westward of the Central Algonquins when the modern story opens were peoples of a language stock known as Siouan, having a culture usually classified as of a "Plains" type very different from that of the Woodland peoples. Yet one important Siouan tribe known as the Winnebago lived in the Great Lakes forest region and had close cultural affinities with the Central Algonquins. Actually they were the nearest neighbors of the Menomini, so that they will come continually into the tribal story.[1]

In 1669 a Jesuit father, Allouez, visited the region and gave an account of the location of the various tribes as of that date. His evidence, together with that of other writers who followed and confirmed his observations, has been fairly generally accepted by anthropologists in constructing their schemes of tribal distribution in pre-white times. Thus Jenks, in a study of the wild rice culture of the lakes people, writes:

> (The Winnebago) were at Green Bay when Nicollet came there in 1634, living in the wild rice fields at peace with their Algonquian neighbors, the Menomini, Sauk, Fox, Maskotin, Ottawa, Ojibwa, Potawatomi, and Kickapoo.—Jenks, *Wild Rice Gatherers*, p. 1052.

Unfortunately for those who have accepted this as showing the aboriginal tribal picture, a number of early documents have become available indicating that the Indian peoples had been "shuffled" around greatly in the four decades immediately preceding the visit of Allouez. One of the principal students of the area, Miss Kellogg of the Wisconsin Historical Society, has suggested on the basis of this evidence a very different tribal distribution at the date mentioned in the quotation above. She writes:

> At the time of his (Nicolet's) voyage the Sauk, Foxes, Mascouten and others were still in Michigan; the Potawatomi had not yet taken refuge at the Sault (St. Marie); the Menominee and their kindred the Noquet[2] were, in all probability, the only Algonquian tribes in Wisconsin, which was peopled by Indians of Siouan origin . . . Winnebago.—Kellogg, *The French Regime in Wisconsin*, p. 95.

[1] For a general picture see Wissler, C., *The American Indian;* note also Bushnell, D. I., *Tribal Migrations East of the Mississippi*, Smithsonian Miscellaneous Collections, vol. 89, no. 12, 1934.

[2] The Noquet were a small Indian group of whom little is known. They were related either to the Menomini or, perhaps more likely, to the Chippewa and lived at the Baye du Noque, on the northwest shore of Lake Michigan. They died out or were absorbed in the main Chippewa people in early post-white times. See *Handbook of American Indians*, p. 842, also *Jesuit Relations*, vol. liv, p. 133, also index volume.

The most important documents on which the student of this very early period must depend are the *"Relations"* of the Jesuit missionaries, written and published every year from the early seventeenth century until well into the eighteenth century. They are regarded by historians as for the most part very reliable records. An amount of evidence can also be drawn from two other documents, a *"Memoir"* by the trader Perrot and a *"Histoire de l'Amérique Septentrionale"*, by La Potherie, said to have been based mainly on information given by Perrot. But these are more doubtful sources, published some years after the events recorded.

There is every indication that the Siouan Winnebago and the Algonquian Menomini occupied the area west of Lake Michigan and in the vicinity of the present Green Bay for a long period before the first coming of the whites. Like the Menomini, the Winnebago claim it as their ancestral home, and archaeological findings appear to confirm this.[3] The relations between the two peoples in these early days were described by La Potherie as follows:

> In former times the Puans (Winnebago) were the masters of this bay, and of a great extent of adjoining country. This nation was a populous one, very redoubtable, and spared no one. . . . The Malhominis (Menomini) were the only tribe who maintained relations with them, (and) they did not dare even to complain of their tyranny. Those tribes believed themselves the most powerful in the universe; they declared war on all nations whom they could discover.

This pictures the Winnebago, with the Menomini apparently their tributaries, as dominating the region. Indeed, their campaigns were serious enough to embarrass even the Huron tribesfolk who lived a considerable distance to the east, for the voyage of Nicolet to the region in 1634 was to arrange a peace with the Winnebago on behalf of that people (*Jes. Rel.*, xxiii, p. 275).

The Menomini always claim to have enjoyed friendly relations with the Sioux or Dakotah tribes to the west. In this they differ from the rest of the Central Algonquian tribes, the Ottawa, Chippewa, Sauk, Fox, Potawatomi, and so

[3] Radin, P., *The Winnebago Tribe*, pp. 76–103.

on, who were notably hostile.[4] On the other hand, the traditional evidence and early records indicate that the Menomini
were generally speaking hostile toward these other Algonquian tribes.[5] It might be suggested that the Menomini
moved west to their present territories in early days—or
alternatively remained in the west while the others went east
—and, achieving a balance of relationships with the adjoining Siouan peoples, became unfriendly to their own kindred
peoples.

On the basis of historical, traditional and linguistic evidence the Central Algonquian tribes may be divided into
some four types. The Menomini stand alone as one, particularly as regards language.[6] The second is represented by
the Sauk-Fox-Kickapoo group of tribes, and these are
linguistically closer to the Menomini than the third type,
comprising the Chippewa-Ottawa-Potawatomi tribes. The
fourth type consists of a group of peoples generally called
Illinois.

According to rather scanty records, supported by tribal
memories, the Sauk and Fox tribes appear to have been
originally one people living somewhere toward the eastern
coast. In the course of wars with Iroquian tribes, they were
pushed westwards, "the Sauks up the St. Lawrence to the
Lakes", "the Foxes to the Grand River".[7] The Sauk at first
occupied territory around Saginaw bay, but were in time
driven thence by the ancestors of the present Chippewa, Ottawa and Potawatomi tribes.[8] They then settled between
lakes Huron and Michigan, where in time they became inter-
married with the Potawatomi tribe to the north.[9] The Fox
appear to have taken up quarters to the south of Winnebago-
Menomini country, near to the Illinois, but whether at the

[4] See for example *Jes. Rel.*, liv, p. 191; liv, p. 223; Perrot in Blair, *The Indian Tribes of the Upper Mississippi Valley*, pp. 163–170.

[5] See Skinner and Satterlee, *Folklore;* also La Potherie.

[6] See Bloomfield, ''Menomini Language,'' in *Proc. Intl. Congress of Americanists*, 1924, p. 336.

[7] Forsyth's *Memoir*, in Blair, *Indian Tribes*, ii, p. 184.

[8] See under ''Sauk'' in *Handbook of American Indians, Bulletin 30, Bur. of Amer. Ethnology.*

[9] Perrot, in Blair, i, p. 270.

time of Nicolet's visits they were living along the eastern shores of Michigan or away toward the Mississippi is difficult to surmise. The same may be said of the Kickapoo and Mascouten peoples who seem to have had affiliations with them.[10]

Concerning the third group of tribes the following may be quoted:

> According to tradition the Ottawa, Chippewa, and Potawatomi tribes of the Algonquin family were formerly one people who came from some point north of the Great Lakes and separated at Mackinaw, Michigan.—Mooney and Hewitt, in *Handbook of American Indians*, part II, p. 168.

Just how early this migration of northern tribes took place is hard to say. The indications are that their breaking up into three sections was a comparatively recent event.[11] When whites arrived, the Chippewa were located round Sault St. Marie, the point of lake Superior's outflow, and to the north and west of this; the Ottawa were eastward on Manitoulin island; and the Potawatomi occupied the northern part of the peninsula between Michigan and Huron lakes. The French in their contact with the first of these groups, the Chippewa, gave separate names to various sections, as "Saulteurs" to those round the Sault, "Outchibous" and "Marameg" to those further north, and perhaps "Noquet" to those nearest the Menomini at the Baye du Noque.

The Illinois, who lived southward of Menomini country, were described to the early Jesuits by tribesmen visiting the white settlements of the lower St. Lawrence as the second largest nation in the lakes region, being surpassed in the number of their villages only by "the Kiristinons" or Cree peoples away to the north. The Illinois comprised a number of groups such as the Miami, Kaskaskia, Peoria and Tamaroa. According to the first records, they had hostile relationships with the Winnebago and their Menomini allies.

The tribal geography of early times as here reconstructed from the scanty evidence is summarized in sketch map 2 of

[10] Kellogg, *French Regime*, p. 95.
[11] Warren, *Ojibways*, in *Minnesota Hist. Colls.*, vol. v, p. 81.

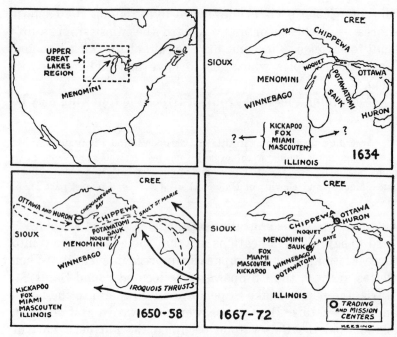

DIAGRAM 1. Distribution of Tribes, 1634–1672.

Diagram 1. What, then, happened after 1634, the date of Nicolet's visit? First the account which Nicolet himself gave of the tribes may be quoted:

We enter the second fresh-water sea (Michigan), upon the shores of which are the Maroumine (Menomini), and still further, upon the same banks, dwell the Ouinipigou (Winnebago) a sedentary people, who are very numerous. In the neighborhood of this nation are the Naduesiu (Sioux), the Rasaouakoueton (Mascouten), and the Pouutouatami. These are the names of a part of the nations.—*Jes. Rel.*, 1640, xviii, p. 231.

In 1658 another geography of the tribes appears in the *Relations;* it starts from a village on northwest Michigan lake:

Father Gabreuillettes . . . conferred the name of St. Michel upon the first Village. . . . Its inhabitants are called, in Algonquin, Oupouteoua-tamik (Potawatomi). . . . They have for neighbors the Kiskacouueiak and the Nequaouichiriniouek (the two groups of the Ottawa tribe). There are in this village about a hundred men of the Tobacco nation (a Huron people), who took refuge there to escape the cruelty of the Iroquois.

The second nation is composed of the Noukek (Nouquet), Ouini-
pegouek (Winnebago), and Malouminek (Menomini). . . . About two
hundred Algonquins, who used to dwell on the Northern shores of the great
Lake or the Fresh-water sea of the Hurons, have taken refuge in this
place.—*Jes. Rel.*, 1657–58, pp. 79–80.

This document offers a picture of movement. There are
refugee tribes in the region. The Potawatomi and Ottawa
are now located to the north of the Menomini territories.
Iroquois tribesmen are on the warpath.

In 1604 the settlement of New France had been established on the lower St. Lawrence river, and furtrading, exploration and mission work were being pursued with vigor
among friendly Indian peoples both Algonquian such as the
Montagnais, and Iroquoian such as the Hurons. These
tribes, with the French as allies, frequently clashed with
others to the south, in the present state of New York, known
to history as the Iroquois League or Confederacy. Shortly
after Nicolet's visit to the "upper country", this latter Iroquois group took to the warpath, armed with muskets supplied by the Dutch traders of the New Netherlands. The
historical records show that for some thirty years they
ravaged the areas to north and west, driving out or extermi-
nating all tribes within striking distance, and continually
harassing the tiny French colony on the St. Lawrence.

Between 1635 and 1653, the bands of the League laid
waste all the Huron country. Those among the Hurons who
were able to escape fled, together with French missionaries
and traders who were among them, either to the lower French
settlements or away west to the upper lakes. The Iroquois
also pressed into the territories of the Central Algonquian
peoples right to the shores of Michigan. Before their
ferocious assault the Potawatomi, Ottawa, and Sauk retreated round the lake to the north, and the Illinois, with
perhaps the Fox, Kickapoo and Mascouten, likewise round
it to the south. Apparently some of the tribesfolk passed
even beyond the Mississippi, seeking refuge in the tangled
swamps and dense woodlands of the region. The documents
give vivid if meagre accounts of these movements, as seen
from the following:

All these people (the Huron, Wyandot and Ottawa) have forsaken their former country and withdrawn to the more distant Nations on account of the fury of the Iroquois.—*Jes. Rel.*, xxxv, p. 185.

The Pouteouatami, the Ousaki (Sauk) and the nation of the Fork[12] also live (at Green Bay), but as foreigners, driven by their fear of the Iroquois from their own territories, which lie between the Lake of the Hurons and that of the Illinois (Michigan).—*Jes. Rel.*, lv, p. 183; also see p. 159.

These (the Fox) withdrew to these (west Michigan) regions to escape. . . .—*Jes. Rel.*, liv, p. 223.

All the Outaouas (Ottawa) were dispersed toward the lakes. The Saulters and the Missisakis (Chippewa peoples) fled northward.—Perrot, *Memoir*, in Blair, i, p. 276.

After the people who formerly lived near the Western sea (Winnebago?) were driven away from lake Michigan by their foes, they (the Illinois) sought a refuge on the shores of this Lake; and when the Iroquois expelled them thence also, they finally withdrew to a spot seven days' journey beyond the great river (Mississippi) . . . the Poteouatami, Ousaki, and other tribes . . . driven from their own abode, the Lands toward the South, near Missilimackinac (Mackinaw), have sought refuge at the head of this bay (Green Bay). Beyond it, and farther inland, may be seen the . . . Mathkoutench (Mascouten), with an Illinois tribe called the Oumami (Miami), and also the Outagami (Fox).—*Jes. Rel.*, lv, pp. 101–05.

The picture offered by these and similar documents is of great tribal movements. Ottawa and Huron refugees fled westward along the south shores of lake Superior, even moving temporarily up to the headwaters of the Mississippi in Sioux country, but later returning to make their headquarters first at Chequamegon bay on lake Superior and then at the Sault St. Marie.[13] The Potawatomi and the Sauk settled on the northwest shores of Michigan, where together with other tribes they succeeded in repelling an Iroquois attack; about 1665 they moved south to Green Bay where

[12] The writer has been unable to trace this people, other than that they seem to be the group mentioned by Gabreuillettes as refugees from north of Huron. Were they a group which La Potherie calls "Mantoue" and which he reports as massacred by a combination of tribes in the region? See La Potherie in Blair, i, p. 306.

[13] See Perrot in Blair, i, pp. 159, 173, 189; La Potherie in *ibid.*, p. 307; *Jes. Rel.*, xli, p. 79; l, pp. 249ff; liv, p. 151.

Allouez found them.[14]   Once peace had been established with the Iroquois in 1664, the other tribes, Fox, Mascouten, Miami, and Kickapoo likewise began to settle in the region.   An idea of these changing distributions can be gathered from Diagram 1, maps 3 and 4.

What effects had all these tribal movements into the west of Michigan upon the earlier dwellers in the territory, Winnebago and Menomini?   The records indicate that both tribes, while sheltered by the stretching waters of Lake Michigan from direct Iroquois attack, were well nigh exterminated by these incoming peoples.   La Potherie tells how a union of the nations was formed against the powerful Winnebago in order to gain revenge for former aggressions; how "they made frequent expeditions" against them; "then followed civil wars among the Puans (Winnebago)"; "maladies wrought among them more devastation"; they lost some hundreds of warriors during a storm on a lake— whether Michigan or the smaller Lake Winnebago near Green Bay is not made clear—during an expedition against the Fox; finally "all the nations who were interested" combined in a campaign against them:

So vigorous was their attack that they killed, wounded, or made prisoners all the Puans (Winnebago), except a few who escaped, and who reached the Malhomini's village, but severely wounded by arrows.—La Potherie, *Histoire*.[15]

The Menomini evidently suffered through war and pestilence along with their allies.   Incoming whites spoke of them as being a mere remnant living in a single village. Father Allouez tells in 1669 how they had been "almost exterminated by the wars," while Perrot, through La Potherie, says that they were "no more than forty in number", presumably in warrior strength, the basis of all early calculations.

14 The Sauk are described as for a time "wandering and scattered in the forest without any fixed abode."—*Jes. Rel.*, li, p. 45; see also under Sauk, in *Handbook of Am. Indians.*

15 The Jesuits also report this decimation of the Winnebago. In *Jes. Rel.*, liv, p. 237, it is told how a remnant were later freed from the captivity into which they were carried and allowed to re-establish their nation near the present Lake Winnebago. See also *Jes. Rel.*, lv, p. 171; lvii, pp. 249ff.

It .can well be understood, then, why the Algonquian tribes were able to settle without opposition around La Baye (Green Bay) and the Fox valley, as noted by Allouez, at the termination of the Iroquois aggression. The stimulus to this gathering of the tribes is made clear by the records—a desire to trade. Already the Ottawa and Huron, and to some extent the Potawatomi had experienced the benefits of commerce with the French. Once peace was made with the Iroquois and the channels of communication with the settlements of the lower St. Lawrence were again opened up, these tribes aspired to become trading intermediaries between the whites and other tribes of the region. The Ottawa and Huron made Chequamegon Bay and later Sault St. Marie a rallying center to which came many Indian ''nations'' even from distant parts to trade furs for goods, especially guns. From about 1665 the Potawatomi sought to make a like center at Green Bay. La Potherie tells how:

> These peoples (the Potawatomi) . . . sent deputies in every direction to inform the Islinois, Miamis, Maskoutechs, and Kikabous that they had been at Montreal, whence they had brought much merchandise; they besought those tribes to visit them and bring them beavers. Those tribes were too far away to profit by this at first; only the Outagamis (Fox) came to establish themselves for the winter at a place thirty leagues from the bay. . . . The Pouteouatemis took the southern part of the bay, the Sakis (Sauk) the northern; the Puans (Winnebago) as they could not fish, had gone into the woods to live on deer and bears. When the Outagamis had formed a village of more than six hundred cabins, they sent to the Sakis, at the beginning of spring, to let them know of the new establishment that they had formed. . . . The Miamis, the Maskoutechs, the Kikabous, and fifteen cabins of the Islinois came toward the bay in the following summer, and made their clearings thirty miles away, beside the Outagamis toward the south. These peoples, for whom the Iroquois were looking, had gone southward along the Mississippi. . . . Before that flight, they had seen knives and hatchets in the hands of the Hurons who had had dealings with the French, which induced them to associate themselves with the tribes who already had some union with us.—La Potherie in Blair, pp. 316–22.

Thus came about the concentration of tribes at the Bay which almost immediately attracted the eyes of French traders and missionaries, apparently a distribution of peoples very different from that· existing thirty years previously. The whole is a picture of population movement that had parallels in other isolated countries as a result of the coming of new weapons and of trade.

Two features of the Menomini experience at this time can be especially noted here. In the first place, the tribe apparently enjoyed a complete isolation from direct Iroquois attack, because of its sheltered position west of the stretch- ing waters of lake Michigan. This character of isolation from eastern influences as a result of geographic factors was to play an important part in shaping the further Me- nomini history, for all alien encroachment came similarly from the east. Secondly, the fact that the tribesfolk were decimated and disorganized when whites and white influen- ces first touched them directly seems to have rendered them particularly susceptible to change.

The elaborate tribal movements glimpsed in the docu- ments above are of far more than merely historical interest. Actually they complicate greatly the task of reconstructing the aboriginal cultures of the Indian tribes of the Upper Lakes region. Peoples hitherto isolated from one another were in contact; former enemies were in refuge together, and later were associating freely in the trading centers; stable communities were overthrown and presumably their traditional modes of living were disorganized; conditions appear to have been such as to favor particularly a levelling down of aboriginal cultures. The full significance of these factors, so far little taken into account by ethnological work- ers in the region, will appear in the later sections. The problem of reconstruction is still further complicated by the fact that, because of the scanty data and the limited value of the contemporary records, any very exact picture of pre-white and early tribal distributions and relationships in the area can apparently never be painted. It must remain sketchy and impressionistic rather than having the sharp accuracy which science looks for. How these factors make difficult the delineation of a specific Indian culture in the region will appear in the next section, which deals with the Menomini culture at the first coming of the whites.

II. THE OLD TIME MENOMINI

The Menomini of pre-white days occupied an unknown number of villages on or near the Menominee river. Dwelling by the waterways, they were seemingly a fairly sedentary people, with their economic life centered around fishing, gathering "wild rice" (*Zizania aquatica*) and hunting. They comprised a number of patrilineal totemic descent groups apparently linked into two moieties, Bear and Thunderbird. Situated at the approximate meeting place of three "culture areas", the plains, northern woodland, and eastern woodland areas, the tribe shared to some extent in the cultural characteristics of each, though as noted earlier they are dominantly affiliated with the Algonquian-speaking tribes to the east.

THE PHYSICAL SETTING

The Menomini region is geologically a part of what is termed the "glacial drift" of the North American continent, pressed flat by the encroachments of the polar ice cap in past ages. It is cut by a network of streams, with numerous small lakes and swampy areas, the whole drained by river systems leading eastward into lake Michigan and westward into the Mississippi. The western shore of Green Bay, into which the Menominee river empties, is "low and sandy with frequent harbors separated by shallow stretches"—the harbors being the mouths of the various rivers flowing eastward. The climate is one of extremes, the country being warm and fertile in the summer, but in winter having frozen lakes and streams, and frequent snowfalls.

The greater part of the area was covered in early days with forest, mainly conifers and mixed hardwoods, though here and there were open sandy areas and to the south were rolling plains. Many of the trees played important roles in the tribal economy, notably birch, basswood, oak, cedar and hickory. The forest produced a variety of nuts, berries, and edible roots, also numbers of plants that had a place in

18

the religio-medical lore of the Menomini. Perhaps the most characteristic growth of the region was the "wild rice", which grew so profusely as almost to block up some of the waterways from navigation by canoe. Both forest and stream were stocked with game—mammals such as the bear, deer and wolf, birds like the eagle and crane, and fish, particularly the sturgeon.

Exactly how much of this area of northeast Wisconsin and the adjacent part of Michigan actually was the ancient territory and hunting ground of the Menomini cannot now be known, in view of what was set out in the last chapter. The system of land holding, too, is rather obscure, though evidence from later days indicates that nothing like the western conception of individual rights in real property existed; the tribe held its lands doubtless by the law of the strong arm, allowing its constituent families and individuals to use them under some convenient set of rules now unknown— perhaps even sharing them with friendly tribes. It is possible, however, to reconstruct with some certainty the main uses to which the resources were put, the material culture and economic organization of the tribe.

MATERIAL CULTURE AND ECONOMICS

Very full records exist as regards Menomini foods. Not only are there early records and extensive references in the tribal lore, but also in many aspects their use has been maintained tenaciously until recent times.[1] In general the seasonal cycle of food getting followed a pattern common to the Woodland Indians, being with local variations known to the other Algonquian and to the Iroquoian and Siouan tribes of the forest area.

Hunting and fishing are referred to extensively in Menomini folklore, and, if frequency of repetition counts for anything in the case of such a source, hunting would seem to have easily predominated. It may well be, however, that its importance compared with fishing became unduly mag-

[1] Hoffman, *Meno. Inds.*, pp. 272–73, 286–91; Skinner, *Mat. Cult.*, pp. 142–207.

nified in later times as a result of the furtrading economy. Early documents give the impression that fishing was the main winter occupation, and that at no time of the year did the people move far from the lake shore and streams. Only in later times, apparently, when the furtraders required winter pelts, did the practice arise of moving far inland for an extensive "winter hunt". Hunting was done variously by individuals, families and small congenial groups as need for food arose. But there were also larger organized hunts for deer and buffalo. The Menomini claim, and documents confirm, that herds of buffalo frequented the region north of lake Winnebago up to a few generations back.[2] In hunting, a variety of all important magical aids were used in the form of charms, "hunting bundles", and rituals to ensure the cooperation of the Powers and to ward off unfavorable influences. Reverence was paid to particular animals, notably to the bear and others from which mankind was supposed to have descended. A kill of game provided not only food but also a supply of skin, bone, sinew and other materials for manufactures. Fish were caught by netting, trapping, spearing from canoes or from the banks of streams, and by constructing weirs across the watercourses. La Potherie tells how:

> The Malhominis (are adroit) . . . in spearing the Sturgeon in their river. For this purpose they use only small Canoes, very light, in which they stand upright, and in the middle of the current spear the Sturgeon . . . only Canoes are to be seen, morning and night.—*Wis. Hist. Colls.*, xvi, p. 9.

In winter, fish were speared or netted through holes in the ice—a favorite Menomini sport that has survived to recent times.

Two foods, the modern Menomini claim, were given by the spirit Powers to be forever their special privilege— maple sugar and wild rice. Both are seasonal products,

[2] Buffalo were seen in considerable numbers along the Fox and Wisconsin rivers by early visitors. See *Jes. Rel.*, lv, p. 195, lix, pp. 111–13; also Powell's *Recollections* in *Proc. Wis. Hist. Society*, 1912, p. 177, and Skinner and Satterlee, *Folklore*, p. 448.

the former manufactured from the maple sap during a short period in the spring and the latter harvested when ripe in autumn.

All living Menomini say that maple sugar is an ancient Indian food, and ethnologists have accepted it as such. In the spring-time, it is told, the various families camped in their favorite sugar groves, gathered the maple sap and rendered it, with appropriate ceremonial, into sugar. The manufacturing process is described fully by the ethnologists Hoffman and Skinner. Nevertheless a careful study of the early records forces the author to doubt that this product goes back to pre-Columbian days. Actually no mention other than of the sap seems to occur in documents of the seventeenth century amid dozens of descriptions of Indian foods.

Up to 1722 only four references to the maple tree were found: (a) in 1634 it was said of the Montagnais tribe that "When they are pressed by famine they eat the shavings of bark of a certain tree which they call *Michtan*, which they split in the spring to get from it a juice, sweet as honey or as sugar. I have been told of this by several but they do not enjoy much of it, so scanty is the flow" (*Jes. Rel.*, vi, p. 273); (b) in 1671 a Jesuit father among the Ottawa tells how he inadvertently baptized someone with "Maplewater, which I took for natural water" (*Jes. Rel.*, lvi, p. 101); (c) La Salle and his followers in 1688 wrote how at fort Chicago "We discovered a kind of manna . . . a sort of tree, resembling our maple, in which we made incisions, whence flowed a sweet liquor . . . which being boiled and evaporated, turned into a kind of sugar" (*Journal of Joutel,* in Cox's *La Salle,* ii, p. 277); there is no mention of it here as being known to the Indians; (d) in 1689 the voyager Lahontan told of the tree, and speaking of the Indians in general, said that "Scarce any body but Children give themselves the trouble" of collecting the sap (Thwaites, *Lahontan,* i, p. 367). In 1722, some two hundred years after the first white contact, there is given, in relation to the Abnaki tribe

in the east, what seems to be the first description of the
sugarmaking process as described by the later ethnologists
(*Jes. Rel.,* lxvii, p. 95). This startling discrepancy in the
records suggests that the sap was known but in pre-white
times it was really a starvation or else a luxury food. The
aboriginal character of the shoulder yoke, used to carry the
maple syrup in vessels, is also doubtful as it was well known
in European countries at the time. Presumably, along with
sugar manufacture, it was learned from the French.

There can be no question, however, as to the antiquity
of wild rice as a food. The first whites constantly mention
its use; in 1673 a full description of how it was harvested
and prepared was given by a Jesuit father, Marquette, techniques still employed into the twentieth century. The Menomini claim to have used wild rice for their food more than
any of the other tribes of the rice area, and indeed the name
Menomini itself is usually translated to mean "wild rice
people." "Whenever the Menomini enter a region", the
tribal elders tell, "the wild rice spreads ahead, whenever
they leave it the wild rice passes". Certainly in pre-white
times wild rice was the most important of seasonal foods,
and an essential basis for ceremonial feasts and offerings.
Presumably in a normal season enough was harvested and
stored to carry throughout the year.

The early Jesuits spoke frequently of wild rice as a
food, and their references give some clue to its distribution. The Sioux peoples of the lakes and the Cree to the
north, together with the Menomini and Winnebago are mentioned as using it, but apparently not the Ottawa, Sauk,
Chippewa (?), Potawatomi (?), or the more southern tribes,
Illinois, Fox, etc. (See for example *Jes. Rel.,* li, p. 53, li, pp.
57–59, also *Journal of Marquette,* in Kellogg, *Early Narratives,* pp. 230–31.) It is possible that not until the incoming
tribes settled in the region did they take over wild rice as
later described by Jenks. The southern tribes were an
inland rather than a waterside people. Certainly various
Sioux-Chippewa wars for possession of the wild rice beds

of the south Superior region appear to have been mainly, if not entirely, post-white.

Agriculture appears to have had a very minor place in the old Menomini economy; it was far less important than among some of the Algonquian tribes to the east. La Potherie remarks that "they raise a little Indian corn, but live upon game and Sturgeons". Whether or not tobacco was cultivated is in doubt; the distribution of the practice among surrounding tribes in early times would suggest it, but tribal tradition denies. But uncultivated varieties, bark of the red willow and sumac leaves, were in great use. Tobacco was an essential part of all religious and ceremonial observance, the incense beloved of the Powers.

Several quotations concerning the economic staples of other tribes are included here for sake of comparison:

Sioux: "They cultivate fields, sowing therein not Indian corn, but only tobacco; while Providence has furnished them a kind of marsh rye." *Jes. Rel.,* li, p. 53.

Cree: "(They) are much more nomadic . . . no fields . . . living wholly on game and a small quantity of oats which they gather in marshy places." *Jes. Rel.,* li, pp. 57–59, lv, p. 99.

Chippewa: "They harvest some Indian corn . . . fishing."—Perrot in Blair, i, p. 102.

Ottawa: "The Outaouaks raise Indian corn . . . They live there on fish and corn, and rarely by hunting."—*Jes. Rel.,* liv, pp. 163, 167.

Potawatomi: "(They) engage in Hunting and Fishing. Their country is excellently adapted to raising Indian corn." *Jes. Rel.,* li, p. 27.

Iroquois: "The Iroquois were not hunters; they cultivated the soil. . . . The Algonkins on the contrary, supported themselves by their hunting alone, despising agriculture." Perrot, in Blair, i, p. 43. (An extreme statement of course.)

Fox: "(They) are given to hunting and warfare. They have fields of Indian corn."—*Jes. Rel.,* li, p. 43.

Miami and Mascouten: "They do not fish, but live on Indian corn . . . and on game."—*Jes. Rel.,* lv, pp. 213–15.

Illinois: "The Illinois . . . raise corn . . . have squashes . . . and a great many roots and fruits. There is fine hunting there." *Jes. Rel.,* liv, p. 189.

While this list does not comprehend all the tribes, and obviously such descriptions are incomplete, they appear to show the main emphases of the different regions. The Menomini were at the point where three types of economy met— the western game area, the northern wild rice area, and the eastern and southern agricultural area; being coastal and river people, they also did much fishing.

Several other food products rounded out the Menomini diet. A cycle of berries ripened in the forest during the summer. Various wild fruits, vegetables and fungi were collected. In the fall the nuts of the forest were stored for winter, the Indian here competing with the squirrels, chipmunks and other nut gatherers that make the autumn woods a hive of provident industry.

Few clothes were worn by the Menomini. The materials used for garments were the skins of animals, particularly of the deer. These were made into breechcloths, leggings, and moccasins. Probably, too, an upper garment of fur corresponding to the blanket of later days was used in cold weather. It would seem that all forms of upper garments found among western Woodland tribes by ethnologists in later times are of post-white origin.[3] The most outstanding impression to be gathered from the comparative materials is the capacity of the Indian to bear exposure to the weather. The explorers and Jesuits refer continually to the scant clothes worn even in the severest winters. As to the exact form of garments used in pre-white times, it seems that the patterns of Indian dress changed so rapidly as a result of white influences, direct and indirect, that the only safe accounts are those of the very earliest visitors. Even

[3] Hoffman, p. 264; Skinner, *Mat. Cult.,* pp. 109–40.

by Champlain's time trade goods had preceded him inland. Cartier, an earlier voyager, met a number of tribes both Algonquian and Iroquoian, and gives several descriptions of clothing. He says of the eastern woodland peoples:

> Instead of apparell, they weare skinnes upon them like mantles; and they have a small payre of breeches . . . as well men as women. They have hosen and shoes of leather excellently made. And they have no shirts; neither covered their heads . . . a few old furs which they throw over their shoulders. . . . In winter they wear leggings and moccasins, and in summer they go barefoot. . . . Both the men, women and children are more indifferent to the cold than beasts.—Cartier's *Voyages,* Canadian Archives, pp. 168, 61, 181–85.

The only clear description of the dress of Indians in the upper country refers to the Illinois, and would indicate that the same would in general apply:

> The Illinois are covered only around the waist, otherwise they go entirely nude. . . . It is only when they make visits . . . that they wrap themselves in a cloak of dressed skin in the summer-time, and in the winter season in a dressed skin with the hair left on.—*Jes. Rel.,* lxvii, p. 165.

What variations from this the Menomini may have shown is not indicated. However their nudity apparently worried a visiting Jesuit father who persuaded them to "cover themselves" in his presence (p. 60).

Two aspects of "dress" definitely old were oil and grease rubbed on hair and body, and a variety of colors applied with particular meanings on ceremonial occasions.

Beyond these general facts little is known to make possible a reconstruction of the old Menomini dress. What elaboration of ornament and pattern was customary, what was correct in hair and headdress, and what were the forms of decoration, including perhaps tattooing, cannot be ascertained with any certainty. Also quite obscure are the distinctions made, if any, between sexes, among various ranks, and for different occasions. The memories of the tribesfolk are quite vague on such details, and with influences coming from other tribes in more recent times, and especially the impress of white dress and decorative patterns through both imitation and direct acquisition from the trader, any exact reconstruction is rendered impossible. It will be shown later that the sashings, garterings, tassels and ornamentation referred to in the writings of Hoffman and Skinner and on display in museum cases are for the most part at any rate of no great antiquity.

Menomini house styles, on the other hand, being a close and apparently ancient adjustment to the special conditions of the physical environment, have changed little until very recent times. There were two main types of house, a rectangular bark cabin for summer use and for winter a dome lodge of mats or bark. Both had a wide distribution among the Woodland peoples, and were particularly suited to the hunting and roving life of the forest Indian. Various less permanent structures were made for short camps, for use on the trail, and for drying or storing food. Ceremonial and religious structures, usually temporary, were also erected, such as the ''sweat lodge'', women's lodge for periodic seclusions, places for dreaming and fasting, and the lodge of the ''juggler'' or magician.

The Menomini house, according to ethnological accounts, had raised beds round the walls. An old document refers to bedding of skins and boughs, but not actually to beds; here, too, there may have been white influence. Actually a number of the most conservative Menomini today still refuse to sleep on beds, preferring the floor, perhaps a reflection of older usage. In the center of the house was a fireplace. The position of honor for a guest was at the rear opposite the door, while close by the sleeping place of the head of the house would be hung the sacred objects of the family.[4]

The Menomini appear to have been on the fringes of three types of housing. Eastward and northward, in the forest area, the main material used for house construction was bark, though mats of reed were also known (*Jes. Rel.,* viii, p. 105, iii, p. 77). To the west was the plains area, where the ''Cabins are not covered with bark, but with Deer

[4] See Hoffman, pp. 253–56; Skinner, *Mat. Cult.*, pp. 83–107.

skins'' (*Jes. Rel.,* li, p. 53). Again the tribes to the south and southwest of the Menomini, having little bark, use ''rushes woven together in the form of mats'' (*Jes. Rel.,* lv, p. 195, lix, p. 129). The only mention found by the writer concerning frame beds in lodges was interestingly enough in one of the earliest records, where Champlain speaks of ''benches'' in the houses of Indians on the lower St. Lawrence.—*Voyages,* ii, p. 120.

The travel and transport adjustments of the Menomini were also ancient and well suited to life in the area. The Indian ''roads'' were rivers, streams and lakes with their portages, and trails blazed where necessary through the woods. The main aids to Menomini travel on land were the moccasin, already spoken of, the snowshoe for winter wear, and various forms of burden straps, baskets and bags. Two forms of canoe appear to have been used for water travel, the birchbark and the less fragile wooden dugout. All these were taken over direct from the Indian by the early whites because of their usefulness.[5]

The canoe is referred to very frequently in the early records, though it is hardly explicit as to whether the birchbark or the dugout is referred to. Of the Menomini, father Marquette wrote: ''They go in Canoes through these fields of wild oats.'' Apparently the birchbark canoe was used throughout the eastern region, but not the dugout. The tribes around the great lakes used canoes, Ottawa (*Jes. Rel.,* xlii, p. 219), Chippewa (liv, p. 131), Cree (li, p. 57), Potawatomi (liv, p. 197), ''Sioux of the lakes'' (liv, p. 193), but apparently not the Algonquins south and southwest of the Menomini: the Fox (*Jes. Rel.,* li, p. 43, liv, p. 189, and La Potherie, in Blair, i, p. 299), Miami and Mascouten (*Jes. Rel.,* lv, p. 195), and Illinois (li, p. 47, lix, p. 137). Away to the south of Illinois country the first explorers found tribes using ''wooden canoes'' (liv, p. 191). This last suggests that the use of the dugout may have been diffused from the south into the wild rice region, either at a period earlier

[5] See Hoffman, pp. 263, 292; Skinner, *Mat. Cult.,* pp. 209–22.

than the occupation of the intermediate area by these Algonquin tribes who were not maritime peoples, or else in later
times.

Menomini weapons and tools followed patterns widespread in the region. Passing over for present various
magical aids in the form of charms and rituals, the known
varieties are as follows: bows and arrows; ball headed and
gunshaped clubs, often spiked; knives of stone, shell, bone
and perhaps copper; and axes with grooved heads of stone.
Only the bows and clubs are familiar to the Indian of today.
The others are known through archaeological evidence alone,
as they were supplanted rapidly by the metal implements of
the whites. According to the older Menomini, the type of
weapon or tool to be used for any particular occasion was
often determined by a medicine man, or by the dream revelations of the individual concerned.[6]

These weapons and tools are fairly frequently referred
to in the early descriptions of tribes in the region. One
interesting artifact that has not been included in the Menomini list for want of evidence is the shield as a protective
weapon. Shields of hide are mentioned as used by the Illinois (*Jes. Rel.,* lx, p. 161), also shields of hide or of wood
"principally cedar" by peoples in the east (Champlain's
Voyages, p. 513, *Jes. Rel.,* i, p. 269, iii, p. 91, xiii, p. 265).
With the coming of the gun and of metal weapons, however,
the shield lost its effectiveness and became obsolete in the
woodland area, though not in the plains area.

Further manufactures of the Menomini seem to have
been as follows: preparation and tanning of skins; weaving
bags and baskets of vegetable fibre, bark, and buffalo hair;
preparing twine, rope, and thread of vegetable fibre, skin,
and sinew; matmaking from reeds, flag and bark; manufacture of simple pottery; preparation of dyes, such as yellow
from sumac and red from hematite; making a variety of
household utensils—woodwork such as bowls, spoons and
troughs, shell dishes and spoons, bone needles and awls,

---

[6] See Hoffman, pp. 273–84; Skinner, *Mat. Cult.,* pp. 310–30.

gourds, birchbark buckets and baskets, skin pouches and bags, stone vessels and pounders, bowdrill and firemaking apparatus; construction of drums, tobacco pipes, and other religious and ceremonial objects. Most of these artifacts were made by women, but a few were exclusively men's work, as for example preparation of sacred artifacts and of fishing and hunting equipment. Almost all bear the stamp of great age, being referred to in the lore and early records and tenaciously remembered, some even retained, right to the present day. An element of doubt intrudes itself, however, as regards the antiquity of woodwork, and the use of birchbark and copper among the Menomini. There is evidence to suggest that at least they had not the important place in Menomini material culture which the ethnological writings and museum collections of later days would indicate. It may well be that wood and birchbark work was stimulated in post-white times through an extensive contact with eastern tribes which will be reviewed in due course.[7]

As with other aspects of material culture the Menomini appear to have been on the fringe of three areas of distribution. Already it has been seen that the Menomini were on the edge of the main woodlands, hence of the bark area. Northward and east, bark-work appears to have been well developed, as seen from such references as *Jes. Rel.*, i, p. 285, iii, p. 83, liv, p. 155, lxvii, p. 137. When, however, father Allouez visited the tribes at La Baye in 1669 he remarked, contrasting his experiences among these eastern and northern tribes with the new:

> The Savages of this region are more than usually barbarous; they are without ingenuity, and do not know how to make even a bark dish or a ladle; they commonly use shells.

Such a reference could well have application to the refugee Fox, Miami and Mascouten, Kickapoo and Illinois, but the puzzle is to know whether it includes such other tribes of the region as the Potawatomi and Sauk and espe-

[7] Hoffman, pp. 258–64; Skinner, *Mat. Cult.*, pp. 224–309.

cially the Menomini and Winnebago.   If the Menomini were
grouped at that time with the peoples immediately to the
west where skinwork was dominant (as *Jes. Rel.,* lx, p. 197),
or with those to the south and southwest where rush, wood,
and bone appear to predominate as materials for manufacture (as *Jes. Rel.,* lv, pp. 195, 217, lix, p. 129) then their use
of birchbark must have been intensified in post-white times
through contact with the eastern and northern tribes.   Apparently shells, which were plentiful in Wisconsin, were
used "commonly" for utensils.   The Illinois, from the
accounts given by the Jesuits, seem to have been influenced
by tribes having a high development of woodwork, either to
the south or perhaps further east before their westward
migrations.   Once more it is difficult to estimate how far
the Menomini culture of the time had been affected by these
influences, or to what degree the woodwork found among the
tribe in later times was a result of post-white diffusions from
Iroquoians.   The only direct evidence of the Menomini use
of skins in these earliest records is found in the journal of
Marquette where he speaks of "A Skin made into a bag,"
used for husking wild rice—*Jes. Rel.,* lix, p. 95.   Another
matter worth more investigation than it has received so far
is the antiquity of copper working in the great lakes region.
All contemporary references speak of copper as being very
sacred:

> Pieces of pure copper . . . they keep as so many divinities . . .
> wrapped up, among their most precious possessions.—*Jes. Rel.,* l, pp. 265–
> 67; see also Champlain, ii, p. 209.

At first sight it would seem that archeological evidence has
given sure ground for assuming a fairly wide use of copper
in pre-white times; but in the Menomini region at any rate
practically all copper artifacts discovered are of "comparatively recent" origin (see Fox and Younger, in *Wis. Archeologist,* vol. 17, number 2, 1918).

The precise nature of ancient Menomini art and decoration as relating to these various material objects is obscure.
In later times, there was noted an elaborate geometric and

realistic art, comprising porcupine quill work, appliqué, carving, etching, and painting. But it will be shown that this is in large measure a product of contact with Europeans and of influence from the Chippewa and other tribes. Actually the only art forms which can be established fairly definitely as dating back to pre-white times are simple markings to be found on pottery fragments, and designs on "medicine bags" and pouches passed down through many generations because of their religious significance. They show a fairly well developed geometric art, and perhaps indicate the use of certain highly conventionalized figures representing sacred beings; but there is nothing like the elaborate floral and other realistic patterns of later days.[8]

The early records for other tribes tell little about the art patterns. Apparently the first visitors did not feel any appreciation of this phase of Indian life. Most spoken of are painted designs on face and body, also the more permanent markings of tattooing. This latter practice was carried on by Iroquoian tribes such as the Huron and Neutral, also the Illinois (as *Jes. Rel.*, lxvii, p. 165) though in the latter case it may have been the result of influence from tribes to the southward. The documents mention among tribes to the east the use of porcupine quill (Champlain's *Voyages*, ii, p. 27, *Jes. Rel.*, i, p. 281, xliv, p. 293), shell ornaments (*Champlain*, ii, p. 128, *Jes. Rel.*, i, p. 281), and feathers (*Jes. Rel.*, xliv, p. 285, lix, pp. 115 on), though what special significance these had to the wearers cannot be known. As regards the Huron it was said: "They sometimes wear on the bottom of their garments little ornaments made from Bear's claws, that they may the more easily kill those animals and not be hurt by them." (*Jes. Rel.*, lx, p. 117.)

Father Marquette mentions seeing among the Illinois "belts, garters, and other articles made of the hair of bears and cattle (buffalo), dyed red, yellow, and gray" (lix, p. 123). This is a suggestive glimpse. It may be mentioned here that the early records show how the coming of trade goods, beads, bells, jewelry and like articles proved an im-

[8] See Skinner, *Mat. Cult.*, pp. 252–76.

mediate stimulus, particularly to personal decoration; see for instance *Jes. Rel.,* xliv, p. 291.

Before the whites arrived a certain amount of exchange appears to have been conducted between neighboring Indian tribes. Some students claim on the basis of archeological finds that many valued articles passed long distances, including shells, unworked flint, catlinite, and copper. Such evidence, however, has to be treated with caution, particularly as once the tribes settled down in peace under white domination the opportunities for intertribal trade were greatly increased. The mere finding of a conch shell in a burial mound within the great lakes region gives no guarantee of its pre-Columbian antiquity, the more so because so many obviously intrusive articles are found by archeological workers.

It seems fairly sure that the Menomini were able to get catlinite from the Sioux quarries in Minnesota, and perhaps copper from the lake Superior region; but whether this was by direct visitation, by intertribal trade, or by ceremonial gift exchange is unknown. The Winnebago claim to have obtained from the Menomini certain manufactures in stone and wood, apparently by trade. But no very developed system of exchange is found expressed in the folklore, or recorded in the early documents. There is some evidence, however, for postulating a considerable traffic between certain Indian groups. Thus Perrot records an exchange of products of the hunt and of cultivation between Algonquian and Iroquoian peoples (in Blair, i, p. 43); the Jesuits also make fairly frequent references to this, including one to market gatherings occasionally held in the northern wilderness (xliv, p. 243). Of the lake Superior region it was said in 1665:

> This lake is, furthermore, the resort of twelve or fifteen distinct nations —coming, some from the North, others from the South, and still others from the West . . . partly to obtain food by fishing, and partly to transact their petty trading with one another, when they meet.

Yet the trade relations between tribes were so obviously stimulated by the coming of whites and white goods into the region that such records cannot be regarded with any certainty as showing pre-white conditions (see *Jes. Rel.*, liv, pp. 191, 195).

Such transactions as ceremonial gift giving, offerings of tobacco, or passing over of goods in exchange for services, involved only a limited number of the concepts of the modern bargain. The use of wampum as money certainly appears to have been a post-white innovation in Menomini country, and the evidence points to the fact that it attained little other than a ceremonial significance.[9]

Concerning the division of labor among the Menomini there is much safer ground for reconstruction. A wealth of allusion exists in the folklore, and much evidence is given by the Jesuits and early traders. As regards specialization along sex lines, Perrot tells in his *Memoir* how Mä''näbus, the great Algonquian culture hero, better known under the name Hiawatha, instructed newly made humans thus:

> Thou, man, shall hunt, and make canoes, and do all things that a man must do; and thou, woman, shalt do the cooking for thy husband, make his shoes, dress the skins of animals, sew, and perform all the tasks that are proper for a woman.[10]

The pattern of what a man must do and the tasks proper to a woman seem ancient, well defined, and widely distributed, with local modification, among the Woodland tribes. It may be summarized as follows:

> *Man*—hunt and fish; conduct warfare; perform tribal, family and individual ceremonials in order to ensure the cooperation of the spirit Powers; prepare sacred artifacts; manufacture canoes, weapons, tools, nets, snares, wood bowls; cut and chop wood.

> *Woman*—cook; conduct the household and rear children; do all agricultural work; collect berries and wild foods; gather firewood; carry water; carry goods when traveling, such as the mats for the lodge; dress skins, make clothing, weave mats and bags and prepare household utensils.

[9] For a full discussion of wampum, see *Handbook of American Indians*, Bulletin 30, Bureau of American Ethnology, pp. 904–09. It is to be suspected that wampum was altogether a post-white innovation west of lake Michigan, introduced mainly through the medium of the French who had taken over its use from tribes in the east. Tobacco, the ''correct'' Menomini offering, is still in use, but wampum has long since disappeared even from memory.

[10] Perrot, *Memoir*, pp. 39–40, also a list on pp. 74–75; see too *Jes. Rel.*, iii, p. 101; xxxviii, pp. 255–57; lxvii, pp. 165–67. The name Mä''näbus is variously rendered by ethnologists, *e.g.*, Mä'näbŭsh (Hoffman). Mä''näbus is used by Skinner.

Within the group, too, certain supernaturally sanctioned privileges and responsibilities were bestowed upon individuals, usually through inheritance, as in the case of chiefs, medicine men, and war leaders. This leads on to a consideration of the social and political life of the Menomini.

SOCIAL AND POLITICAL ORGANIZATION

All early records refer to the tribe as living in a "village" at Menominee river. This settlement appears to have had permanent "cabins", but whether it was stockaded as were, at least in post-white times, the "forts" of the Iroquois, Ottawa, Huron, Sauk, and Fox, is not apparent.

The comparative material shows how closely community life relates to economics; the hunting and fishing peoples tended to be variously less stable than the predominantly agricultural groups. The Winnebago are referred to as "sedentary" (xviii, p. 231), having before their later downfall many villages (see Radin, P., *Winnebago Tribe, Ann. Report of the Bureau of American Ethnology*, 1915–16). In contrast to this the tribes around the Sault St. Marie and to the north are referred to in the records as "nomadic," "wanderers" (*Jes. Rel.*, liv, pp. 131, 139), while the Cree are even described as having "no villages" (li, p. 57). The Potawatomi, Sauk, and Fox appear to have moved their settlements according to the seasonal cycle (liv, pp. 205, 221, lvii, pp. 291–99); but just how far such movements, as also those of other tribes mentioned above, were the result of a disorganization of earlier more settled modes of life during the Iroquois aggressions can hardly be known. The Illinois, Miami and Mascouten appear to have had permanent villages. Just where the Menomini fit into this picture is difficult to say. Skinner tells that they moved inland from the lake for each winter season, but his descriptions appear to relate to post-white times when the Menomini had changed their mode of living considerably under the stimulus of the fur trade.

Again it is not clear whether fortification was customary. By 1730 the main Menomini village is referred to as a "fort," and later another Menomini settlement is noted on a map as being a "castle." There is some evidence that the Iroquoian peoples built strong palisaded villages (see Kellogg, "The Stockaded Village," in *Wisconsin Archeologist,* January 1919, for the collected documents). Yet this, if really ancient, did not apply to all the Iroquoians, for the early Jesuits said of the Hurons: "They are not careful to . . . enclose their villages with palisades" (x, p. 95). Later, however, the fathers themselves actually "set to work to fortify the village of the Hurons . . . (and) erected for them bastions" (x, p. 53, xxxv, pp. 85, 87), this in the time of Iroquois peril. When the Huron and Ottawa refugees reached north Michigan they were able to repel the Iroquois attack by means of impregnable fortifications. In contrast to this none of the first descriptions of villages in the upper country speak of stockades. It is only later that palisaded forts come to be mentioned among the Sauk, Fox, Winnebago and other tribes. The inference is that at least these peoples learned the art in post-white times, though whether this came from the Hurons or direct from the French leaders who themselves built a number of forts in the region cannot be clearly ascertained.

In the previous chapter it was shown how, because of war and invasion, the Menomini were a remnant of their former strength. Just what wider distribution they may have had previously, and how many villages they occupied will apparently never be known.

Any direct questioning of the Menomini today on this point yields little satisfaction, as the memories of even the oldest and best informed Indians go back only a fraction of the time. At most, certain hints may be gained from the ancient sacred lore. This, too, reveals something of the social organization.

A story recorded by Skinner and Satterlee mentions that the tribe was originally divided into "two bands". One collected earlier by Hoffman makes this more explicit:

One time the Kĭnĕ'ŭᵛ and his people lived on the southern shore . . . while the Owä'sse and his people lived on the northern shore . . . nearer the mouth of the river.[11]

The "Kĭnĕ'ŭᵛ and his people" here referred to were a num-

[11] *Meno. Inds.,* p. 217. The reference is of course to the Menominee river.

number of totemic groupings associated with mythical beings called "Thunderers" or "Thunderbirds" (Kinĕ′ŭᵛ, the Golden Eagle, was supposed to be their general representative), and the "Owä′sse (Äwä′sê) and his people" were a like set of groupings associated with the mythical ancestral "Bear" who emerged at the mouth of the Menominee river (p. 6). This suggests a dual organization or moiety system. A similar division appears in the sacred origin myth of the tribe, as shown by the following extracts from the version given to Hoffman (*Meno. Inds.*, pp. 39–41):

> The Bear (came out of the ground and) . . . was made an Indian. . . . He found himself alone, and decided to call to himself Kinĕ′ŭᵛ, the Eagle, and said, "Eagle, come to me and be my brother." Thereupon the eagle descended, and also took the form of a human being. While they were considering whom to call upon to join them, they perceived a beaver approaching. The Beaver . . . was adopted as a younger brother of the Thunderer. . . . (Then) the Sturgeon . . . was adopted by the Bear as a younger brother and servant. . . The Elk was accepted by the Thunderer as a younger brother and water-carrier . . . (and) the Crane and the Wolf became younger brothers of the Bear (also the Dog and Deer which were associated with the Wolf in a sub-group). . . . The Good Mystery made the Thunderers the laborers . . . (and) also gave (them) corn. . . . (They) were also makers of fire. . . .
>
> The Thunderers decided to visit the Bear village (at the Menominee river), . . . and when they arrived at that place they asked the Bear to join them, promising to give corn and fire in return for (wild) rice, which was the property of the Bear and Sturgeon. . . . The Bear family agreed to this, and since that time the two families have therefore lived together.

Other traditions add that the Bear people supplied the civil leadership, and the Thunder people leadership in war, likewise that the former occupied the east side of the council fire and the latter the west side. Apart, however, from such glimpses nothing was known, even to the old people of Hoffman's time, as regards the sociological functions of the two groupings. Final supporting evidence of this moiety organization is that the "Pagan" Menomini have been rather clearly segregated into Bear and Thunder settlements since coming on the reservation, indicating how the general framework of the system has been persistent even though the details have passed from usage.

A story still widely current is that long ago two "villages" or groups of Menomini quarrelled and fought, with the result that one of them moved from the ancestral region. The usual version says that these folk passed west, and are today living in one of the western states (though which is obscure, as different narrators favor one or other of eight or nine states), where they still allegedly "speak the Menomini language".[12] Hoffman records this, but he also gives what appears to be an older version telling how the two groups again became reconciled and resumed relations. This may be a localized version of a general myth; alternatively it may refer to a historically recorded dichotomy of the tribe which occurred towards the middle of the eighteenth century, this to be referred to later (p. 77).

Within each moiety was a number of patrilineal descent groups (phratries, gentes, or clans according to the terminology preferred) which in the mythology lead back to the spirit beings of air, earth, and water that formed the original ancestors of the tribe. Here again the changes of modern times make it impossible to get more than a very general picture. The origin myth above gives such an outline; yet Hoffman found that even the oldest men knew little of the structure and purpose of such groupings and their subgroupings, and today there is only the most fragmentary knowledge. An early document which purports to give the clan systems of various Indian tribes[13] lists the Menomini as divided into the following: "the large-tailed Bear, the Stag, a Kiliou—that is a species of Eagle". In 1877 Powell, official interpreter to the tribe and himself of part Menomini blood, wrote of the tribal totems: "the White Beaver, the Wolf, the Turtle, the Crane and the Bear were the principal clans—there were several lesser ones, such as the Turkey, etc."[14] Hoffman collected from his informants, one at least

[12] The theme of this story, however, is not uncommon among Indian tribes, as need not be wondered at in view of the fact that tribal dispersions over the continent must have involved a frequent hiving off of groups.

[13] "Census of Indian Tribes", (author unknown) *New York Col. Docs.*, lx, 1736.

[14] *Proceedings Wis. Hist. Soc.*, 1912.

of whom was born as early as 1827, two distinct versions: first, that there were "three phratries", with 8, 13, and 3 "gentes" respectively; and second, that there were "five phratries" with 5, 6, 4, 3 and 4 gentes respectively; he was also informed that "originally there were a greater number of totems". Skinner in 1910–11 was given a list of ten "gentes", divided into 21 "subgentes", but later he revised this list to "seven phratries" composed of 19 "gentes"; in addition he collected the names of several groupings which he calls intrusive as coming in modern times from other tribes, and even of some which were created and assumed by mixed blood children of white fathers.

It will remain for a later phase of the study to unravel the causes of such extensive disintegration of the very fundamentals of the Menomini social patterns so relatively early in the history of contact. The obvious confusion revealed here makes any comprehensive reconstruction of the old system impossible beyond saying that there were apparently at least seven main totemic descent groups included within the moieties, and these were in turn subdivided into further units.

The organization and functions of these groupings can be inferred in a general way from study of tribes in the region the ancient systems of which have been much less broken down, as for example the Winnebago and Fox.[15] But the direct evidence is fragmentary. They were evidently aggregations of individuals tracing descent in the male line to the totemic ancestors, and doubtless the linkages between the groupings were mythologically defined. It is said that an exogamic principle was practised but how it related to moieties, phratries, and gentes is uncertain. Each group had a number of names or honorary titles; some indeed are in use today. The Äwä'sê (Bear) and Kině'ŭ' (Thunder) groupings provided the leadership in their respective moieties, but what other hierarchical arrangements existed be-

[15] See Radin, *The Winnebago Tribe*, Ann. Rep. Bur. Am. Eth., 1915–16; Eggan, F.(ed.), *Social Organization of North American Tribes* (includes bibliographic references).

tween and within the groups or what specific functions may have pertained to them cannot be ascertained. At most well informed individuals today can give glimpses into the backgrounds of their own special kin group. Thus a member of the Wolf group, in speaking to the writer of the related sub-groups within it as being Wolf, Dog, and Deer, told how the Wolf came first because in the beginning "the Wolf permitted the Dog and the Deer to join him and become human".[16] The aspect of culture in which the totemic system has persisted most tenaciously is in the supernatural connection of the "pagan" folk with spirit powers and ancestors; thus each individual has his totem painted, usually upside down, on a grave-stick at his place of burial. (See Plate IV, p. 163.)

Students of the works of Hoffman and Skinner are likely to be confused by the fact that, along with material on these totemic groupings, they refer to a "band" system among the Menomini. Neither succeeded in showing the relation between the two types of organization. The band system, however, will be seen as a development in social organization emerging during the fur trade era, and not really ancient. The forces bringing it into being were likewise those which broke down the older system. In turn, the band units became obsolete as soon as a more or less sedentary reservation life was adopted.

The relation of the moiety and other totemic groupings to the village organization is naturally impossible to unravel in view of what has been said above. Nevertheless evidence is available to show the general features of community life. The Jesuits and other early whites spoke of dealing with a council of elders, and also of special leaders in war and in religious matters. In later times the Menomini asserted that the council comprised the "hereditary chiefs" or heads of the descent groups (presumably the eldest living males), with the head of the Bear group as "chairman".[17]

[16] He added that "the Deer comes last because both the Wolf and the Dog hunt it—in fact you could say that the Deer is the feedbag hung on the end!"
[17] Skinner, *Social Life*, p. 22.

It seems doubtful, however, whether the council among
the central Algonquins was so elaborate as among the Iroquoians. The accompaniment of speeches with "collars" of
wampum and progressive gifts as among the latter was
known among the Menomini by 1730, but was apparently a
practice learned in the east and brought west by the French
in their dealings with the tribes. Among the Menomini the
main ceremonial observances of the council appear to have
been connected with tobacco, as in a reception to Perrot on
the occasion of his first visit, to be quoted later (p. 54).

Besides this civil leadership there were said to be war
chiefs who won prestige through individual dreams or because of their prowess, though from such positions the civil
leaders were not barred. These persons acted as keepers
of the tribal war medicines, as public spokesmen for the
hereditary leaders, as masters of ceremonies during public
celebrations, and as "police" and guardians of the wild rice
at harvest time. War among the Menomini seems however
to have been rarely a general affair of the whole tribe but
rather a matter of small parties and sudden actions. Doubtless every youth strove to win a reputation as a warrior, and
early documents characterize the Menomini as brave fight-
ers. The warparty can be noted as an important social unit
in the old time life.

Such a political structure, however, does not appear to
have been elaborate. The Jesuit father Allouez speaks of
the Menomini as a people who "have neither laws, nor police,
nor magistrates to check disorder". Perrot refers to the
Algonquins as having as a characteristic weakness "the lack
of subordination which has always prevailed". He further
says (*Memoir,* pp. 144–45):

Ambition and vengeance are two passions which imperiously possess
the minds of the savages; self-interest carries them still further. . . . The
savage does not know what it is to obey. . . . The father does not venture
to exercise authority över his son, nor does the chief dare to give commands
to his soldier. . . . If the chiefs possess some influence over (their men)
. . . it is only through the liberal presents and feasts which they give.

This picture of individualism is, however, tempered in another of Perrot's descriptions which reveals the intimate face-to-face community life with its less overt controls over social activity; he writes:

> The Harmony which subsists among the savages is in truth displayed not only by their words, but in their actual conduct. The chiefs who are the most influential and well-to-do are on equal footing with the poorest, and even with the boys—with whom they converse as they do with persons of discretion. They warmly support and take in hand the cause of one another among friends; and when there are any disputes they proceed therein with great moderation. . . . Seldom are there quarrels among them. When some erring person commits an evil deed . . . the entire village takes an interest in the settlement. . . . If any person encounters a grievous accident or a great misfortune, the entire village takes an interest in it, and goes to console him.

The Jesuits gave many similar accounts of Algonquian life; thus of the Montagnais, one of the tribes whose daily round was intimately described by the fathers, it was said:

> You note, in the first place, a great love and union, which they are careful to cultivate by means of their marriages, of their presents, of their feasts, and of their frequent visits. On returning from their fishing, their hunting, their trading, they exchange many gifts; if they have thus obtained something unusual . . . they make a feast to the whole village with it. Their hospitality toward all sorts of strangers is remarkable. . . . I do not know if anything similar in this regard is to be found elsewhere. (viii, 127).

This seems in marked contrast to the very individualistic picture of Menomini society as described by Skinner in later days. Perhaps the difference could be explained somewhat by reference to a remark made by Perrot just a century later.

> At the present time, it is evident that these savages (who have intercourse with the French) are fully as selfish and avaricious as formerly they were hospitable.—in Blair, i, 134.

As with innumerable small groups the world over the force of public opinion, and the benefits to be gained by adherence to the rules surrounding economic, social, ceremonial and like activities, these backed in many cases of course by supernatural sanctions, made for relatively harmonious community living. A "code of blood vengeance" is frequently referred to in the tribal lore and mentioned in some of the early records, and this doubtless came into play after inter-tribal or inter-group killings in order to even up unbalanced scores—an example of the much-discussed "reciprocal" principle in primitive law.

Far more is known about the smaller groupings within Menomini society, the household and immediate kinsfolk, than about these larger units. The lore and early documents give some intimate glimpses, while what appear to be ancient patterns of individual and family living have persisted right to modern times.

The first recorded description of a Menomini household is given by a trader, Radisson, who visited the upper lakes region in 1654:

> We came to a cottage of an ancient witty man, that had a great familie and many children, his wife old, nevertheless handsome. They weare of a nation called Malhonmines; that is the nation of Oats.

This description could be applied directly to a number of Menomini households today, for the patriarchal home is by no means extinct. Especially familiar is the term "witty" for the Menomini old and young are inveterate jokers. The Menomini "family" was a larger and more inclusive kinship group than that typical of modern white society, and appears to have been the basic unit of economic life and effort. According to early Indian censuses of the region women outnumbered the men considerably, one document says by "four to one". Whether this represents the normal condition in pre-white times, or came about as a result of the decimating wars spoken of in the last chapter must remain a matter for speculation. Polygyny was practiced, according to a statement by the Jesuit father Allouez, but its extent is not known; the stability of marriage ties is also obscure. The Jesuits were somewhat more specific about marriage customs as regards some of the other tribes than in their descriptions of the Menomini. The Fox, for example, were said to have "commonly four wives, some having . . . as many as ten" (*Jes. Rel.,* liv, p. 219). The permanence of

marital ties appears to have varied.   Thus Perrot says that
while the Iroquois make little of the marriage tie, the
"Outaouas marry their wives in order to remain with them
throughout life."   (In Blair, i, p. 64; he also gives an account of marriage customs.)   The reason he gives is that if
a man should put away his wife without cause, all her relatives would set upon him.   Father Allouez received a very
bad impression of the peoples of the upper country:

> All the devotion of the men is directed toward securing many wives,
> and changing them whenever they choose; that of the women toward leaving
> their husbands; and that of the girls toward a life of profligacy.—l, p. 291.

He attributes this situation to the orgies that end their
sacrifices and ceremonials.   The first observers among the
Illinois found that facial disfigurement was the usual punishment for "unfaithfulness", but apparently this applied
only to women.

Marriages were arranged between kin groups, perhaps
as the result of liaisons arising from nightly courting adventures of the young men such as are spoken of in folk tales;
reciprocal presents were exchanged by the relatives.   A
young married couple usually lived in the lodge of the hus-
band's parents.   Children were given very great freedom.
Each household or its constituent individuals possessed an
amount of property, such as ritual objects, canoes, and
ornaments—but here again the details are obscure.

The Menomini kinship structure and terminology have
been recorded in outline by Skinner, and need not be repeated here;[18] the information he collected bears the marks
of great antiquity.   Among noteworthy features are: a
largely classificatory system of terminology; the importance
of the mother's brother, sister's son relationship; rigid distinctions between parallel and cross relatives; restraints in
regard to parents-in-law; and the prescription of a "joking
relationship" between certain classes of relatives.   Kin

[18] *Soc. Life*, pp. 32–34.   For its place within the wider scheme of Indian
kinship systems, see Olsen, R. LeR., *Clan and Moiety in America*, and Spier, L.,
Distribution of Kinship Systems, University of Washington, 1925.   Compare
also Eggan, F. (ed.) *The Social Organization of North American Tribes*.

linkages of course merged in the wider setting into clan (gens) ties, and the mythical totemic ancestor and apparently indeed his living animal replicas (bears, wolves, etc.) were counted as kinsmen.

Religion and Ceremonial

Very naturally the religious and ritual life of the Indian peoples, including the Menomini, aroused great interest among early observers, especially the Jesuits. Their comments, together with extensive references in the ancient mythology and other lore, open the way to a fairly sure characterization of the essentials of the old system of beliefs and practices.

Even so, reconstruction presents some difficulties. Apart from elements in the data collected by Hoffman and other ethnologists which are obviously of post-white origin (to be seen later), there is the possibility that more subtle changes have taken place here as in other aspects of Menomini life. Pertinent to this is a quotation from a missionary journal of the nineteenth century, the *Annales de la propagation de la foi,* as follows:

> Today the Outaouais (Ottawa) and the other tribes of the West— Maloumines, Sakis, Renards, and Ouinipegs (Menomini, Sauk, Fox, and Winnebago)—cite, as belonging to their primitive beliefs, certain facts of which neither Perrot nor the Jesuit missionaries found, even one hundred years ago, the slightest trace in the traditions of those peoples.—Vol. iv, quoted by Tailhan in his edition of Perrot's *Memoir* (1864).

Our safest starting place therefore is undoubtedly the Jesuit records. The following are the main references:

> (The Menomini and other tribes of the upper lakes) all acknowledge various sorts of divinities to whom they offer frequent sacrifices. These People have Gods as had the Pagans of old,—having them in the skies, in the air, on the earth, in the woods, in the water, and even in hell. . . . Those of our savages who are regarded as intelligent among their fellows hold the belief that, besides the sun and thunder,—which they recognize as the Gods of the Sky and of the air,—each species of animals, fishes, and birds, has a special genius who cares for it, watches over its safety, and protects it. . . .
>
> There are certain animals to whose genii they pay far more respect than to others. . . . It passes belief what veneration they have for the Bear;

for after killing one in hunting, they are wont to hold a solemn feast over it with very special ceremonies . . . (a description is given). To secure their favors, they practice devotions of various kinds, of which the following is the most customary and the most important. They pass four or five days without eating, in order that, having their heads weakened by this fast, they may see in their dreams some one of those Divinities, on whom they think, depends all their welfare. . . . They are taught from The age of four or Five years to blacken Their faces, to fast, and to dream . . . being led to believe that thus they will be successful in fishing, hunting, and war . . . (Besides Dreamers there are) Jugglers.—*Jes. Rel.*, lvi, pp. 121–129, lvii, pp. 265–67.

In the same accounts another list of the outstanding "deities" includes, besides the sun, the thunder (thunderbird) and the bear, a mythical being called "missipissi," the underground panther, and "Michabous" or Mä'näbus, the famed Algonquian culture-hero sometimes called Hiawatha or the Great Rabbit; one of the early travellers speaks, too, of "a kind of monstrous serpent", doubtless what Skinner later called the horned hairy snake.[19]

It is unnecessary to reproduce here the fairly extensive material concerning these and other Powers, major and minor, given by Hoffman and Skinner. Supernatural forces played a vital role in the Menomini universe. Just as the original totemic spirit beings metamorphosed into man so it was believed that humans could change into, or marry animals, and vice versa. A newborn infant showing unusual characteristics or behavior would be specially watched on the chance that it might be a reincarnated ancestor, or even some deity (perhaps a "Thunderer" in the case of a boy or one of the "Sky Sisters" in that of a girl); the truth might be discovered either through the dreams of the parents or else by calling in a medicine-man. It will be seen later that the fear elements in Menomini belief have tended to remain tenaciously: included were the dread of spirits unappeased, of unlaid ghosts, of "witchcraft", and of the non-observance of essential customs such as the segregation of women during menstruation, the usages connected with tobacco, and

---

[19] Extensive references to such "Powers" among other Indian peoples is found in the Jesuit and other records, and all seem to have been known more or less widely over North America. See *Handbook of American Indian Tribes.*

the right disposal of remains or portions of animals at certain feasts to ensure success for future hunts.

Most of the benefits and regulations of human living, according to the sacred lore, came by way of the primal activities of the culture-hero, Mä'näbus. Through him the deities gave to humans not only the tribal rituals but also the right to use Power in the form of "medicines" such as roots, herbs, shells, and charms:

> The way of the Indian in the past, and his custom was this, that he did things even as the spirit powers gave it him to do. And it was that nephew of us all, Me'napus, who first was given these herbs and roots, in all their various forms and as they taste. Then he in turn gave them on, that all the Indians might use them whenever they were ill, and grow well from their use of them. And as the Indian knows it, is to use these herbs in curing people. Now this earth is the grandmother of us all; it is from her that these roots spring forth which this Indian is to use.—Bloomfield, *Menomini Texts,* p. 9.

The religio-medical lore of the Menomini has been set out in some detail by Dr. Huron Smith; it would seem that most of the medicines, as the white man calls them, and the particular songs and rituals appropriate for their gathering, preparation, and use, are of great antiquity. This lore was always the sacred possession of individuals who had received it by "purchase" or else through dreams, and in turn passed it on to others at a worthy price.

As indicated in the Jesuit accounts above, the central experience of Menomini religion was the dream revelation. Another Jesuit writer says of the Indians in the region:

> They look upon their dreams as ordinances and irrevocable decrees, the execution of which it is not permitted without crime to delay. . . . A dream will take away from them sometimes their whole year's provisions. It prescribes their feasts, their dances, their songs, their games,—in a word, the dream does everything.—*Jes. Rel.,* x, pp. 169–71.

It was indicated that children from an early age were encouraged to fast and dream. The special crisis for boys and girls came at puberty in what ethnologists speak of as the "dream fast". Each was placed by the parents in a special structure at a secluded spot where, after perhaps eight or ten days of starvation, with face blackened, or after several such vigils, he or she might receive supernatural visions or visitations. By these, or rather by their interpretation, was determined in large measure the future destiny of the individual in the sight of the Powers and of fellow tribesfolk, his or her rights and duties in the religious sphere, fortunes for good or evil, and adult status generally. Further dream fasts would also be undertaken throughout life whenever revelations were desired, particularly as regards food getting and warfare. This importance of individual dreams seems to have given a marked personal character to religion and ritual, on the one hand excluding the possibility of developing highly institutionalized religious forms and on the other giving a potential of variation that was to be significant in the course of modern change.[20]

Various material aids were used in religion and magic. The so-called "sweat lodge" with its steam bath was apparently a means of purification as well as of personal enjoyment. "Medicine bundles", receptacles of skin or matting containing an assortment of medicines and charms, and used with accompanying rituals and songs in order to secure success in hunting, war, and the like, undoubtedly go back to antiquity, as being mentioned in the early documents. Tobacco was all-important when approaching the Powers, and sacred pipes, drums and other artifacts had a place in ceremonial. It is told that the Indian gave his most precious possessions in religious sacrifices; his food supply would be disposed of freely for ritual feasts; and he would endure the utmost personal rigor and discipline when the favor of the supernatural was sought.

The most puzzling question connected with this phase of Menomini life is the extent to which the tribe had a super-individual structure of religion. Undoubtedly those persons who were notably favored by the Powers in their dream revelations were called upon by others to "consult the Demon", as the Jesuits put it. "Dreamers" and also "Jugglers" are spoken of in the early records, while as seen above the skills

[20] Refer to *Jes. Rel.*, liv, pp. 139–43 for a contemporary account of the dream fast among peoples of the upper lakes region.

of the "medicine-man" were passed from generation to
generation according to dream revelations or else through
purchase by novitiates. There were also ceremonial feasts,
games and dances in which presumably large groups par-
ticipated.

In the later days observers found among the Menomini and
some of the other Woodland tribes an elaborate secret society, in Menomini terminology called the Mitawin or "Grand
Medicine Lodge", also two less organized cults, the Wa'bano
and Je''sako, and traces of a malevolent association of
"Witches"— to the English-speaking Menomini of today a
dealer in black magic whether male or female is known by
the word "witch".

The Mitawin lodge has been adequately described, with
its elaborate rituals of initiation, renewal of magic, and
other ceremonies not unlike those of the Masonic lodges of
white peoples.[21] It is puzzling to place, however, because it
combines features that bear marks of great antiquity with
others obviously intrusive. The student of the very early
documents will find no references to anything approximating to such an organization; yet in later times it occupied a
central place in the religion of the Menomini and other tribes
among which it existed. Either this important institution
was kept entirely from the Jesuit fathers and other recorders, a strange happening since they set out in considerable
detail the religious observances of a number of the tribes
concerned, always emphasizing the unusual, or else it had
not developed to its later elaborate ritual, or at least had not
been diffused geographically as widely as at present. The
Menomini lodge appears to have always been subordinate to
the lodge of the Chippewa, using their language considerably
in the ceremonial and referring to them as a higher authority on the lore, the inference being that the institution was
taken over in part or wholly from that tribe. A tempting
hypothesis, at least suggested by certain records, is that it
represents a religious cult comprising both Indian and white
elements which arose in the early days of contact, and so is

[21] See Hoffman, pp. 66–137; Skinner, *Med. Cer.*, pp. 15–184.

akin to many such religious movements that have emerged
in frontier regions the world over where indigenous and
alien cultures have come together—Africa, China, the Pacific Islands, and so on.

The first reference to the Mitawin in the early records
seems to be in the Jesuit *Relations* of 1636 (x, pp. 205–09),
which tells of a "brotherhood" having as its central ceremony "killing . . . by charms which they throw at each
other". The group concerned was the Huron tribe, but the
ritual was being performed among them for the first time, as
the result of a dream; the performers comprised "eighty
persons including six women" invited from a neighboring
tribe, possibly the Ottawa. The same ceremony is referred
to nine years later (*Jes. Rel.,* xxx, p. 23) as "the most celebrated in the country". Nothing like it, however, appears
in the records of religious practice among the tribes among
whom by the first decades of the nineteenth century it was
strongest: the Chippewa, Potawatomi, Sauk, Fox, Winnebago and Menomini. In 1718 there is a reference to what
may be the lodge among the Potawatomi as follows: "Often
the old men dance the *medelinne;* they look like a band of
sorcerers. All this is done at night" (*Memoir,* in *Wis. Hist.,
Coll.,* xvi, pp. 367–68, author unknown). An interesting detail is that the central sacred object in the ritual is a cowrie-
shell, this not found in the inland region but a popular object of trade in early days of white contact. A final point
is that the Mitawin is not mentioned in the older folklore of
the Menomini—a fact which leads Skinner to classify it as
an institution "of later date" in the tribal history.[22] All in
all, therefore, there is at least a strong suggestion that the
lodge represents the first of a number of religious and mystical movements among the Indian peoples that were reactions to mission and other white encroachment, the best
known of which are the Tecumseh "rebellion", the Ghost
dance, and the Dream dance. Based essentially on an Indian
mythology and paraphernalia, it nevertheless may bear the
marks of white influence especially in its set organization

[22] *Folklore,* p. 228.

and elaborate ritual. It might be pictured as being developed among one tribe about 1630 and "catching on" with remarkable rapidity; then later assuming, just as has the Dream dance to be seen in due course, all the earmarks of a permanent and ancient institution.

Passing now to other religious groupings known to later days, the Wabano can be noted as comprising a number of medicine-men who claimed immunity from fire, also other special powers. The Je'sako, apparently the "Jugglers" of the Jesuit records, were diviners and doctors who worked in a special lodge or "jugglery" where they consulted the spirits. Both the Wabano and Je'sako, also the "witches", seem to have worked more or less entirely as individuals, and probably represent the older Indian religion back of the Mitawin. Those practising the black art were considered to be in league with the evil Powers, and could change shape, make themselves invisible, steal the luck of hunters, and despatch objects or spirits into the bodies of victims at will.

Among essential ceremonial elements in Menomini religion were games and dances. It was written of the men of the neighboring Illinois tribe that "when not engaged in war or in hunting, their time is spent either in games, or at feasts, or in dancing".[23] The chief Menomini games were lacrosse, played by the men; shinney, and bowl and dice, both women's games; also the so-called "moccasin" and cup and pin games (see Skinner). All had sacred meaning, being played in honor of deities, to comfort departed relatives, to cure sickness and for similar religious purposes. They were also widespread among the tribes of the region.

There are recorded in the early documents a number of different kinds of feasts, most elaborate among which seem to have been the "bear" feast held at the killing of that sacred animal, an "eat all" feast, and special feasts at times of success in food getting. According to Skinner the Menomini had numerous ceremonial dances, including those he has called war, braves, victory, and scalp dances, periodic dances in honor of sacred bundles, a youth's first gamekill

23 *Jes. Rel.*, lxvii, p. 167.

feast and dance, harvest, all animals, rain, dog, and tobacco or calumet dances. The last mentioned is especially interesting, since Perrot, the first visitor to the tribe, tells how the Menomini warriors "danced the calumet to the sound of the drums".[24] Perrot also observed that songs sung at feasts and dances were the peculiar possession of individuals, and could not be sung freely by everyone, a fact confirmed by later writers. The fundamental of all chant, dance and ritual was the rhythmic beat of a drum, accompanied usually by rattles or striking of sticks. These all have frequent references in the early documents, as singing (*Jes. Rel.*, vi, pp. 183–85), dancing (xliv, p. 303), drums and rattles (vi, pp. 185–87). Two kinds of drum seem to have been used, namely the "tambourine" and the "water" drum. One rather unappreciative father describes the Indian singing as being much as if "the demons and the damned were to sing in hell".

The beliefs and ritual associated with death can appropriately close this sketch. These have proved among the most tenacious elements of the old culture. A corpse was painted with red to signify happiness at the privilege of the soul in departing to the spirit land. Burial took place apparently within the day, sometimes on a scaffolding, sometimes beneath logs on the ground, or perhaps in a mound. The ghost was believed to linger round the grave indefinitely and to be capable of having influence on the living; but the soul or personality, it was thought, passed on a four day journey to the spirit land. To help the latter as attendants en route, the souls of warriors slain in battle to the number

[24] The first records of the Calumet or "tobacco pipe" dance speak of it as practised by the Illinois and certain Siouan tribes. Apparently it was unknown among the Chippewa, Ottawa and other Algonquins to the east, for father Allouez described it as something unique when he first met with it in 1666. (*Jes. Rel.*, li, pp. 47–49.) Perrot said of the Calumet: "The savages believe that the sun gave it to the Panys (Pawnee), and that since then it has been communicated from village to village". (Blair, i, p. 186.) Presumably it spread east to the Ottawa and other tribes as a result of later intercourse. For a full description of the Calumet ceremony, and the beginnings of its use by whites as an object of mediation, refer to Marquette's experiences among the Illinois, in *Jes. Rel.*, lix, p. 115 on.

of four or more were customarily invoked in the course of the funeral ceremony by persons who could claim to have killed such; likewise appropriate weapons and utensils for the journey were placed with the body. A widow is said to have observed a period of four years of mourning, while close relatives were for a time ceremonially unclean. In spite of fears connected with the dead, visits of mourning were made to the burial place, and offerings of food, feastings, games, and other ritual activities were consummated there to keep the ghost contented with its lot.[25]

Summary

Such a critical survey, necessary as it is for scientific accuracy, reveals many gaps in the evidence available for reconstructing the old Menomini life, and offers various puzzles as to whether this or that cultural element bearing apparent marks of antiquity is really old. As, in the chapters that follow, the modern changes are traced, it will be possible to understand further the problems here raised, and the circumstances under which some phases of Menomini culture tended to persist while others became obsolete or were modified. The scene is now set for the white man to walk, or rather paddle, upon the stage.

[25] See Hoffman, p. 239; Skinner, *Soc. Life*, pp. 63–71. No early references to Menomini death, burial and mourning customs could be found, but there is an amount of material concerning other tribes. Two main types of burial are spoken of among tribes to the east, bark burials on a scaffold, and earth burials, especially in the flexed position. One clan of the Ottawa was said to have burnt their dead (*Jes. Rel.*, lxvii, p. 157). Scaffold burial seems to have been predominant among the Iroquoian tribes, but merely as a preliminary to the real earth burial at the important periodic "feast of the dead" (*Jes. Rel.*, x, pp. 143 on). The Menomini say that in old days a corpse was taken out through the wall of the lodge, and every effort was made to keep the spirit from frequenting the homes of relatives. The Jesuits described just such ceremonies among the first Indians they met with on the continent (as *Jes. Rel.*, l, p. 261). To the Menomini, just as to whites, "black is a sign of grief and mourning".

III. THE PERIOD OF FRENCH ASCENDANCY

For some two hundred years after the first white man entered Menomini territory the Indian tribes of the great lakes region were under the influence of governments whose dominant interest in the area was the wealth represented in its furbearing animals.

The incoming European wanted furs; he also wanted to use the Indian as a fur getter. The Menomini region became in turn the political possession of France, Britain and the newly formed United States. Such changes in white domination, however, meant on the whole little to the Indian. To him the furtrader, regardless of nationality, became a satisfier of new wants. Over these two centuries the white man used the Indian and his environment, and the Indian the white man and his trade stores, fairly much to the satisfaction of both parties. This mutual exploitation resulted in certain adjustments by those whites who went among the Indians, and a vast readjustment by the Indians as a result of new and stimulating contacts. The breaking down of isolation from the non-American world, and also of such isolation as was existing between Indian tribes themselves, had far reaching effects.

For the first century, that is until 1760, the Menomini were exclusively under French influence, and for most of that time their territory was counted as a political possession of France. The impact of the French discoverers, traders, Jesuit missionaries, and later soldiers and political leaders upon the tribe, also incidentally upon the other tribes of the region, forms the theme of this section.

EARLY DISCOVERERS AND TRADERS

The emergence of new needs, particularly a desire for guns and ammunition, quickly prepared the Indians of the upper country for French penetration and commerce. Under circumstances already reviewed, Chequamegon Bay and

later La Baye (Green Bay of today) became gathering
places for traders and Indian peoples, particularly the latter
place after a portage route was discovered between lake
Michigan and the Mississippi river along the Fox and Wisconsin rivers.

The first recorded visit of a white man to the ancestral
Menomini village on the river Menominee was that of the
trader Perrot:

At that time (probably 1667) there was war between the Tribe (Potawatomi) and their neighbors, the Malhomines (this following some inter-
tribal killings). . . . Perot, who was desirous of making their acquaintance,
offered to mediate peace between them. When he arrived within half a
league of the (Menomini) Village, he sent a man to tell them that a
Frenchman was coming to visit them; this news caused universal joy. All
the youths came at once to meet him, bearing their weapons and their warlike adornments, all marching in file, with frightful contortions and yells;
this was the most honorable reception that they thought it possible to give
him. He was not uneasy, but fired a gun in the air as far away as he could
see them; this noise, which seemed to them so extraordinary, caused them
to halt suddenly, gazing at the sun in most ludicrous attitudes. After he
had made them understand that he had come not to disturb their repose,
but to form an alliance with them, they approached him with many gesticu-
lations. The Calumet was presented to him; and when he was ready to
proceed to the Village, one of the savages stooped down in order to carry
Perot upon his shoulders; but . . . he . . . refused. . . . He was escorted
with assiduous attention; they vied with one another in clearing the path.
. . . The women and children who had heard "the Spirit"—for thus they
called the gun—had fled into the woods. The men assembled in the cabin
of the leading war Chief, when they danced the Calumet to the sound of
the drum . . . (he presents them with a gun and a kettle, offers French
alliance, and seeks the peace he has come for with the Potawatomi. After
ceremonials, in which the father of a murdered man renounces blood vengeance, this man says:) that he attached himself wholly to the French . . .
that he asked only the protection of the French, from whom they hoped for
life and for obtaining all that is necessary to man.—La Potherie in *Wis.
Hist. Colls.,* xvi, pp. 35–36.

The Menomini also have their stories passed down concerning the arrival of the white man. According to a version
given several years ago by one of the best informed old
people of the tribe:

At one time . . . a certain man was addressed by the Spirit: "Now
then, very soon now you will see someone coming here over the water. He

will be the father of you all; all manner of things he will give you, for all too great is your want." Thereupon he assembled the people and told them. . . . When the time came, they all assembled. Then truly, at noon, something came sailing toward them far out upon the water. When it had come near, the people were frightened. When they arrived, then in the shallow water the white man launched little wooden boats and embarked in them and landed from them. "Spirit people are these whom we see!" said the Indians in fear, and went off in all directions to hide in the brush. "Do not be frightened, my children!" said the white man. As though from old did he understand his words, who had been spoken to by the Spirit. All came and stood there, looking at those people.

Then the others gave them all kinds of things to eat, and gave them kettles; garments to wear, and hatchets, and all manner of things they gave them, including guns. They were frightened when they heard a gun. When it went off with noise, the Indian flung it away and ran for dear life. So now the Indians lived well, possessing all these things, such as garments, knives, kettles, and hatchets. With these things now they had a good life.— Bloomfield, *Menomini Texts*, pp. 77–79.

The boats here mentioned of course reflect a later memory, for the first whites used Indian canoes; the logical white mind, too, may not credit the prescience of "a certain man." Yet the tale is rather typical of such interpretative memories passed down in the Indian lore.

In both accounts there is an interesting reference to the profound impression made by the gun. Another outstanding memory of first contact preserved in Menomini story is of the second great magic of the trader, liquor. It is still related today, with all the humor and action that goes into a Menomini tale, how none of the chiefs would touch this mysterious firewater, so three old men were selected to experiment. At first these reeled and fell apparently dead, but, soon reviving, they told of visions seen and delightful sensations experienced. Later documents will show clearly that the chiefs and people were more than convinced of its desirability from then forward. It is often referred to by the Indians as the "milk" given by the governor, their parent, to his children; it came also to have an important religious significance, as an aid in securing the all important dreams and visions.

The coming of Perrot and others to the Menomini region was made possible only through the establishment of peace between the French and the Iroquois. From 1663 a new era had commenced for the French colony in America. Troops were sent across the Atlantic to crush the Iroquois, and agricultural settlers to develop the valley of the St. Lawrence. Just what havoc the Iroquois had wrought upon the tribes allied to the French and upon the tiny group of French missionaries, traders and colonists cannot be realized except through the perusal of such documents as the *Jesuit Relations*. Devastation, torture, cannibalism, slaughter and annihilation of whole villages and even tribes, ravages right up to the gates of Montreal itself, had "reduced to extremities . . . this poor afflicted land." In 1664 a vigorous invasion of Iroquois territory brought their envoys suing for peace. The same year New Netherlands, the main base of supply for firearms, was ceded to Britain, then the ally of France. This marks the real turning point in the history of the upper country and of the Menomini, for as the bands of Potawatomi, Sauk, Fox, Miami, Mascouten, Kickapoo, Huron, Ottawa, Chippewa and others settled down, they, together with the Menomini, Winnebago, and many other tribes but dimly heard of on the western prairie formed a great potential group for French trading and mission activity.

In 1668 Perrot and his fellow traders took the first cargo of furs from La Baye. Three years later the tribes of the lakes region became French "subjects" by a formal act of annexation performed at Sault St. Marie. Apparently the traders, and in some tribes the Jesuits, had acquired sufficient influence to persuade some fourteen Indian "nations" to be represented at this ceremony, to receive gifts, and sign their marks to the mysterious document. Among them were the Menomini.

A period began in which traders, officially licensed, or unlicensed, flocked to the northwest. For the most part they came and went without record, bringing in goods and carrying out to New France or even to the British posts the precious furs so desired in Europe. In 1673, Joliet and Marquette made their official exploration of the Mississippi river, crossing by an age old Indian trail, the Fox and Wisconsin rivers. Five years later two famous explorer-exploiters were sent into the upper country, Duluth and La Salle. This marked a recognition by the French of a new phase in the furtrade. Instead of flotillas of western Indians making the long journey to barter in the lower settlements, goods were now being taken inland by white traders who wintered with the Indians and established trading forts at strategic points. Their chief stocks in trade were firearms and brandy, through which they stimulated the Indians to hunt the furbearing animals, particularly the beaver, ever more vigorously.

In these early days, La Baye became one of the main trading centers both for licensed whites and for the outlaws called "coureurs du bois", and the valley of the Fox became a concentration point for many tribes. It was calculated in 1677 that some twenty thousand Indians lived within a short radius. But the limited resources of the area could not support so many for long, and their bands, especially those of the Miami and Mascouten, soon began to scatter once more.

La Baye was made, too, a center of mission effort. Before considering the work of the Jesuits among the Menomini an incident of the time may be mentioned to illustrate the rather precarious nature of Indian-white intercourse and the way misunderstandings could arise between the two peoples. The records show that a quarrel took place between whites and Indians in which some servants of the Jesuits were killed, and interestingly enough the Menomini were accused of the deed. La Potherie writes of this:

The Nations at Baye des Puants (*i.e.*, Bay of the Winnebago, that is Green Bay) no longer dared to go down to Montreal after the Missionaries' servants had been assassinated upon their lands; for they were persuaded that our customs must be like their own, which allow them to avenge a death not only upon the evildoer, but also upon his nearest Relatives, his Friends, or his neighbors. Some of the more courageous among them exposed themselves to this danger; but, seeing that the murders they had committed on every side were left unpunished, they conceived a contempt for our Nation, and continued to plunder and massacre all stragglers, whom they found.

A contagious malady suddenly appeared at the Bay, which caused great mortality. . . . In the midst of this affliction, our Missionaries found themselves in great danger; for, since the Savages are extremely superstitious, they imagined that the Fathers had cast upon them some spell of witchcraft, in order to avenge the death of their People.—La Potherie in *Wis. Hist. Colls.*, vii, p. 101.

At this crucial time of misunderstanding which so threatened French prestige, the trader Perrot was sent to the Bay and his influence was sufficiently strong to quell the disaffection. Restitution was later gained for the dead, thus making the lives of whites in the northwest safe once more.

The Work of the Jesuits

On the heels of the discoverers and traders, even in some areas ahead of them, came Jesuit missionaries from France to work among the Indian tribes. Starting on the east coast in 1610, their missions and their influence moved westwards, especially after the peace of 1664. Their work was facilitated by the fact that the dialect of the Chippewa became a *lingua franca* among the lake tribes as a result of the need for a language of common intercourse.

The Jesuits had a short but enthusiastic contact with the Menomini and other tribes of La Baye. The first father to arrive among them was Claude Allouez, in the spring of 1669. Apparently one of the reasons for his coming was a request by the Potawatomi that he should "curb some young Frenchmen who, being among them for the purposes of trading, were threatening and maltreating them." Allouez has left an interesting account of his visits to the various tribes. Of the Menomini he wrote:

On the sixth, I paid a visit to the Oumalouminek . . . and found them at their River in small numbers, the young people being still in the woods. This Nation has been almost exterminated by the wars. I had difficulty in understanding them, but in time made the discovery that their language is

Algonquian, although much corrupted. They succeeded in understanding me better than I understood them. After making a little present to the Elders, I proclaimed the Gospel to them, which they admired and heard with respect. On the ninth, the Elders invited me to their council, and there made me a present, with an expression of thanks for my having come to visit them. . . . "Take heart," they said to me; "instruct us often, and teach us to speak to him who has made all things."—*Jes. Rel.*, liv, p. 235.

Allouez returned the following year with his father-superior, and arrangements were made for a permanent mission station on the Fox river. This was started in 1671, and with Allouez came a younger co-worker, father André, who was allotted as his sphere of work the coastal tribes including the Menomini. Allouez wrote in his further reports:

All these Nations have their fields of Indian corn, squashes, beans, and tobacco. . . . The Savages of this region are more than usually barbarous; they are without ingenuity, and do not know how to make even a bark dish or a ladle; they commonly use shells. They are grasping and avaricious to an extraordinary degree, and sell their little commodities at a high price, because they have only what is barely necessary. The season in which we first arrived among them was not favorable to us; they were all in a needy condition, and very little able to give us any assistance, so that we suffered hunger . . . (yet two pages further on he remarks:) Bustards, Ducks, Swans, and Geese are in great number on these Lakes and Rivers—the wild oats on which they live, attracting them thither. There are large and small Stags, Bears, and Beavers in great abundance. . . . To all the advantages of this place may be added the fact of its being the great—and the only— thoroughfare for all the surrounding Nations, who maintain a constant intercourse either in visiting or trading. Hence it was that we turned our eyes thither, with a view to placing our Chapel in the midst of more than ten different Nations, who can furnish us over fifteen thousand souls to instruct.—*Jes. Rel.*, lvi, pp. 67, 69, 121–29.

The work of André, which was predominantly among the Menomini, continued for some fourteen years. His first experiences among the tribe are related as follows:

The Father had already assailed them vigorously on account of their vices, and especially their superstitions, during several months which he spent with them last summer; but wishing to devote the whole winter to the work, he set out on the 15th of December, to repair thither. . . .

(After nearly losing his life in the ice) he reached the spot where the Savages were,—one of whose chiefs offered him a bag of acorns, to regale him well after so much toil. This was not to be refused, being a present of no small account among these people, who have no more delicious dish during the winter, when they are unsuccessful in hunting or fishing.

The Father's first care was to visit all the cabins, teach the children, and explain on every occasion the mysteries of our religion. The days were all too short for satisfying the holy curiosity of all these people, who did not give him leisure even to take his meals until very late; or to perform his devotions, except in some remote spot, whither they persisted in following him. . . .

The reason why he was so eagerly sought was found in certain spiritual songs that he was wont to have the children sing to French airs, which pleased these Savages extremely. . . . This success . . . made him resolve to assail the men through the children, and to combat idolatry with souls of extreme innocence. In short, he composed some songs against the superstitions that we have mentioned, and against the vices most opposed to Christianity; and after teaching the children to sing them to the accompaniment of a sweet toned flute, he went everywhere with these little Savage musicians, to declare war on Jugglers, Dreamers, and those who had several wives. . . . It must not however be thought that one can repress . . . decry . . . throw reproach . . . and wage open warfare . . . without receiving occasional affronts among people who have neither laws, nor police, nor magistrates to check disorder.—*Jes. Rel.*, lvi, pp. 129 et seq.

Equally important are the actual letters of André written from the field. The following are the main and typical selections:

They are taught from The age of four or Five years to blacken Their faces, to fast, and to dream of some false God. . . . I found no better way of compelling Them to clean their faces than to show them The painting of the Devil, to whom they made themselves similar. . . .

I have had no trouble this year with the savages. None of them have been angry with me because I decried the false divinity of the sun, of thunder, of the bear, of missipissi (the underground panther), of michabous (Mä'näbus), and of Their dreams, nor because I spoke against superstitious feasts and Against the Jugglers. They had no objections to cover themselves before me. . . . There were even some who fasted without blackening themselves, telling me that they fasted because they thought God would make Them spear fish. . . . Several sturgeon and bear feasts were also given, but in a fashion that led me to entertain good hopes for the adults.—*Jes. Rel.*, lvii, pp. 265–87.

Among the Savages of these countries, they (the Menomini) have manifested the most affection for Christianity, especially after an unexpected blessing that God granted them in connection with their fishing. . . . (He recounts how the people had on a pole a sacrifice to the Sun, since sturgeon were not entering the river as expected. He persuaded them to allow him to replace it with his crucifix.)

On the following morning, sturgeon entered the river in such great abundance that these poor people were delighted. . . . After that, their confidence in Prayer and their desire to learn it made them so docile and so attentive to me that I was astonished; and although, as a rule, I called only the children to me to pray, the adults themselves listened to me very attentively, and repeated in a low tone what we said aloud, while either praying or singing. But it was chiefly in the evening, when neither the men nor the women were any longer engaged in fishing, that we gathered greater numbers together to pray to God in the chapel. All the elders, except three, came there. Several women were very assiduous in their attendance, a thing that I had not yet observed. . . . I had ample evidence of (their fervor) in the obedience which they showed me, and in their docility in removing the black from their faces and in breaking their superstitious fast . . . and before setting out for war, they offered no feasts to the devil, nor did they dream any dreams, according to their ancient custom. But they addressed themselves to God, saying: "We obey thee; we love Prayer; grant us life." I myself was astonished at such universal obedience. . . . I had previously employed every means imaginable to induce them to abandon (these superstitions) ; all my efforts had until then been almost fruitless. . . . The chief juggler . . . showed that he took pleasure in my instruction. This man had an exceedingly great confidence in thunder as a powerful divinity; and, far from hiding when he heard it rumble, he did all that he could to meet it. One day, when it rained, he ran about in the woods, entirely naked, crying aloud and invoking the thunder in his songs. . . . I told him that he had reason to fear lest God, who uses lightning, as a hunter does his gun, should discharge it at him, and make him die instantly. He promised me that he would no longer invoke the thunder.— *Jes. Rel.*, lvii, pp. 273–89.

These quotations will suffice to illustrate the type of work and approach made by André, and the resulting achievement;[1] they also provide the fullest records available of a contemporary nature for the study of Menomini life.

André stayed in the region apparently until 1684, this about the time the incident of the killing of the mission servants took place. But the peak of Jesuit effort in the northwest was the period 1679–80. From then on, the number of workers in the field dwindled, and the personnel declined in worth and fervor.[2] The work became stereotyped, while

[1] Father Marquette also comments on the Menomini mission in *Jes. Rel.*, lix, 95.

[2] This decline was due mainly to historic quarrels between that Order and the Pope and a decided break between their supporters and those favoring trade exploitation in New France.

their avowed policy of keeping the Indians in "their sim-
plicity and ignorance, only to be taught to worship the true
God" was doomed to failure in such an age of expansion;
their influence became increasingly negligible, except in Versailles politics.

It seems certain that no mission work of importance was
done among the Menomini for a long period after 1684,
though the station on the Fox river to the south of their territory had a resident priest until considerably later. When
in 1831–32 the Roman Catholic missions again commenced
work with the tribe, they reported that "the oldest Menominees say that they saw no 'black gown' for more than a
hundred years."

CONTINUED FRENCH CONTACTS

Westward discovery and exploitation, under the leadership of such exceptional personalities as Perrot, Duluth,
La Salle and Tonty, had by 1680 made of the upper great
lakes region a rich hinterland for New France. At this time
of excellent promise, the French hold upon it suddenly became dangerously threatened. Once more the Iroquois confederacy took to the warpath, cutting the essential artery
of communication, the St. Lawrence river.

The warparties of the league had not been altogether
idle in the intervening years, but their activities had been
against southern and eastern tribes. As their nearer forests became denuded of game the Iroquois hunters had to
rove further west for their trade furs. This brought them
once more into the territory of the Illinois. In 1680 a clash
occurred, actually at the time the Frenchman Tonty was
among the Illinois, so that he had to retreat north. As a
result La Salle gathered together a confederation of western
tribes into the present state of Illinois, mainly bands of
Mascouten, Miami, Kickapoo, Shawnee and the Illinois themselves. This may be noted as another step in the outward
movement of the peoples who had pressed earlier into the
territory of the Menomini and Winnebago.

The detailed events of the next twenty years need not be treated here.   At first the French and the western Indians were opposed by the Iroquois tribes alone, but in 1689 the latter were joined by the force of British arms and commerce, England being then at war with France.   French prestige ebbed and flowed among the tribes in the west according as French fortunes varied in the east.   Time and again it seemed that the Iroquois, in command of the essential artery of communication, would be able to expel the French from the upper country; three times British trading expeditions penetrated to the heart of the French west; the western tribes coquetted with the Iroquois and the British.   Yet disaster was averted for the French by the personal ascendancy of the handful of trading, fighting fort builders such as Perrot and La Salle.   Only when in 1694 the French were able to relieve the joint Iroquois-British pressure in the east did they regain fully the confidence of the western tribes, and restore the interrupted fur trading operations.

During this period the Menomini as in earlier days were geographically isolated from the eastern peril.   As a result they do not figure prominently in the records.   But each year their representatives together with those of the other tribes of the upper country, would journey to Montreal to hold council with and receive presents from "Onontio," their "father," the French Governor.

In 1684 reference is made by Duluth to the arrest and execution of a Menomini and a Chippewa for murder. Apart from showing how by this time the code of white justice was being brought somewhat to bear on Indian life, the record is interesting as including a list of trade goods presented to the father of one of the Indians concerned, these rather typical of the presents given by the French at the time:

Blankets, guns, powder, lead, mitasses (leggings), tobacco, axes, knives, twine for making a beaver net, shirts and two sacks of wheat to keep them till they should kill some game.—Letter Duluth, in *Wis. Hist. Colls.*, xvi, p. 124.

In 1689 the well known traveller Baron Lahontan visited La Baye and the Fox river. He reported that:

Villages of the Sakis, the Pouteouatamis, and some Malhominis are seated on the side of that River, and the Jesuits have a House or College built upon it. This is a place of great Trade for Skins and Indian Corn, which these Savages sell to Coureurs du Bois, as they come and go.—Lahontan, *New Voyages*, ed. by Thwaites, i, pp. 167–68.

This speaks of an encampment of Menomini on the Fox river, that is considerably south of their main village. No other vistor records any permanent settlement of the tribe there, however, until about half a century later, all referring to them as occupying merely a single village at the Menominee river. The inference would be that the party of Menomini had come south at the time for trade purposes.

La Potherie, writing soon after this, comments upon the problems involved in "managing" the peoples of La Baye:

It was very difficult to obtain from those peoples all the satisfaction which we had desired. Their great distance from us prevents us from reducing them to obedience; and the blustering manner which must be assumed with them was the best policy that could be adopted to make them fear us.—La Potherie, in *Wis. Hist. Colls.*, xvi, p. 148.

He also gives an example of a speech made to the Indians by Perrot, an expert in the "blustering" method:

I love Peace in my country; I have discovered this land, and Onontio (the governor) has given the charge of it to me; and he has promised me all his young men to punish those who undertake to stain it with blood. . . . You have forgotten that your Ancestors in former days used earthern Pots, stone Hatchets, and Knives, and Bows; and you will be obliged to use them again, if Onontio abandons you. . . . I do not take away the War-club or the Bow that I gave you on Onontio's behalf; but I recommend to you to employ them against the Iroquois, and not against other nations. If you transgress his orders, you may be sure that the Spirit who made all, who is master of life and of death, is for him; and that he knows well how to punish your disobedience if you do not agree to my demands.—*Idem*, pp. 159–60.

In 1696, just when prospects were once again bright and the loyalty of the western tribes to the French seemed assured, an extraordinary change in official policy altered the whole situation. In Europe the market for furs suffered a slump, while agitation by an anti-imperialistic party in France decrying the fur trade as ruining the Indians both through the sale of brandy and through the relations of the whites with Indian women received the sympathy of the king. As a result official commands were issued to call in all garrisons, evacuate all posts, revoke all trade licenses, and prohibit the carriage of goods westwards.

Within two years, the order was put into effect, this in spite of strenuous opposition from New France and remonstrances from the Indians themselves. At the annual council held with the governor at Montreal, a Potawatomi chief voiced the feelings of the tribes thus:

Father! Since we want powder, iron, and every other necessary which you were formerly in the habit of sending us, what do you expect us to do? Are the majority of our women, who have but one or two beavers to send to Montreal to secure their supplies, are they to entrust them to drunken fellows who will drink them, and bring nothing back? Thus having in our country none of the articles we require, and which you, last year, promised we should be furnished with and not want; and perceiving only this—that nothing whatsoever is yet brought to us and that the French come to visit us no more—you shall never see us again, I promise you if the French quit us; this, Father, is the last time we shall come to talk with you.

By 1698 the upper lakes region became officially emptied of whites except for three or four missionaries. In reality however the woods still held their coureurs du bois, without doubt in considerable numbers. Shortly after this, a great council of Indian tribes was held at which a peace was formally made between the western tribes and the Iroquois. The latter, realizing their strategic position, quickly adopted the role of middlemen between the British posts and their former enemies, an exceedingly significant fact for the student of possible culture diffusions between the Iroquois and the Central Algonquian peoples. At this time, too, the French colony of Louisiana was founded to the south, so that French penetration recommenced from a new direction.

The Versailles authorities soon found that the western tribes would not bring their furs down to Montreal as had been hoped. When, therefore, a demand for furs commenced once more in Europe, it was realized that the evacu-

ation order in New France had to be revoked. But a new
plan was decided upon, namely to concentrate French
authority at a few strategic points, with strong garrisons and
permanent agricultural colonies of whites. Near to these
the Indian tribes were to be settled, there to be taught
French ways, and ultimately to be assimilated into the local
communities. Three principal posts were so occupied—
Detroit, New Orleans, and Chicago.

The Indian tribes of La Baye were invited to remove to
Detroit. Meantime bands of the Potawatomi, Miami and
Mascouten had already been moving south along Michigan
shores and east into what seem to have been their old tribal
territories. The direct invitation to remove to Detroit was
accepted by some or all of the Fox and Sauk bands, also by
part of the Kickapoo and Mascouten. But there is no evidence of any Menomini or Winnebago taking part in this
concentration, the presumption being that they preferred to
remain on their own lands; an ancestral tie which apparently
was not there to hold these other peoples. The new policy,
however, could end only in Indian troubles. The Detroit
experiment soon produced a fight, in which the most turbulent of the groups, the Fox, were practically exterminated,
even the French taking part against them. The surviving
Fox fled back into Wisconsin where they began a savage
aggression against the French and their Indian allies. The
attitude of the Menomini tribe toward the Fox at this time
appears to have been on the whole wisely neutral.[3]

Thus was demonstrated the failure of the concentration
policy. The Indians showed no eagerness to learn white
ways or to admit the superiority of European culture. So
the former license system was restored, an amnesty was declared for all coureurs du bois, and the old fur trade posts
were reoccupied with commandants and garrisons; that is,
commercial and military domination were renewed as the
keynotes of French policy instead of concentration and
assimilation.

In 1716 an expedition sent by the French against the Fox
met with little success. But a fort was built at La Baye.

3 *Wis. Hist. Colls.*, xvi, pp. 301–02.

Henceforth the Menomini region became a key centre of official activity as well as a mission station and customary rallying point for traders. The Menomini, who in this troubled period had received little mention, again find their way into the contemporary records.

In 1718 Sieur La Mothe Cadillac travelled to La Baye. He reported Mackinac as occupied by Huron and Ottawa, the Noquets near the mouth of Green Bay to be "degraded . . . few . . . incorporated with many others," the Menomini as "on their river," the Sauk at La Baye near the fort, the Winnebago on the lake now known by their name, and the Fox as further inland. He says:

> The Malhominy or Folles Avoines are so called on account of the river on which their village is situated, which produces a prodigious quantity of wild oats. . . . There is no nation in which the men are so well built or have so good figures as in this one. They are not so swarthy as the others, and if they did not grease themselves they would surpass the French in whiteness. The women also are rather pretty, and more gentle than those of the neighboring tribes.—From Magry, in *Wis. Hist. Colls.*, xvi, p. 360.

In the same year was published a *Memoir on the savages of Canada,* furnished by a M. de Sabrevois to his superiors, in which are described Algonquin life and customs; from it comes the following:

> La Baye . . . is settled by the puants (Winnebago) and the folles-avoines (Menomini); there are some French also. The puants and the folles-avoines are not numerous; each tribe numbers possibly 80 or 100 men. The Saquis (Sauk) number 100 to 120 men. The two former nations, as far as I have learned, have the same customs as the outaouacs (Ottawa) and the poux (Potawatomi). As for their language, it is not quite the same; but whoever understands the outaouac tongue easily makes himself understood. . . . All these Nations Are very industrious and have four women to one man.—*Wis. Hist. Colls.*, xvi, p. 371.

Shortly after this date, a "Commandant-General of the Upper Country" was appointed from Versailles; his instructions were:

> To remedy the abuses that are Prevalent, to maintain peace and union among the Savage Nations, and absolutely to prevent the French from selling brandy.—*Idem,* p. 387.

In his memorial of acceptance, the new commandant writes a commentary important enough to quote in part:

The Trade in brandy which My Lords absolutely prohibit, is the Cause of all the troubles among the Savages, among whom there are no laws, and no punishments beyond the will to do harm. The Savages no longer Think of hunting in order to clothe Themselves but only to get drink. Brandy is making them poor and miserable; sickness is killing them off; and they slay one another on very slight provocation, and without any penalty for the murderer except the risk of meeting the same fate. Through this fear they disband and quit their Villages to settle elsewhere in families. . . . They no longer recognize any chiefs. . . .

You order me, My Lords, to establish union among these Nations and I will do my best; but that they can be restrained from pursuing their ideas of revenge, which are often very Capricious, and from exercising their ferocity, is a thing which I believe impossible. It would be necessary to change their natures. It is more expedient for the repose of all the Europeans to let the Savages who have a war between themselves fight it out, rather than to undertake to concern ourselves with their quarrels. We should reserve to ourselves only the quality of Mediators, whenever they have recourse to the Mediation of the French.—*Idem*, pp. 388–89.

Another famous traveller, Charlevoix, visited La Baye in 1721. He writes of the Menomini:

We found ourselves abreast of . . . the entrance to a River on which is the Village of the Malhomines. . . . The entire tribe is comprised of this Village, which is not very populous. That is a pity, for they are fine-looking men, and among the most shapely in Canada. They are even taller than the Pouteouatamis. I have been assured that they have the same origin, and almost the same language, as the Noquets and the Saulteurs (Chippewas); but it is also added that they have, besides, a private language, which they communicate to no one. Certain tales have also been related to me about them—for instance, of a Serpent that every year goes into their Village, and is there received with impressive Ceremonies; this leads me to believe that they meddle somewhat with sorceries.—Charlevoix, in *Wis. Hist. Colls.*, xvi, p. 411.

At this time the Fox were busy organizing a secret alliance of western tribes against the French, in which the Sauk and Winnebago joined, but not the Menomini. Finally in 1728 the French moved to forestall them by sending an elaborate expedition into the Fox valley. Before this show of might, the Fox, Sauk and Winnebago fled, leaving the Menomini the sole occupants of the area. The latter allied themselves with the French and even accompanied the troops "to the number of a hundred men." Though the expedition proved rather futile, it is very important for the study in that it appears to mark a turning point in Menomini history. The tribe, which apparently had been lying low for some decades recuperating its strength, now definitely starts on the warpath again, this time as an ally of the whites against other Indians.

The Menomini as French Allies

The Fox confederation soon crumbled. Before long the French were able to incite the other Indian peoples of the upper country, including the Menomini, to attack this unfortunate group, which apparently they did with a will. At this time a new figure appears in the records, a soldier-trader named Marin. Like Perrot before him, he soon came to dominate the western tribesmen. In 1730 he reported on a visit to the Menomini thus:

On my arrival at the Village of the folles avoines I was very well received with some Calumets, according to custom, by the old men who Had remained in the fort. They said to me: "My Father, we will let you rest today, and tomorrow we will speak to you".

On the following day they began by spreading a mat, and, by a Collar (of wampum), they spoke to me as follows: "Here is a mat, my father, on which we beg you to rest and to be pleased to kindle your fire here and never Extinguish it; for we are resolved to Listen attentively to your word, which is that of our Father Onontio, who no doubt has pity on us since he has Sent you to assist us. Have pity, therefore, my father . . . and look upon us as the faithful and true children of Onontio. We need your help. . . ." This I granted them, assuring them of your protection.

(Here follows a spirited description of a campaign of Marin and his Menomini allies against the Fox; it is a savage picture of the times—cross treachery, cannibalism, torture and like features of Indian warfare.)—Letter, Marin, *Wis. Hist. Colls.*, xvii, pp. 88–100.

The Fox bands now sought to migrate eastward, but were met and decimated by other tribes, the few survivors fleeing back to the Wisconsin forests, where the further extermination of their "Wretched Remnant" was continued. The reason for the official encouragement of this harrying of a small Indian people is revealed in a letter written by the governor of New France:

If this step meets with the success that I expect of it, we shall be in a position next year to make all our Nations of the lakes attack the Chicachas.—*Wis. Hist. Colls.*, xvii, p. 183.

This represents a new phase of French relations with the western Indians; the "chicachas" were the Chickasaw tribe to the south of the lakes toward the Mississippi mouth. Through this tribe the British traders were seeking to penetrate the French monopoly of the west, and it was really against this rival white aggression that New France was seeking to direct its western allies.

In 1731, at the invitation of the French, the disaffected Sauk returned to their old village at La Baye. Two years later an elaborate French expedition, accompanied by "a hundred folles avoine (Menomini) Savages", appeared at the gates of their settlement demanding that they yield certain Fox refugees sheltering among them. In the ensuing negotiations the French commandant was shot down, and after a fierce engagement the Sauk fled once more from La Baye, pursued by the French and the Menomini warriors. All Indian eyes in the west turned to see the French reaction to this fresh disaster. In attempting the final extermination of the Fox they had alienated completely the powerful Sauk, and a new Sauk-Fox combination once more menaced French prestige. An expedition sent against them proved a failure. Shortly afterward the French lost their alliance with the Sioux peoples, obtained by the earlier traders, and at the same time an expedition from Louisiana was destroyed in an attack on the Chickasaw. It seemed again that the empire of France in the New World was slipping from her grasp.

The whole situation appears to have been saved by the personal ascendancy of one man over the western Indians, Marin. In the records of the 1737 council of tribes at Montreal, there is presented the rather amazing spectacle of the Menomini and Winnebago asking the governor to spare the lives of the Fox, and of the Ottawa and Potawatomi begging the lives of the Sauk. Naturally the dazed official did not deny their requests. Peace reigned once more awhile in the upper country, though the Sauk and Fox firmly refused to return to the Fox valley from their refuge in the fastnesses of the middle Mississippi basin.

Meantime the Potawatomi and Mascouten had been settling to the south and southeast of Michigan lake, and the Kickapoo southward toward Ohio. By 1740 the region of La Baye is said to have been almost deserted except for the Menomini; the fort there was important mainly as a trade center and for keeping open the Fox-Wisconsin portage route. However, in the following year, the Winnebago began to return to the area from their exile among the Sioux further west, whither they had retired following on their participation in the Fox conspiracy.

Among the contemporary records is given a "census of Indian Tribes" compiled in 1736, the authorship of which is unknown. It estimates the warrior strength of the Menomini as 160, that of the Winnebago as 80, the Sauk as 150, the Kickapoo 80, the Mascouten 60, the Fox, "migratory and separated", 100. This, if at all accurate, shows the Menomini as now the most numerous of all tribes in the region; apparently they had increased considerably in the decades since first white contact.

In the summer of 1740, Marin, appointed commandant at La Baye, arrived at Montreal accompanied by the representatives of all the western tribes. The speeches of conciliation are recorded in the contemporary documents. Among these, the "words of the Folles-avoines" contrasted markedly with the penitent, promising words of the others; their spokesman said:

It is without any purpose, My Father, that we have come here. It is only in order to see you, as well as our young people who are here.[4] We are glad to have Heard what our brothers have just said, and will report it in our village. My father; if all that has just been said is sincere, it pleases us greatly. . . . My Father, all of us, both old and young, have great joy in seeing you.—*Wis. Hist. Colls.*, xvii, pp. 325–26.

[4] The wording is ambiguous: it may possibly mean that the Jesuit mission had obtained a few of the Menomini children to teach them in some boarding school at Montreal, a policy that they did carry out with some tribes. If this was so it must have been an important cultural influence upon the Menomini. But no documentary confirmation of this could be traced. Probably the words merely refer ungrammatically to the fact that a few young people accompanied the expedition in order to see "Onontio".

The same spirit of loyalty of the Menomini to the French was shown in a recorded speech made at a later council:

> My father never have I done evil, because I have always followed your advice and done your will. It has seemed to me that the French only were my allies.—*Idem,* p. 397.

In 1741 still another new policy was initiated in the fur trade. By an edict from Versailles the trade license system was again abolished, and the posts were ordered to be auctioned to the highest bidder for monopoly exploitation. In the next few years the upper country was again in general revolt. La Baye was chosen as one of the posts at which to initiate the experiment. The lessees of the post, a Montreal firm, were "unscrupulous" and their agents bad. The exorbitant prices and poor assortment of goods brought for the trade became worse as a new British-French war kept trade goods very scarce. An unpopular agent was killed by one of the Menomini, but with difficulty peace was maintained. When the lease of the post lapsed during 1746, no one would bid for it again. Finally two private traders of Mackinac[5] took it over, one of whom was a M. Augustin de Langlade, known later as the "Father" of Wisconsin settlement. Within two years the intercolonial war had come to an end, and the French were able to quell the incipient revolt in the upper country.

Peace in the west, however, always seemed ominous to the French, and their influence, apart from the few dominating personalities and the yearly council at which presents were given, seems to have been superficial. This is illustrated by the failure of French officials in their attempts to control intertribal relationships. An example may be given from the records. A Potawatomi had been killed by a Peoria, with the result that the commandants at forts Chartres and St. Joseph both tried to mediate:

> The efforts of the two commandants did not meet with much success. Last spring a party of Pouteouatamis, Maskoutins, Folles avoines, and Saulteux went to attack the Peorias. . . .—*Wis. Hist. Colls.,* xviii, p. 89.

[5] Now Mackinaw, Mich.; in earlier days this French center was also known as Missilimackinac.

A report by the governor of New France indicates the unsettled state of even the Menomini at this time:

> The folle avoine chief called la Mothe, who came to see me in Montreal, promised me he would make every effort to stop (Menomini bands going on the warpath with the Winnebago against the Missouri). . . . Marin also succeeded so well in appeasing those nations that the folles avoines, in their regret at having formed those bands against my will, wanted to strangle a Saulteux . . . who had induced them to take that step. . . . The Sioux nation . . . is at peace with the Saulteux, Folles avoines, and other nations that wintered on its lands.—Governor's report, *Wis. Hist. Colls.*, xviii, p. 77.

The great anxiety of the French was less concerning immediate relations with the western Indians, than the reaction of the latter to their failure to stop the encroachments of the British through the Chickasaw country in the Ohio valley.

In this critical period the whole west was electrified by a sudden and successful manoeuver on the part of a band of western Indians headed by a young mixed blood Frenchman, in which an important Ohio post was captured and the British with their Indian allies massacred. This youth, Charles de Langlade, son of the Mackinac trader already spoken of and an Indian mother, from henceforth began to supersede even Marin and Marin's son in his ascendancy over the tribes of the upper lakes region. His reputation acquired in this bold stroke was further enhanced in 1755 when a strong military expedition was led from England by General Braddock to oust the French from the Ohio valley. Langlade, together with other leaders, gathered a war party of the western tribes including Ottawa, Chippewa, Menomini, Winnebago, Potawatomi and Huron; these, joined with other friendly Indians and a small white force in the apparently impossible task of holding up the oncoming army, actually succeeded in routing it. During the next two years French-Indian expeditions continued to harass British settlements to the east and south; the west was firmly French; and the Indian allies even entered into the sport of a winter campaign against the enemy.

A set of instructions issued to a new governor at this time are illuminating as showing further the nature of the Indian policy pursued by the French:

His Majesty wishes him to devote all the attention in his power to avoiding war with the savages as much as possible . . . it is not however advisable to endure certain insults from the savages . . . the toleration of which brings on the greatest disturbances. . . . With a view of keeping them occupied and of weakening them, it has been deemed advisable to take every opportunity to foment and encourage wars between them. . . . But, in view of the extent to which these nations are today reduced, and of their dispositions in general, it is better in every way that the French should play the part of protectors and peace makers among them.—*Wis. Hist. Colls.*, xviii, pp. 151–52.

While the western tribes were thus rallied in warfare under strong French leaders, the fur trade was degenerating still further into a system of "favoritism, corruption, and undue profits". The La Baye post was given by a new governor to his brother for personal exploitation; as such it was managed by a commandant who was financially interested. La Baye and the Menomini had fallen again on evil days.

In 1757 a combined French and Indian force gathered for an attack on a British stronghold, Fort Henry, which fell before them. So great, however, was the Indian ferocity in the engagement that public opinion among the whites demanded their withdrawal from the campaign, and this was now done. Disappointed in victory, in disgrace incomprehensible to them, the western bands marched sullenly home. They took back with them a scourge of smallpox, which raged among the tribes through the ensuing winter. The Menomini claimed four years later that they "lost three hundred warriors . . . with the smallpox, and most of their chiefs by the late war . . . against the English".

Without such Indian help, the French power in the east waned, and this added to the defection of the western tribes. The real end to French authority was at last in sight. By 1759 only Detroit, Mackinac and La Baye were flying the French flag in the upper country. In that year the abuses practised by the French commandant at La Baye caused

some of the Menomini to attack the French post.   Different
accounts tell how:

> The Folles Avoines have killed eleven Canadians at the Bay; missed
> the Commandant, and pillaged a storehouse.

> The Indians called Folles Avoines, had killed twenty two French, and
> pillaged the magazine of the post at La Baye. They will soon make
> reparation for what they have done.

The reparation did come, for the journal of Montcalm shows
the severe punishment exacted by the French officials for
this first major aggression of their allies:

> The Folles Avoines have sent as prisoners to Montreal the seven sav-
> ages of their nation, who this winter have assassinated a French family at
> La Baie.   Three of them have been shot on the town square, and the other
> four must go to the war. . . . This submission of an independent nation
> more than five hundred leagues distant does great honor to the French
> name.—All three quotations from *Wis. Hist. Colls.*, xviii, pp. 203–04.

In this same year, 1759, Fort Quebec fell before the attack of Wolfe. The records show that Langlade took part
in its defense with "twelve hundred Indians", including
some Menomini. According to an account by the grandson
of Langlade:

> Some aged Menominees served under him there—among them Glode,
> son of old Carron (of whom more later), O-sau-wish-ke-no, or the Yellow
> Bird, Ka-cha-ke-wa-she-ka, or the Notch-Maker; the old Chief Carron, was
> also there.—Grignon's *Recollections, Wis. Hist. Colls.*, iii, pp. 217–18.

After the battle Langlade and his Indians left for Mackinac.
They arrived just in time to take charge of the French fort
as the commandant and garrison evacuated it. The latter
retreated by way of the Fox-Wisconsin portage to Louisiana,
picking up the commandant and garrison of La Baye as they
went. Thus ingloriously was made the last official French
crossing of the route discovered in the heroic days, and so
ended French dominion in the northwest.

In 1760 Mackinac was entered by a small British force.
The following year La Baye flew the British flag, and by the
treaty of Paris in 1763 New France became British Canada.
This remote fact had little meaning to the Indian tribes of
the upper lakes. But the immediate fact of the submission

of Charles de Langlade, the "bravest of the brave" as the tribesfolk called him, carried with it also the submission of the western Indians.

A REVIEW

While on the whole these records are scanty, predominantly of a political nature, and lacking detail, they give some important glimpses into the tribal life and experience.

Being sheltered by the stretching waters of lake Michigan from the full force of repeated invasions from the east, the Menomini seem to have been the least affected of all the upper lakes tribes by French-British-Indian hostilities. Yet because of their strategic position as regards the early trade centers and the portage route to the Mississippi they were brought strongly under French influence. Clearly they were a mere remnant when white records begin, but their numbers increased once more until by 1736 they were estimated to be the most numerous in the region; furthermore, as close allies of the French, they prospered to a point where they became one of the dominant tribes.

It is feasible that the rehabilitation of the Menomini and their strong bonds with the whites may be explained in part by a considerable degree of intermixture as a result of doubtless numerous alliances, permanent or temporary, between whites and women from the tribe. The descriptions given by Cadillac and Charlevoix, in which the Menomini are singled out as physically different from other tribes, particularly as to lightness of skin, might support this—by then traders and soldiers had been mingling with the tribesfolk for some two generations, this at a time when they were so reduced in numbers and females greatly outnumbered males. It will be seen how continued mixture with whites has been a feature of later days. There may, too, have been some intermarriage between the Menomini and other Indian peoples who were brought into closer contact with them through trade and as war allies in the post-white period.

The records do not mention specifically an important happening in Menomini history that later documents show to have taken place during the time, namely the breaking

away of part of the tribe from the ancestral living area on
the Menomini river.   These folk moved south to settle on the
Fox river near the French trading fort.   This evidently
occurred between 1730 and 1752, perhaps about 1740 when
the region was most deserted by other tribes.   Doubtless
this was profoundly important as disruptive of the older
social organization.   (See Diagram 2.)

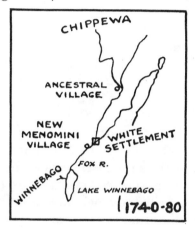

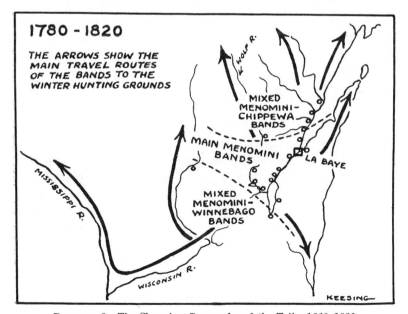

DIAGRAM 2. The Changing Geography of the Tribe 1660–1820.

The indefiniteness of evidence concerning the earliest contacts of the Menomini with whites has been referred to already. Among the first adjustments made, the following were noted or can be inferred: certain fundamental modifications of knowledge and belief to admit of the category "white man"; the great wonder and even fear evoked by the first of the newcomers; the new experiences and possibilities opened up by the goods they brought; the quick adoption of those which appeared to the Indian desirable and improving, with corresponding reorganization of the indigenous arts and crafts and of the values pertaining to them; the stimulation of new wants; and ready adoption of the rules and standards of value set by the whites in commercial transactions.

From Perrot's time on three main types of white influence reached the Menomini, as represented in the activities of traders, missionaries, and soldiers. The first and last of these were not mutually exclusive, while representatives of both the commercial and military groups often took over the role of administrator, thus exercising political influence.

The furtrader profoundly affected Menomini life. Most obvious in their effects were the trade goods which they introduced; to the list on page 63 may be added clothing, liquor, cheap jewellery, ribbons and garters, bells, beads, sword blades, utensils, flint and steel, hoes, mirrors and combs, jews' harps, and pigments, especially "vermillion", some of these of course destined to leave more permanent marks upon the Indian culture than others, as will be seen. In addition to this material cargo of pack and canoe the trader also carried with him commercial ideas and more or less of morality, politics, religion and other imponderables of his homeland. Over against this, however, the trader readily accepted many cultural elements from the Indian either because his own corresponding elements were inaccessible in the wilderness or else because the Indian ones were genuinely better for local conditions. He variously took over canoes, snowshoes, houses, woodcraft, foods, tobacco, wampum, the "council", the language, and (more or less) the social etiquette of the Indian. The Indian, for his part, began a far more intensive exploitation of his resources in order to secure furs for trade. Something of his psychological attitude may perhaps be glimpsed in the following remark of an Indian recorded by a Jesuit writer (*Jes. Rel.*, vi, p. 297) :

> The beaver . . . makes kettles, hatchets, swords, knives, bread; and, in short, it makes everything.

Apparently the changes from a subsistence to a partially trading economy were accomplished with relatively little strain, as based on mutual convenience and appreciation. How thorough they were is indicated by the fact that on the two occasions when furtrade policies were such as to curtail or make oppressive the trade relation (in 1746 and 1758) there were Menomini outbreaks. Though it does not seem to have worried the Indian much as to whether his trader was officially licensed or a coureur du bois, or had affiliations with Montreal or Albany it had become essential to his life that the trader be there. Later it will be seen how, as the game became depleted in the nearer forests, the Indian hunter had to rove far afield for his furs and this brought extensive modifications in social and political organization; but these probably had not become very marked by the close of the French era.

The influence of the Jesuit missionary lay of course primarily in the field of religious beliefs and activities, though records show that the fathers also tried to improve methods of cultivation (especially among the Hurons), battled hard for "decent" clothing, touched the social system at points like birth (baptism), marriage, and burial, and demonstrated methods of treating sickness; doubtless, too, their more or less decorated sacred and symbolic objects presented a potential stimulus to art and craft. Like the traders they accepted much from Indian life. As for the reactions of the Menomini during the fourteen years of contact they had with the "black robes" the following is a summary of what actually appears in the records set out above: at first the "listened with respect", and asked instruction;

their "holy curiosity" met, they came to tolerate attacks on their ideas and allowed father André to work among the children; they "covered themselves", sought to learn what presumably they thought were magic songs, fasted without blackening their faces, and modified their feasts; after the noteworthy sturgeon incident, in which they permitted a crucifix to replace their sun sacrifice, they displayed an extraordinary anxiety to learn, some being baptized, and even women going to the chapel presumably along with the men; finally the principal "juggler" of the tribe agrees not to invoke the thunder.

This brief mission experiment provides an interesting example of cultural conflict and change. The following main points can be made. Even if familiarity with the whites soon dispelled the idea of their being "demi-gods", it seems sure that the Jesuit always moved in the rarified atmosphere of the supernatural; he came under the Indian category of shaman, or medicine-man. Again the interpretations of the Powers which he brought, variously good or evil, living above or below, would be comprehensible to the Indian, also the ideas of prayer, chant, and sacrifice. The Jesuit's pack containing his ritual paraphernalia must have seemed to the Indian a potent medicine bundle. The main differences lay of course in the exact definitions of deity, of good and bad, of the particular acts required to establish contact with things supernatural, and of the value of an elaborated organized "church" such as the individualistic religion of the Indian quite lacked.

In Menomini thinking the essential test of the opposing systems was how they worked. Behind the one lay all Indian experience, but the other was clearly potent in view of the superior material equipment and political dominance of the strangers. All were willing to give the new "medicine" a hearing, some even to venture a trial. The first thrust against the old ways came with the interesting situation of the children being arrayed deliberately against their parents, one of the few examples in the early records of a definite clash within the Menomini culture itself as a result of white influences. No doubt it served to loosen the grip of the old ideas, for before long some were willing to take extreme liberties, such as neglecting traditional activities of a religious nature and repeating the new religious formula in the hope that "God would make them spear fish". The crux of the Jesuit impact came with the sturgeon incident in which the superiority of the new belief and ritual was so to speak convincingly demonstrated.

Presumably the tribe as a whole would have completed the transition to Christianity but for the happenings viewed above. For one thing the tribe was left without any earthly mediator such as was required by the white man's faith. For another, a quarrel took place which resulted in bloodshed; if the Menomini were the aggressors, as the account suggests, it would indicate some serious conflict of which no record now remains. An epidemic followed, and the Indians interpreted this as witchcraft, hence the lives of the missionaries were threatened. Looking back from later times, it would seem that little permanent imprint was left upon the Menomini; nevertheless the ground was doubtless prepared for a resumption of mission work in the nineteenth century, and there are elements in belief, ritual, and art as they appear in that century which may trace back to the Jesuit influences; of this more in due course.

The impact of the soldier emphasized matters relating to warfare and political authority. It was especially potent after the fort was built at La Baye in 1716 and when regular visits were made by the tribesfolk to the lower settlements and they were enlisted in the white man's quarrels. Already mention has been made of the likelihood that Indian fort-building was taken over from the whites, and later it will be seen how military uniforms gave inspiration to Menomini tailors. On the other hand the formal drilling and tactics, the hierarchical ranking and discipline of army life remained quite foreign to the Indian. The French gave up early their attempts to enlist individual Indians in their troops. The loyalty of the tribes was won and maintained through a show of force, or more subtly through the influence of certain outstanding whites and a fairly continuous flow of presents. The traditional war party remained the effective unit in Indian fighting, and when the French desired to stop scalping, "treachery", or cannibalism the only way was to remove the Indian from the fighting line.

These three types of influence represent even together only a circumscribed and specialized amount of white culture, and the response of the Indian to them was likewise limited. On the whole white relationships with the Menomini in this period were predominantly economic and political and except for the brief Jesuit impact there was little real interference or pressure in essential cultural matters. Such change as took place proceeded as a voluntary reorganization from within rather than a superimposition from outside. True, there were certain conflicts arising out of differences in customs and values—examples appeared of differing ideas of justice and of what was fair in war—but these frictions did not produce any vital modifications in either Indian or white ways. That the Menomini gave compensation both times white blood was spilt by them probably shows the effectiveness of the alien control rather than any essential change in their conception of blood vengeance.

A word may be said concerning the general Indian policy of the French authorities. Its keynotes were domination and exploitation. Early in the eighteenth century a policy of assimilation was planned, but after the first experiment failed, indicating that the Indian peoples would not or could not quickly adjust themselves to the patterns of white life, it was given up. Administrative officers were instructed not to interfere with Indian ways, except in situations where French prestige was threatened. Because an essential of fur trade development was peace and order among the tribesfolk a main aim was to achieve pacific relations between hitherto warring groups. Unfortunately for this aim the increasing threat by the British and their Indian allies necessitated the cultivation of a warlike spirit which prevented anything approaching complete pacification.

On the whole, considering the remoteness of the upper country, the French succeeded in dominating the western tribes to a remarkable degree in both peace and war. Little as the representatives of the tribes may have understood what the French meant by the ceremony of annexation in 1671, or appreciated the significance of the political rivalries of whites in North America, they certainly looked to ''Onontio'' and his representatives with respect, and by the end of the period showed a fairly complete willingness to submit to white rule. This political allegiance was of course closely related to economic interests; yet the psychological attitudes created during this time, strengthened as they were to be by decades more of like domination, seem to have had a great deal to do with the fairly smooth submission of the Indian to reservation control and wardship in modern days. In this connection it is significant that such political subordination was more marked among the Menomini than among any other tribe in the region.

IV. BRITISH AND EARLY AMERICAN
INFLUENCES

The British, strictly speaking, had political control of
the Menomini area only from 1761 to 1794, as at the latter
date the region became according to "Jay's treaty" the
possession of the United States. Nevertheless the former
continued to dominate it through a number of traders and
administrators until after the British-American war of
1812–14; not till 1815 did a United States force reach La
Baye.

Yet in reality the majority of the whites in close touch
with the tribes were still Frenchmen, and they and their
mixed blood children were the real mediators between both
the British and Americans in their dealings with the Indian. Only after American occupation did French influence
begin to diminish, and the Indian really come to feel the
pressure of "Anglo-Saxon" control and manipulation of
his life.

The period is important from several viewpoints. In it
the fur trade reached its greatest prosperity, but this peak
was followed by a spectacular decline that disorganized the
Indian way of life stabilized around it. Moreover, British
and American methods of dealing with the tribes produced
interesting reactions, particularly as the latter commenced
to lay the foundation of what later became its Indian policy.

THE MENOMINI AS BRITISH ALLIES

Fort La Baye was occupied by the British for only two
years, being then abandoned as the result of an outbreak
among the tribes of the great lakes region, headed by an
Ottawa chief, Pontiac. The British commander in charge
during the time made various comments about the Menomini in his reports, the most important of which follow:

We arrived at La Bay . . . at a time when there was but one family
in the village—they being gone a hunting, according to their custom . . .
(they) return commonly in the months of April, May, and June, according
to the distance they go, and the openness of the season. . . .

(He has great difficulty in getting from his superiors a supply of wampum.)   The French, in their time, always gave them belts (of wampum), rum, and money, presents by which they renewed their peace annually. . . . (In May the tribe take up residence again; he gives presents and holds council with them.)   They . . . said they were very poor, having lost three hundred warriors lately with the small-pox, and most of their chiefs by the late war . . . they would adhere to whatever instructions the commanding English officers might give them, for the future, as they had always done with the French. . . . (They request "a gunsmith to mend their guns," "rum as a true token of friendship," and "colors and commissions" all of which the French gave them.   He sets out an Indian census including:) Folles Avoines 150 warriors.   They live at La Bay in two towns. . . . The chiefs of the Folles Avoines came and demanded credit for their young men, which the traders here granted on the chiefs giving their word for payment in the spring.—Gorrel's Journal, in *Wis. Hist. Colls.*, i, pp. 25–48.

When Pontiac's rebellion broke out at Mackinac, the British commander approached the Menomini leaders for "their counsel and assistance". They agreed to aid him, and both villages, that on the Fox and that on the Menominee, after liberal presents, sent parties to accompany him thither. Thus again the Menomini took the side of the whites against other Indians. One of the early French settlers of La Baye has reported verbatim a speech alleged to have been delivered by Pontiac to a gathering of the tribes at Milwaukee. The sentiments at least are probably correct:

"My friends! I have come here to consult you. . . . When the white man came across the ocean, he . . . asked to be permitted to settle in a corner and live with us like brothers.   We received and admitted them as such. . . . They then commenced to encroach upon us more and more. Their purpose is plain to me—that they will continue to encroach upon us, until they discover that they have sufficient power to remove us from our country to a distant land. . . . It is now in our power to force the whites back to their original settlements.   We must all join in one common cause, and sweep the white men from our country, and then we shall live happy . . . we shall live as did our forefathers; we shall with our furs and skins obtain all necessary supplies, and—be happy."—Porlier, *A Menominee Tradition*, *Wis. Hist. Colls.*, viii, 228–29.[1]

[1] For a contemporary account of Pontiac's rebellion, see Henry, *Travels and Adventures*. Refer also to documents in *Wis. Hist. Colls.*, xviii, particularly p. 267.

The tribal attitude was the more striking since rumors of a reconquest of the northwest by France were in the air. But the Menomini stood by their new allies; they even sent ninety-nine of their number to a council of the tribes held at Detroit by Sir William Johnson, the British agent in Indian affairs.[2]

The departure of the British garrison from La Baye did not mean that the region was deserted by the whites. Probably soon after this date the Langlades made a permanent home on the Fox river, and so became the founders of the future city of Green Bay; before long a settlement grew up, forming a small patriarchal community such as was to be found elsewhere among the French in Canada.[3] Furthermore, once the Indian outbreak was quelled, Mackinac became a permanent military and administrative post for the upper country. The British wisely continued to put responsibility into the hands of Charles de Langlade, appointing him superintendent of Indians and commander of militia for La Baye region. During the American War of Independence it was not surprising as a result to find that the Menomini and other Indian tribes fought on the British side.

In 1766 Jonathan Carver, a well known traveller, passed across the Fox-Wisconsin portage. He reports seeing some French settlers, and records the two Menomini villages on his map. Still another visitor at this time was Peter Pond, whose account of La Baye is well worth giving as far as possible in its original weird spelling:

We went a Short Distans up the (Fox) River whare is a small french village and there Incampt for two days. . . . The Inhabitans Rase find corn and Sum Artikels for Fammaley youse in thare Gardens. They Have Sum Trad with ye Indans what Pas that way. On the North Part of this Bay is a small Villeag of Indians Cald the Mannomaneas who Live By Hunting Cheafley. They have . . . a Large Quantity of Wilde Rice. . . . I ort to have Menshand that the french . . . Rase fine black Cattel & Horses with Sum swine.

[2] About this time two certificates were granted by the British to "Ogemawnee" and "Okimasay," leaders of the Menomini, in recognition of their loyalty. *Wis. Hist. Colls.*, xviii, pp. 268, 286.

[3] According to the Quebec Act passed by the British such settlers enjoyed the benefit of their own French laws, customs and religion.

He describes his journey up the Fox, noting the wild rice and game. At Butte des Morts he meets a mourning party of Indians, probably of Menomini:

We stopt hear awhile finding Sum of that Nation on the Spot Who Came thare to Pay thare Respect to thare Departed frend. They Had a small Cag of Rum and sat around the grave. Thay flld thar Callemeat (calumet) and began thar saremony by Pinting the Stem of the Pipe (in different directions) . . . after which thay smoaked it out . . . then thay took Sum Rum out of the Cag in a Small Bark Vessel and Pourd it on the Head of the Grave . . . then thay all Drank themselves—Lit the Pipe and seamed to Enjoi themselves Verey well. Thay Repeated this . . . Then Thay began to Sing a Song or two But at the end of Every Song thay soffened the Clay. After Sumtime Had Relapst the Cag had Bin Blead often. (They make some speeches about the excellences of the deceased) . . . Thay Amused themselves in this manner til thay all fell a Crying and a woful Nois thay Mad for a While til thay thought Wisely that thay Could Not Bring him Back . . . that an application to the Cag was the Best Way to Dround Sorrow and Wash away Greefe for the Moshun was soon Put in Execution and all Began to be Marey as a Party Could Bea . . . the men began to approach the females and . . . apeared Verey amaras . . . I thought it was time to Quit and went.—From the *Journal of Peter Pond.*[4]

The political events of this period appear to have affected the upper country but little. In 1778 Spain declared war on Britain and a combined British-French-Indian expedition, including some Menomini, conducted a campaign against Louisiana, by then ceded to Spain. Two years after the signing of Jay's treaty in 1794 the British officially evacuated Mackinac; yet they merely retired to Drummond's island beyond, where, even as late as 1825, the tribes continued to visit them, disregarding the fact that in political terms they were under the United States flag:

British officers continued to receive the tribal delegations that swarmed upon them at the northern posts. As of old, the visitors were given military commissions, gay uniforms, medals, arms, ammunition, and a profusion of miscellaneous presents—liberality in sad contrast with the method of the economic Americans who without doubt were somewhat niggardly toward their red wards.—Thwaites, *Wisconsin,* p. 150.

This unwillingness of the British to yield territories and Indian friendships in the northwest is explained by the

4 Seen at Yale University.

rich harvests that were being reaped by their merchants in the fur trade. In 1787 a North West Company welded together many of the numerous small British furtrading concerns. The wealth of furs gained by this company, together with the Hudson Bay Company, surpassed by far the earlier French exploitation, and marked the climax of fur trading in the area. But as the trader had still to deal through the French or half-breed voyageurs this made comparatively little difference to the Indian.

A number of references to the Menomini are to be found in the documents. There is a short description of the tribe dated 1777, lodged in the Spanish archives of the Indies; this enumerates them as having "two hundred warriors", and names as their chief, Carron.[5]

Both the old chief Carron and his son Claude or Glode, who is the one here mentioned, were named as taking part in the defense of Quebec. The Carron family really play a most important part in the social history of the Menomini. Actually they were interlopers among the tribe, for Carron the elder, or "Vieux Caron" as he was sometimes known, was a French halfbreed from the east who came to the Bay region as an agent of the Langlades. He appears to have gained an ascendancy among the Menomini, marrying into the tribe, and even becoming "speaker" for the head chief, especially no doubt in matters involving contacts with the whites. He, and particularly some of his sons after him, were referred to frequently by writers of the time as "chiefs"; at least they were outstanding leaders in war and council. One of them, Tomau (Thomas) following after Glode, appears to have been virtually head chief of the Menomini from near the end of the eighteenth century until his death in 1818.

In 1779 a British commandant at Mackinac, De Peyster, wrote a rhymed chronicle purporting to be a speech given by him to the Indian tribes in council. In it he speaks of "Carong's brave Menomenies"; incidentally it sets out a list of the main trade goods used and presents given by the British:

[5] *Wis. Hist. Colls.*, xviii, p. 364.

Smoked red-deerskins for warriors' shoes
Item—large birch-bark, north canoes,
Masts, halliards, sails, flags, oars and paddles
Broaches, medals, bridles, saddles,
Large rolls of bark, awls, watap (pine-root), gum,
Lines, spunges, pipes, tobacco, rum,
Guns, powder, shot, fire-steel and flint,
Salt pork and biscuit, without stint;
Rich arm bands, gorgets and nose-bobs,
Made of French Crowns and Spanish cobs;
Lac'd coats, chintz shirts, plum'd hats for chiefs,
And for your beaux silk handkerchiefs;
Paints, mirrors, blankets, moultin, strouds,
To clothe the living and make shrouds,
For those who might in battle fall,
Or die by rum at Montreal . . .
Clothe each child, old men and women,
Give nets, hooks, lines, grease and mandamin (maize),
Knives, scizzars, combs, hoes, hatchets, spears
And Kegs of *milk* (rum) to dry their tears.
                    —In *Wis. Hist. Colls.*, xviii, pp. 377–88.[6]

Another document by this same commandant shows something of the method used to get the Indians to fight as British allies:

The Weenippigoes & Menomies . . . know they are not to have goods sent among them unless they strike the enemy. Should they misbehave I hope you will see the necessity of curtailing their presents.—*Idem*, pp. 393–94.

In 1780 a trader John Long visited La Baye; he writes of the Indians there:

The southern Indians have more villages and are better civilized than the northern (he had been among the Chippewa), the climate being warm and nature more prolific, which enables them to raise the fruits of the earth without much labor. Their houses are covered with birchbark and decorated with bows and arrows and weapons of war. Their beds are bark and mats made of rushes.—*Voyages and Travels*, Lakeside Classics, p. 186.

Long shows on this map the Menomini as still occupying their two settlements, "Monomony Town" on the Menom-

---

[6] It is seen here how the British, in seeking to enlist the Indian as a fur-getter and a fighter, not only gave presents of white goods, but also appear to have actually given his own Indian types of manufactures or else the raw materials, in order to relieve him of the necessity of taking such extra time to satisfy his own needs.

inee river and "Monomony Castle" on the Fox, also the Winnebago as living round lake Winnebago. Apparently the two tribes had their frictions, for in 1794 the records indicate that Langlade, as British agent, had to make peace between them.

By the beginning of the nineteenth century the United States began to take more of an interest in its new territory of the northwest. The first official recognition of the existence of La Baye by the Americans seems to have been the appointment in 1803 of a local trader named Reaume as a justice of the peace. This "erratic" individual appears to have conducted the whole legal and judicial business of the region, even after the American occupation later. Evidently the move was a practical expression of what is known as the "Ordinance of 1787", passed by Congress for the government of its western territories. As a statement of Indian policy for the area the document is worth quoting, particularly in view of the succeeding events in Menomini history:

> The utmost good faith shall always be observed toward the Indians; their lands and property shall never be taken from them without their consent; and in their property, rights, and liberty, they never shall be invaded or disturbed, unless in just and lawful wars, authorised by Congress. But laws founded in justice and humanity shall from time to time be made for preventing wrongs being done to them, and for preserving peace and friendship among them.

In 1800, the Menomini lands were included in an area organized as Indian Territory. Nine years later they were placed within the "Territory of Illinois". By this time a trading house known as the American Fur Company had been founded which bought out its British rivals at Mackinac, establishing the Southwest Company. Before long its agents were competing with the local French and British traders of La Baye for the one all-important source of wealth, furs. Such were the first steps of American penetration into the Menomini region.

A famous American explorer, Lieutenant Pike, recorded in his journal some encounters with Menomini hunters and accompanying traders when voyaging up the Mississippi river:

> On the 27th (of November, 1806) the men . . . returned . . . accompanied by two Indians who stated that they belonged to a band called Fols avoines. Their language was that of the Chipeways . . . (He notes that four traders are with the tribe) Three families of the Fols avoine arrived . . . next day another . . . Chien Blanche, a chief . . . Mr. Pike visited the lodge in the afternoon, and found him seated in the midst of his children and grandchildren, amounting to ten . . . The lodge was covered with mats made of plaited rushes . . .
>
> Several Indian chiefs came in to see Mr. Pike . . . Thomas, the Fols avoine chief gave assurances . . . This chief is of a noble and masculine figure, and an extraordinary hunter: as an instance of this it is related that he killed forty elk and a bear in one day, chasing the former from the dawn till evening . . . He appears very much attached to the Americans . . . a Fols avoine chief, called Shawanoe, and six young men paid a visit . . . (He proceeds to tell of the fine physique of the Menomini; describes them as "close in their dealings"; and tells of feasting and dancing.)—Pike, *Account of a Voyage*, pp. 26–28, 46 ff.

In 1810 another Indian uprising under chief Tecumseh failed to enlist Menomini sympathy, even though bands of most of the other Central Algonquins took his side. An early resident records a meeting between this insurgent leader and Tomau when they were present at an Indian council in La Baye. Tomau spoke after Tecumseh whose words had made a big impression; the account of his address finishes:

> Tomah . . . then paused; and while the deepest silence reigned throughout the audience, he slowly raised his hands, with his eyes fixed on them, and in a lower, but not less prouder tone, continued "but it is my boast that these hands are unstained with human blood!" The effect is described as tremendous. . . . He concluded . . . that he was fully aware of the injustice of the Americans in their encroachments upon the lands of the Indians, and for them feared its consequences, but that he saw no relief for it in going to war.—Biddle, *Recollections, Wis. Hist. Colls.*, i.

The rebellion of Tecumseh is another reminder of the steady pressure of white settlement following the trader out into Indian country, and pushing back the tribes across the Mississippi. From this, however, the geographical position of Menomini country was still keeping them isolated.

In the test of loyalties involved in the British-American war of 1812–14, both the French settlers of La Baye and the Menomini fought on the British side. Langlade had died by that time, but his place had been taken by a British trader, Dickson. A combined force of British, French, and Indian militia crossed the Fox-Wisconsin portage to capture a newly placed American fort at Prairie du Chien. When, after the peace of Ghent, the British formally evacuated the Menomini area, the French and Indian residents saw with chagrin its occupation by the "Bostonnais" or "Long Knives" as the Americans were called.

First Menomini-American Contact

In 1815 a United States government trading post and Indian agency was established at La Baye, the name of which was changed to Green Bay. The following year troops took up quarters there, clearly a strategic move designed to close the main line of communication "by which traders may introduce goods into the Mississippi and Missouri country from the British dominions". On their arrival the Americans made overtures of friendship to the Menomini. In spite of opposition by the French residents the tribal leaders realized the wisdom of once more being willing to change their nominal political allegiance, or at least saw that opposition was futile:

> The officers . . . visited Tomah, a Menominee chief, whose quarters were some half mile distant, and asked his consent to build a fort. He replied that they were too strong for him, even if he wished to oppose them; and added that they might build a fort wheresoever they pleased, but asked as a favor that they would not molest the French settlers.—See French, *History of Brown County.*

Green Bay settlement at this time comprised some forty-five to forty-eight families, practically all being French traders and their employees and mostly married to Indian women, particularly of the Menomini tribe. Their patriarchal community was ruled by the leading traders, and among them "Reaume law" and the "coutume de Paris" prevailed. With the advent of the United States authority and American people into the settlement and the region, these folk were called upon to make drastic adjustments.

Some of the first experiences of an Indian agent appointed to take charge of the "Green Bay Agency" are revealed by his correspondence:

> I wrote the Secretary of War last fall, I had taken from the Chiefs their British medals, arm bands and Flags, and had promised to replace them . . . I have received no answer on this subject, I also requested a moderate supply of presents for the chiefs and their families. The Indians from fear more than from principle, appear friendly; it will for some time require strong measures to destroy the British influence in this quarter . . . (According to another document a considerable number of Indians, including "584 Fullsawwynyes," had visited the British at Drummond's island just previously.) I have prohibited the landing of every description of spirits in this agency, for the purpose of trade or Barter . . . I have taken the liberty of enclosing to you the Copy of a treaty made at St. Louis with the Menominee tribe of Indians. The fellows who have Signed this treaty, have no influence or character with the Indians, and I am confident this treaty has been made without the knowledge of the principal chiefs, and of nine-tenths of the nation.—*Wis. Hist. Colls.*, xix, pp. 466–67.

The treaty referred to appears to be one containing merely a statement of peace and friendship between the Menomini and the United States (p. 129); it did not have to do with land as did later treaties. This however was not the first Indian treaty affecting tribes in the area that is now Wisconsin. The United States Government had already worked out a definite technique of dealing with tribes within its borders by making agreements with their chiefs and leaders as if they were independent nations. Already as early as 1804 the Sauk and Fox had, for due compensation, ceded their interests in lands south of the Fox river, and twelve years later a similar cession was made by the Ottawa, Chippewa and Potawatomi. The tribes of the distant northwest were thus feeling the first touch of the pressure that was to close in upon them within a short space of years.

The government venture into trade by the establishment of a fur post at the Bay and other centers was a failure from the first. The French and British traders, "from the ascendancy which an uninterrupted intercourse of many years has enabled them to acquire . . . supported by extensive family connections" with the Indians, had control of the trade. Furthermore the United States government was entering into competition not only with these foreign interests but also with a powerful political element within its own borders, the Southwest Company. Before long laws were passed by Congress forbidding entrance to all foreign traders and capital, and in 1821 the government factory closed its doors as a result of further legislation. By that time even the local traders and habitans were on the verge of ruin from their powerful American rivals.

Some extracts from a series of letters by the local residents show the status of the fur trade at the time, also the effect of the new conditions, including the rise of a ramshackle "Shanty Town", at Green Bay upon Indian life:

1820—All is dull in regard to business . . . the Hunt in general is faild all threwout this part of the Country, & we do not here of one particular Spot about where the Indians makes any kind of a Hunt its worse than last year . . . the Indians about here is numerous more I believe than usual just waiting till the Lake Froze to go to their usual Hunt Spearing Fish.—Lawe, at Green Bay, January.

1823—As to getting Corn . . . I will say that I have already attempted it, but one cannot do here as one would wish. The Savages given over to Drink makes it difficult, part are Attracted by the keepers of the canteen and others. They have their Stores well Garnished for they have a privilege . . . Very little hunt has been made, and the Whiskey . . . has too much influence.—Grignon, at Green Bay, September.

1824—The Indians around here has made no Hunt they have made a great deal less hunt than ever they have made & besides that the very good intentions they have towards us in trying to cheat & defraud us as much as they can as even the few Peltries they do kill they take it to the Shanty Town (the "disreputable" end of the settlement) to trade either by Night or take a New route round . . . by day . . . even the very best Indians that . . . would be able & willing to pay His Credit to us, after paying if he had any Peltry remaining he would . . . trade it with these Shanty Men . . . they are now so much taken up with these people . . .

The Winter has been so Open & mild this Year that the Lake is not yet taken (frozen) . . . there has not been a single Speared Sturgeon has been brought to the Bay this Year, the Indians is all a Starving & it is quite a famine for them. There is not a Single bit of Ice at the Follavoine (river) . . . the nets has catch'd but few fish I do not know what is going to become of us.—Lawe, at Green Bay, February.

The Indians has made 100 per Cent less hunt than I ever know them to make, and about the Bay there has been a great deal more opposition than ever.—Lawe, April; all are from *Wis. Hist. Colls.*, xx, pp. 148, 307–08, 331–32, 337.

These show not only the hard times that were being faced by the French trading community but also some of the closing scenes of the furtrade era in the region. Though into modern days a certain amount of hunting has been done, the fur trade from this time lost its predominant place in the economy of white and Indian; the stretching forest lands were wanted for other purposes.

In 1818, the Menomini area was included in Michigan territory. Three counties were created in what is now Wisconsin, Green Bay being the seat of Brown county. The years from 1820 were a serious time of transition for the group of older French families. A British scheme had before this been afoot by which they, together with their Menomini allies, should be removed bodily and resettled in Manitoba, Canada; but this had lapsed at the death of its sponsor, Lord Selkirk. In the year mentioned a Commissioner was appointed to investigate private land holdings by whites in the region.

Heretofore, Indian titles having been acquired by them through either consent or purchase at an early day, the settlers at Green Bay and Prairie du Chien occupied their fields much in the manner of an Indian village, the lands being alternately in common, and improved parts as each should please, and this by the common consent of the villagers. As a rule the holdings were . . . narrow strips running far back from the river, which was the common highway . . . Exact boundaries were of small account . . . and Wisconsin Creoles had characteristically failed to obtain definite title to their plots.—Thwaites, *Wisconsin*.

But the new administration demanded exactness of ownership, and individual title in land unknown either to French or Indian. The residents had to submit to an examination by the Commissioner. Fortunately, because of his wise handling of the situation, there was not much friction. In 1821 the Quebec law was replaced officially by Michigan law. Two years later Congress established a circuit court, the first session being held at the Bay soon after. An at-

tempt was next made to regulate the marriage of French
and Indians. Some thirty-six "offenders" against the
new American code for the region were formally indicted
and notified that they would have to be married by civil or
church law;[7] this aroused fierce indignation, and after pro-
tracted litigation the mutual consent marriages were up-
held. As early as 1821 a postal service and office were
established; the Catholic missions opened again, closely followed by other denominations; and before long a school was
commenced. Meantime lumbering was being started in the
rich forests and military roads replaced Indian trails and
the age-old water highways. White influences of a far more
comprehensive nature than ever before were coming to
Menomini country. Indeed Green Bay was bidding fair to
be the capital of the newly forming territory of Wisconsin,
and the records show it as a center of contrasts with its
"soldiers and officials, bourgeois, humble habitans, and ever
present blanketed Indian".

For the Menomini and other tribes of the region, these
were days of unsettlement and considerable disorganization.
The fur trade around which their life had stabilized in these
many decades was passing, and they did not settle down
readily under American rule:

In August last a party of Winnebagoes fired upon Captain Whistler,
(also upon others). Dr. Maddison . . . was treated with insolence by
the Winnebagoes . . .

The drover (of a herd of cattle for the fort supplies) . . . was attacked
by several young Chippewa Indians . . .

A soldier of the garrison . . . was assaulted within a short distance of
the Fort, stabbed and supposed at first to be mortally wounded. The out-
rage was perpetrated by several Menominee Indians, and their object . . .
(was) said to be to obtain a small quantity of Whiskey, which the soldier
had in his canteen . . .

[7] The older mode is thus described by Lockwood (1816); "The traders of
Green Bay mostly married, after the Indian manner, women of the Menominee
tribe, there being no white women in the country . . . The coutume de Paris
so far prevailed . . . that a part of the ceremony of marriage was the entering
into a contract in writing . . . If they desired to be divorced, they went together
before the magistrate . . . he, in their presence, tore up the marriage contract."
—*Early Times, Wis. Hist. Colls.*, ii, pp. 104, 121.

The Winnebagoes . . . proceeded to Drummond's Island; obtained British presents . . . I have (since) found on an eminence . . . the English flag erected and flying.—*Wis. Hist. Colls.*, xx, pp. 139–40.

In 1820 the Reverend Jedediah Morse visited the Bay as a special government Commissioner to investigate Indian affairs. He reported:

We found the Winnebagoes and Menominees . . . in a state of considerable agitation; the former in consequence of the recent murder of two of our men, at Fort Armstrong . . . the latter, on account of an unauthorized treaty, professedly in behalf of the Government of the United States, which the Indian agent had just completed with the Menominees for the purchase of a large tract of their most valued land, on both sides of Fox river . . . Nearly all the real, acknowledged chiefs of the nations were strongly opposed . . . Divisions and contentions immediately succeeded this sale, between those who signed, and those who were opposed to the treaty, one immediate consequence of which was, the murder, while we were at Green Bay, of one of the signers . . . Happily . . . this treaty . . . has not been ratified. The joy expressed by these poor Indians on receiving intelligence that this treaty was not to go into effect, was correspondent to the extreme grief and depression, which they had previously felt.—Morse, *Report to the Secretary of War,* p. 15.

This report contains much information supplied by local residents concerning the Menomini, important portions of which will be quoted in the summary chapter that follows. Concerning Menomini leadership he said:

The chiefs of this nation are principally young men, and have less influence than their predecessors, on account of their age, and because the white people have not given them that attention and support, which they were wont formerly to receive from them.

He specified the contemporary leaders as being "Mancantaubee", the son of Tomau, and "Shakautcheokemau", or the Great Bear, otherwise Oskos (Oshkosh), a grandson of the old hereditary chief of that name who was called by whites the "Old King", together with "Iwyemataw", a brother of Tomau. The first two of these were young men apparently just out of their 'teens. Actually the leader mentioned earlier, Tomau, had died in 1818, and the old chief or "king", impotent with age, died in 1821. In this difficult period of transition, therefore, the Menomini were without men combining experience and authority to guide their policies and to mediate with the whites. Shortly after the visit of Morse the first named youth died. There began a hot dispute among the tribe as to whether the position of paramount chief should go to another son of Tomau, Josette, who was the representative of the powerful Carron family, or to Oshkosh with whom the prestige of the hereditary leadership seems to have rested (as head of the "bear" clan). Finally in 1827 a Commission appointed by the President settled the issue by naming Oshkosh, with Josette as second chief.[8]

The Menomini were indeed needing capable leadership at the time. In 1821 there came to Green Bay a large delegation of chiefs from tribes to the east seeking land on which to settle. They were headed by a Reverend Eleazor Williams, a "clever but erratic quarter breed" who later achieved notoriety by claiming to be the lost Dauphin of France. The full history of this Indian movement has been traced by Hoffman and need not be repeated here.[9] The tour was backed by missions for philanthropic motives, and also by speculators who wanted the Indian lands in New York state. Through the plausible arguments of the leader, the Menomini and the Winnebago were induced to complete a treaty with this delegation by which, for $500 cash and $1,500 worth of goods, a strip of land four miles wide was ceded to them on the Fox river. Apparently unsatisfied with this the delegates treated still further. The Winnebago withdrew from the council, but the Menomini, yielding to arguments, promises, and, it is said, threats in the name of the government, agreed to accept the New York tribesmen as joint owners with themselves of all Menomini lands.

This extraordinary cession was regretted bitterly within the year. Apparently the Menomini had not understood what was involved in such a land transaction, and so followed some ten years of confused discussion during which

8 For additional data on Menomini chiefs and leadership, see Hoffman, *Meno. Inds.*, pp. 44–60.

9 *Menomini Indians*, pp. 21–30.

Congress tried several times to intervene. The final settlement of the question will be discussed in a later section. Here it may be said that from this time on considerable numbers of New York tribespeople moved to Wisconsin. Williams and his own "mission band" of Oneida Indians, part of one of the Iroquois nations, took up residence immediately on the Fox river, while the Stockbridge and Brothertown (or Munsee) tribes, really a remnant of the Mohegans or Mohicans whom the Iroquois had removed earlier from their original territory in Massachusetts and Connecticut, settled east of Lake Winnebago;[10] other Oneida bands established themselves near Green Bay. Thus came about once more an Iroquois invasion of the Menomini region from the east, this time as a portentous result of the pressure of white aggression and settlement upon the very people who before were the aggressors.

By 1825 the first outposts of extensive white settlement, as contrasted with those of white exploitation and administration, reached the area. Certain lead mines in the southwest of the present Wisconsin, for long spasmodically worked by Indians, French and Spanish, were properly opened up by enterprising Americans with the help of Negro slave labor. In that year about a hundred whites were legally and illegally mining there. This number quadrupled in the next two years, and from then on a "lead rush" to the region took place. This early industrial migration was followed by a migration of agriculturalists. The Sauk, Fox and Winnebago peoples were soon rudely pushed aside from their hunting grounds, as formally they had a right to be according to the land treaties. But the opening up of the lead mines directed the main stream of white immigration well south of and past Menomini country. When, therefore, the pressure of settlement culminated in Indian outbreaks among these tribes (p. 133) the Menomini were still found fighting on the white side; and when in turn their own lands became wanted, they were then too isolated and outnumbered to resist by force of arms a similar encroachment.

10 The "last of the Mohicans" are therefore now to be found in Wisconsin.

A REVIEW

Clearly the French had broken in the Indian peoples very thoroughly to white political domination, thus opening the way for comparatively easy control by their successors. Indian-white relations in the Menomini region were dominated by several outstanding figures, and the British commandants of Mackinac, and afterwards of Drummond's island, secured the continued loyalty and cooperation of the tribes by means of a steady flow of presents and honors. But with the coming of the Americans these rather haphazard paternalistic and personal relations tended to break down. Instead, a system of institutionalized control was established, which developed later into the Office of Indian Affairs. Though the Great Father in Washington was to emerge importantly, it will be seen that he has in general handed out rules and regulations rather than gifts. Even today the older Menomini recall stories they heard in youth about the "good old times" when the sovereigns of England cared for their Indian children and sent them presents.

Administration still continued mainly in the hands of the military. Yet the lack of commercialism such as marked the French system doubtless gave an air of more disinterested authority. The victory of American diplomacy, and later of American arms, appears to have inspired a considerable respect among the Menomini and other tribes. Nevertheless the anomalous situation arose of their acknowledging allegiance to the United States yet continuing to visit the British. In due course, it will be seen, these visits were stopped and by 1832 the Menomini were fighting under the Stars and Stripes.

The exploitation of furbearing mammals waxed in intensity during the period, and the trading business was stabilized with the formation of the permanent white settlement at La Baye. Likewise an elaborate system of giving credit became more general. The influence of the furtrade upon Menomini economic and social life will be analysed in the next chapter. By the third decade of the nineteenth century this whole enterprise reached a state of collapse.

The center of furtrading moved west to the Pacific coast and north into upper Canada, leaving the Menomini and other tribes to work out their destiny among a growing body of white colonists; timber and agriculture become the keynotes in place of hunting and warfare, and questions relating to the ownership of natural resources emerge as profoundly important.

This period in Menomini affairs can be placed in the perspective of history by quoting from a historian and an economist:

Under American domination, it was impracticable for Wisconsin long to remain a game preserve for the redmen, as had been contemplated by both its French and its British owners.—Thwaites, *Wisconsin*.

The lands of any country are important for the human opportunity they represent . . . For long ages the lands of Wisconsin made their mute and ineffectual appeal to the natives. Then came a few French who were intent mainly upon such trade as the wild life of forest, stream, and swamp would yield when exploited by native huntsmen and trappers. Small haphazard settlements grouped about the trading posts . . . were all the French contributed toward the actual taming of the wilderness . . . The British occupation of the territory . . . was practically an extension of the furtrading era and need not, any more than the French, concern this story of the agricultural development of Wisconsin.—Schafer, *Agriculture in Wisconsin, Wis. Domesday Book*.

Such is the orientation of the period from this time on, and such was the new situation that was to demand Menomini adjustment.

V. AFTER TWO CENTURIES OF CHANGE

With the Menomini thus poised at the brink of their modern adventurings, it will be profitable to break into the moving stream of history and assess, so far as the materials permit, the tribal situation at about 1830–40.

The new economic and social order appears to have had in it the possibilities of considerable population growth, though warfare, the privations of the winter hunt, and still more the enervating effects of a summer around the trading posts could be reckoned as negating influences. Actually population estimates of the early nineteenth century indicate that the Menomini were more numerous at this time than at any stage of their history, earlier or later. Commissioner Morse in 1820 enumerates a total of 3,900 Menomini, of whom 600 were "warriors", 900 women, and 2,400 children. Some calculations make the figure much lower, others higher.[1] At least 1830 forms about a peak point in numbers, for in 1834 the tribe was swept by a disastrous small-pox epidemic and in 1849 by a cholera epidemic. Around the latter date all records speak of the "tragic" decline in population during the previous two decades—a decline which was not to be stayed until the twentieth century.

One important factor making difficult such calculations, other than the problem of counting heads accurately, was that a considerable mingling was taking place among the tribes. In 1820 Judge Reaume told Morse that "the Menominees, in great part, are of mixed blood, Ottawas, Chippewas, Pottawattamies, Sacs, and Foxes, with whom they intermarry" as a result of the "intimate intercourse between all these tribes, who have a common language" (i.e., lingua franca), Chippewa, and frequently "hunt together in the interior". A census of 1824 states that the Menomini bands north of the Fox river were closely asso-

[1] For example, an official "census of Indian tribesmen" dated 1821 gave 1,990; a "census of Wisconsin Indians" in 1824, 2,528; other figures are 3,000 in 1836; 2,464 in 1842; 4,200 in 1844; 2,500 in 1847, and 2,300 in 1849.

ciated with the Chippewa, and those to the Southwest with the Winnebago.[2] This fraternizing among the Indian peoples, stimulated by common economic, political and military interests, had become so free that, in spite of occasional clashes by warparties over local troubles, the older tribal distinctions seemed on the way towards becoming obsolete. Already this intercourse has been referred to as complicating greatly the task of reconstructing what is really old in the culture of this and that tribe. The levelling process was, however, stopped abruptly in the first half of the nineteenth century. With the land treaties and subsequent movements of the Menomini and other tribes to reservations, all Indian families and individuals were called upon to declare their particular tribal ties, hence a thorough segregation into exclusive units took place once more.

Along with this mingling of the tribes there were also established close relations between the Indian peoples, especially the Menomini, and the whites. The region was still a remote frontier, a census of 1824 showing that the number of whites in the Green Bay region was less than 160 (about 130 men, 7 women, and 22 children). Yet these numbers are no measure of the profound influence that they exercised—especially the handful of leading French and British traders who were thoroughly established. On the whole the Menomini had been peculiarly fortunate in the types of white men who had dealings with them; their paternalistic and personal relationships with the Indian, their sympathetic observance of custom, their utilization of the tribal leadership, and the periodic distribution of presents and honors all were well suited to win the loyalty and cooperation of the Indian.

Almost all of the white residents, too, were married into the tribes, notably to Menomini women—always a potent channel of influence on the frontier. From such unions and others less permanent came ever increasing numbers of children of mixed descent. Already the certainty that such mixture was extensive has been referred to, but unfortu-

2 *Wis. Hist. Colls.*, xx, pp. 349–50.

nately its extent cannot be traced at all exactly. The mission records of Mackinaw (p. 120) show that the "half-breed" families of La Baye were in many cases large. When in 1849 all "half-breeds" were given the opportunity of buying out their rights in the tribe's resources some three hundred availed themselves of the offer; at that time the number of those having white blood was without doubt considerably greater. Some of these persons of mixed descent will be seen as very influential in Menomini affairs, notably the Carron family, of which more shortly.

A minority of the Menomini during this time continued to occupy the ancestral lands on the Menominee river, but the majority spread out over a far wider territory. First they split into two settlements, as noted earlier; then, toward the end of the eighteenth century, they subdivided into a scattering of "bands" or hunting units. Each of these made its summer headquarters at some customary spot not far from La Baye settlement, either at or near the mouth of one or other of the various rivers debouching into Green Bay, or else on the Fox river. In winter it ranged inland after the furbearing game, even in some cases as far as the Mississippi headwaters. Because of the advantages accruing from nearness to the main trading post and of the Fox portage the original tribal area had become by 1830 merely a northern outpost. (Diagram 2, p. 77.)

Morse, after his visit, defined the Menomini territories as "the Fox river to the south, as far as Winnebago lake; Bay du Noquett to the north; Menominee river to the northeast, and Mississippi to the west", and indeed the land treaties recognized also certain rights held by them in territories south of the Fox as far as Milwaukee. Obviously such definitions of title refer to rights which became established in post-white times, presumably at the periods when other tribes were driven out, or drifted from the region.[3]

[3] In *Wis. Hist. Colls.*, xix, pp. 470–72, a list of the Menomini summer-time settlements places them on the Menominee, Oconto, and Wolf rivers, Green Bay, Winnebago lake, the Fox river at Big and Little Kackalin, Butte des Morts, and Vermillion islands, also in "scattering villages on the Islands and Rivers of the Bay".

Again, the system of tenure must been seen as following Indian custom, the land being held according to usehold rights
rather than anything like the exclusive property ownership
which developed in Europe. Contact with the French and
British had apparently done little towards familiarizing
them with the latter; indeed the habitants of La Baye had
made no attempt to establish titles to the lands they occupied until forced to do so by the United States authorities. This will explain why the Menomini and Winnebago so readily assented to the desire of "their Brothers
in New York to sit down among them" *i.e.,* merely to use
the land, as they thought. But they were soon to learn
through increasingly bitter experience the meaning of legal
definitions of land ownership and of survey pegs and fences.

The Menomini contacts of the time, of course, extended
far more widely than the region named above. Apparently
to go to the lower St. Lawrence, Detroit, St. Louis, or
similar places either with peaceful or warlike intent had
become nothing very unusual, at least to the men. On such
trips the tribesfolk were able to meet and observe the ways
of distant Indian peoples and also of the whites other than
on the extreme frontier.

Considering now the economic changes of these centuries, it is obvious that the Menomini had moved far from
the old subsistence economy. Though the "man-land" relation remained close, there had come in between the people
and their physical environment the trader, representative
of the world's markets. In earlier times the Indian had
hunted furbearing mammals only so far as they were needed
for food, skins and other products. Now they had to get
pelts for trade, and these had be at their best and thickest,
which meant intensive fall and winter hunting. Furthermore, the constant exploitation brought about a scarcity in
the nearer forests necessitating long trips over an ever widening territory, with corresponding modifications in the
social and political system. In addition, the availability
of various artifacts through trade tended to discourage,
and in some instances rendered obsolete, corresponding In-

dian manufactures, causing a reorganization of time and effort. The rhymed chronicle of de Peyster (p. 89) is highly significant as showing how the whites, by providing the Indian with raw materials or with manufactured articles were seeking to release his energies along channels of intensive hunting and warfare under their direction. Along with this new wants were stimulated, bringing the Indian standards of living more into line with those of the larger world. All this meant that the Menomini and other tribesfolk had left their old self-sufficiency to become, so to speak, one group of specialized workers in the larger commercial economy. Their region might be likened to a great open-air fur factory, an industrial establishment managed and financed by the whites and the part-whites, in which the Indian, through the urge of his new wants and tastes, was driven to work.

In the late eighteenth and early nineteenth centuries the Indian was apparently used to the utmost limit possible under the circumstances in exploiting the fur resources, and the trade became wealthy, highly organized and, especially near the beginning of the end, intensely competitive. It has sometimes been said that, in becoming increasingly reliant upon the trader, the Indian "had lost his proud independence as a son of the forest";[4] but this seems to be merely a sentimental appraisal by whites of what to him appeared an improvement, and does of course to the whites themselves.

Various writers have seen disadvantages in the dependence of the Indian upon the trader and especially in the system of credit by which the Indian, departing for his winter hunt, had his potential catch already mortgaged on account of debts contracted during his summer of "idleness" around the trader's post, and the goods and equipment advanced to him for his expedition. This, says the historian Thwaites, caused him to be constantly in debt to the traders and so was his "undoing".[5] Yet the responsi-

[4] See, for example, Kellog, *French Regime in Wisconsin*, p. 38.
[5] Thwaites, *Wisconsin*, pp. 196–98.

bility and worry of this mutual relation appears to have weighed far more heavily upon the trader than upon his debtor, judging by the records set out above. Granting that the Indian may often have been imposed upon and given a poor deal, it is wrong to see this system as fundamentally any more unsound or disadvantageous than, say, the set-up of modern business and financing. It will be seen later that many Indians still find the credit system a simple and convenient procedure as regards their commercial dealings. Of course new risks were introduced beyond those existing in the old life; the failure of the hunt, possible withdrawal of the trader, or the cutting of communications with the sources of supply away east. Over against this, however, some of the hazards of the former economy were negated; as where, in the winter of 1817-18, the women and children who would otherwise have starved were provided for.

The furtrade of course did not bring the Indian into touch with more than a segment of the larger commercial and industrial order of Europe. Obviously he continued to meet many of his needs, as for example those concerned with food, clothes, shelter, and transportation, in the Indian way. The division of labor between the sexes remained much the same; men continued to be the hunters and warriors, even if in a different setting, and women's tasks continued to keep them busy; if in some respects they now could lean on the store to provide some of the artifacts they previously had to manufacture there were other activities to fill in the gaps, such as making more elaborate clothing. Where the Menomini received money, such as the silver coins distributed by the British at Mackinac and the "French crowns and Spanish cobs", he was as likely as not to use them for the manufacture of ornaments. The way the tribesfolk were to handle the money coming to them through land sales in the decades immediately following shows that their ideas about its value and use were exceedingly vague.

Their commercial experience lay in the limited field of exchanging furs for trade-goods, and also to a lesser extent in bartering whenever the whites wanted supplies or Indian manufactures. Of the latter it is an interesting sidelight upon cultural change that, in the early days of trade when the Indians came to realize a new worth in their everyday goods, they did what some at least of the Pacific Islanders did at the same stage of innovation, namely put exorbitant prices upon their products in order to wring as much as possible of desirable things from the newcomers. Thus La Potherie says that the Menomini were "selfish to the last degree, and consequently characterized by a sordid avarice", while Allouez wrote as a result of his first attempts to barter with the peoples of La Baye that "They are grasping and avaricious to an extraordinary degree, and sell their little commodities at a high price". Naturally such first kinks in the trade relation were soon smoothed out.

The new economic equilibrium produced in these first two centuries, based primarily of course on mutual exploitation, appears to have been satisfactory to both Menomini and white. The agents of trade fitted with apparently no great strain into the tribal organization. Apparently their ideas and those of the Indian coincided fairly well as to what was worth keeping and what should be modified in the traditional life, so that the readjustments were on the whole not forced upon the Indian from outside, but were a voluntary changing from within under the stimulus of new wants. They appear to have come about relatively quickly, then, reaching more or less of a new functional integration or balance, to have lasted right up to the end of the furtrading era.

Turning now to a closer study of the material aspects of Menomini living, it is obvious that there had been both change and conservatism. While some phases of material culture will be covered in more detail in a later chapter where data from museum collections and ethnological records will be surveyed, the evidence of the contemporary records can be analysed here.

Put to the tests of usefulness and convenience, many of the tools and other artifacts brought by the traders proved immediately superior to the local products, and so were quickly adopted. This process appears at first sight to have been very simple; the earlier bone, stone, wood, hide, or other object was discarded and the metal or cloth artifact brought by the trader used in its place. Actually, on further study, it is seen that such innovations tend to alter, even revolutionize every aspect of the culture. A change from the bone awl to the steel awl, for example, or from the crude pottery or skin kettle to the iron utensils of the whites was no small event; it had repercussions comparable with those evident in western countries through, say, the invention of the automobile. Apart from the mental readjustments involved, there came about an inevitable decline in the crafts of bone and pottery work and in the prestige of those expert in them; the use of the ready made article gave an extension of leisure, with consequent reorganization of time; possibly there were stresses between conservative and progressive people; often the old form of object was maintained in ceremonial usage long after it was discarded from common use.

Again, such artifacts as passed into Menomini culture were more or less made over in accordance with their new context, accumulating meanings and uses that they did not have before, and losing more or less the functional significance they had in white culture. The ordinary trade thimble provides a simple but clear example. A study of old artifacts in museum collections shows that the thimble lost entirely its association with sewing, and became an ornamental or even a sacred jingler attached to medicine bags and other artifacts, presumbably replacing some less effective form of jingler used previously. Such an object in reality ceased to be a white man's thimble and became an Indian jingler (Plate V, p. 204). Often in the cultural transfer a cultural element was modified in form as well as in meaning and use; the steel awl was set into a bone handle, a kettle was beaten to a new shape and used as a receptacle in a sacred bundle. Processes of this kind were, of course, at work in spheres other than that of material culture but it is perhaps here that they appear most clearly. A further implication of this is that even where elements of the old culture appear to have been preserved unaltered, they really have undergone change in the sense that the larger context within which they were a functional part was being greatly modified.

Of the cycle of food-getting, Morse wrote in 1820:

> In the spring they subsist on sugar and fish; in the summer on fish and game; in the fall on wild rice, and corn, and in the winter on fish and game. Those who are provident, have some rice during the winter.

This appears to correspond to the ancient cycle, subject to what has been said about maple sugar (p. 21) and also to the qualification that doubtless in the furtrading era hunting became magnified as over against fishing as a cold weather activity. The records show, however, that with the decline of the trade around 1821 fishing came back strongly as a winter pursuit. It is perhaps worth emphasizing that, since pelts were good only in winter, there was a minimum of interference with the rest of the traditional cycle of food-getting, garden culture, berry gathering, harvesting the wild rice, and so on.

The Menomini had become, of course thoroughly familiar with, and appreciative of certain foods of the white man, notably salt pork, flour, biscuits, and coffee. Yet these were only occasional luxuries outside of the normal food cycle. Indeed, during this time, the white men in general took over the foodstuffs of the Indian. Not until permanent settlements were founded and farming took root was the customary menu of whites demonstrated to the Indian, and even that included a number of foods native to America.

In attempting to reconstruct the pre-white life, it was noted that the clothing and personal adornment of old days cannot be known in any detail. The records show that from early times a miscellaneous array of white garments and clothing material was received by the Menomini as presents, and, presumably, in the course of trade. Included were military uniforms and such special decorations of the period as are set out in de Peyster's chronicle. The most universally accepted article of clothing with the Menomini as with other tribes was the blanket; what in white culture had been primarily a bed covering became in the context of Indian culture a cloak. The animal skins formerly used as wraps now went to the trader, and in any case the blanket represented an improvement. Apart, however, from these facts there is little in the documents to aid in reconstruction. In the nineteenth century this lack is remedied as quite good information becomes available. One of the first white women to live in the area writes:

> I used to think that all Indians dressed alike. It was a mistake; each tribe dresses differently. The Foxes wear dressed deerskin, soft and white, one half of their heads shaved clean, with a great bunch of cock's feathers on the top. The Sioux dressed in deerskin, colored black, worked with porcupine quills, their hair brushed up and tied on the top of their head in one large square cushion. The Winnebagoes had their blanket daubed with paint, and large rosettes of colored ribbons; hair in two square cushions on the back of the head. The Chippewas and Menomenees dressed plainly, with nothing by which they could be distinguished.—Mrs. Brevoort Bristol, *Wis. Hist. Colls.*, viii, p. 305.

This reference to plainness of dress meets with confirmation from Kemper who in 1834 reported seeing at Green Bay Menomini men "nearly naked some with nothing but a dirty ragged blanket". In 1849 a Quaker who visited the tribe as a government commissioner wrote of their chiefs assembled for a council at Green Bay:

> . These sons of the woods were not, as one might have expected, dressed out in holiday trim. On the contrary their clothing was scant, not very cleanly and a good deal worn. There was no dirty finery about it nor any relics of finery . . . Few made much attempt at decoration. A son of the Sachem . . . was the most of a dandy. Red, green, and white streaks traversed his visage, and bright red knee-bands, inwrought with white beads in curious devices, edged with part-colored fringes . . . On his muscular arms were displayed glittering bracelets of tin, and a plume of dyed feathers surmounted his head, the raven locks of which were glossy with grease. His father, the Head Chief, wore no ornaments, except the broidered kneebands . . . (A certain chief) painted himself, apparently anew, every day, throughout the holding of the Council . . . Few of the chiefs wore any ornament or covering on the head, except a band to secure their long hair . . . In bad weather, the blanket was drawn up, in the manner of a hood . . . (The Menomini and Oneida women) wore the long, black glossy tresses

neatly parted . . . but confined by a fillet only. Their heads . . . were always bare, except when a blanket . . . was drawn over them. They were dressed in garments of blue cloth:—leggins . . . a narrow and short frock, and an anomalous sort of upper covering . . . The only decoration, was a little embroidery and lace, on extra occasions, about the ankles.—in *The Friend,* xxiii, Nos. 1 to 21.

Far better than these written descriptions are several portraits in colors of Menomini tribesmen, the work of the artist-traveller Catlin who in 1830 and 1836 visited the region. These show what was presumably the everyday dress, a blanket, breechcloth and leggings of deerskin, and moccasins, likewise the ceremonial dress with fairly elaborate ornaments such as a feather head-dress, necklaces, amulets, garters, and porcupine quill or bead work in geometric designs. (Plate I.)

The Quaker commissioner of 1849 noted that several of the Catholic converts had adopted the "long French surtout" and hats to distinguish them from their "pagan" fellows. But this seems to have been very temporary. More significant, perhaps, is that the Indian garments seem undoubtedly to have been modified to conform to the ideas of "decency" held by the whites. Not appearing in the quotations given above, but known from museum evidence to be set out later, is the additional fact that in the first half of the nineteenth century some of the Menomini women began to copy a type of dress worn by white women of the day, a full gathered skirt and waist. This in time became adopted more or less universally as the female costume among the Menomini and many other tribes. The fashion was probably popularized, if not actually started, along with various forms of elaborate ornamentation, by the Indian women married to the white traders, and received impetus among the Menomini through a sewing school conducted by a woman teacher (p. 160); it can still be seen among older Menomini women today. Museum evidence also indicates that the Menomini at the time with which this chapter deals were on the verge of a period of great elaboration in ornament and artistic decoration that was to leave its marks especially upon the ceremonial dress—of this more later.

PLATE I

SOME MENOMINI AT 1835–36

Sketches based on paintings by Catlin. (Note: Catlin's paintings give mainly an impressionistic outline rather than the detail of dress, ornament, etc.)

PLATE II

CHIEF OSHKOSH

Portrait by Samuel M. Brookes about 1852—reproduced by permission of the State Historical Society of Wisconsin.

Where clothing had been thus subject to change, Menomini housing evidently remained little affected in the new order. Their lodges were well suited to the natural conditions and their roving life. Apparently the trading posts and forts of the French and British, the few permanent log cabins at La Baye and other centers, and the more elaborate homes observed during visits to the eastern cities gave no stimulus to change.[6] Furthermore, whenever the whites had to be on the move, they would use Indian lodges or structures much like them.

In the same way the Indian modes of transportation, long proved suitable to the forest and water enviroment and in the case of the snowshoe to winter travel, remained virtually unchanged. Though the whites made a partial adaptation of the light birchbark canoe in the form of a larger "batteau", and sails were sometimes used, it was not until the early nineteenth century that ships of a white type appeared on Wisconsin lakes and rivers. One important innovation did come to affect Indian travel and transport, the use of the horse. For the full story of the arrival of the horse in America and its spread from Spanish Mexico across the southwestern plains into the woodland region, reference should be made to the well known paper by Wissler.[7] In the journal of Peter Pond, dated about 1774, the French settlers at the Bay are referred to as having "fine black Cattel & Horses", apparently from the east. It is relatively unimportant to debate the question as to whether the first Menomini horses came from the great plains tribes to the west or from the French; yet the fact that the Menomini used the type of saddle, bridle, and like equipment that is more or less uniform among the tribes of the whole region, and also the horse motif in much the same way on flutes, dishes and other artifacts, probably indicates the former as correct. Horses however were not of much use in the dense forests of north-

[6] Unless of course the rectangular form of lodge (p. 26) represents a post-white innovation; something, however, that can hardly be demonstrated one way or the other.

[7] "The Influence of the Horse in the Development of Plains Culture", *American Anthropologist*, N. S., vol. 16, pp. 1–25, 1914.

ern Wisconsin except as pack animals, and probably the Menomini employed them less than any other of the great lakes
tribes.   Certainly no revolution in Menomini culture took
place after their advent such as happened among the tribes
of the open prairie. (Plate VI, p. 205.)

Perhaps the greatest changes in material culture came
about in tools and weapons.   Most of the Indian artifacts
appear to have been superseded as fast as supplies of the
more effective ones of the whites could be obtained, especially metal objects like hatchets, knives, spearpoints, awls,
needles, scissors and fishhooks. The bow and arrow was kept
to more tenaciously, even when guns were available. This
is said to have been because as a weapon it worked silently,
and in the dense forest the approach of a hunter to his quarry
or a warrior to his enemy was usually at sufficiently close
quarters to make it effective; again the arrow was particularly suitable for the killing of small game and was lighter
to carry.   The guns traded to the Indians, too, were clumsy
flint-locks, more or less obsolete even in their day, and almost as dangerous to the user as to his victim, while powder and shot were obtainable from the trader only at a heavy
price.   Though in the early period the coming of guns to the
Iroquois was the paramount factor in bringing about extensive tribal movements and a general upset in the earlier
inter-tribal equilibrium, as happened indeed in other comparable areas of western penetration, these weapons seem to
have later been mainly used only as the white man distributed them to their Indian allies in campaigns against common enemies.   The warclub also seems to have survived in
use up to the nineteenth century, though whether it had then
a practical or mainly a ceremonial significance is not clear.
Menomini warriors are reported as carrying both clubs and
spears in a campaign of 1832 against the Sauk and Fox,
while Catlin painted clubs in the hands of certain of his sit-
ters.   The insertion of a metal knife-blade or spear-point
into the wooden head made it indeed a formidable weapon.

Other Menomini manufactures appear to have followed
the general process emerging, namely that those which were

the best adjustments to the Indian environment and life were held to, while those less effective or able to be obtained more conveniently through the trader tended to be superseded. At the same time all elements of the available white culture which were useful and desirable were adopted. Skin tanning and its techniques for example, appear to have altered very little other than that the old hide scrapers probably of stone were replaced by pieces of metal set in a wooden handle. The Menomini continued to twist rope, cord, and thread in the old ways, but in time the native article tended to give way to the yarns, cotton and silk of the trader. Pottery, shell utensils and the bowdrill disappeared, and in their place were used metal utensils and flint and steel. The old dyes and paints were to some extent replaced by trade pigments. Receptacles of fibre, wood, birchbark, skin and reeds were still being made, also mats; but buffalo hair work was declining and perhaps obsolete by then, because of the difficulty of obtaining and working the material.[8]

Some interesting problems of cultural reconstruction emerge here. Already in the study of the old life reference was made to the difficulty of knowing how far wood, bark and copper were used in the old manufactures. There is the startling assertion by Allouez in 1669 that the tribes of the Bay region were "without ingenuity and do not know how to make even a bark dish or a ladle; they commonly use shells", this either to be rejected or else reconciled with the fact that elaborate bark and wood work was found among these peoples in modern days. Allouez was familiar in the east with tribes using these materials freely, hence his surprise when he reaches the western tribes. The implication is that the Menomini bark and wood crafts were at least considerably elaborated through diffusions from the eastern Indians, Algonquian or Iroquoian, in post-white times. A study of museum collections today indicates that—as with artifacts connected with the horse—such wooden objects as bowls,

[8] Here, and in the four paragraphs that follow, evidence from later ethnological records and museum collections is drawn upon in order to round out the analysis.

spoons, the shoulder yoke used in the manufacture of maple sugar, and the many forms of birchbark work show little variation in form between the tribes. At least it is fair to surmise that these represent the end results of a considerable levelling out in the material culture of the Indian peoples coincident with the extensive contacts of post-white days.

One particular wooden artifact widely distributed may be separated out for special mention, the weaving heddle. Its antiquity as an Indian invention may be questioned in a practical way by saying that a visitor to the Public Museum at Milwaukee can see in adjoining rooms what is apparently the same artifact, first in the collections of Menomini and other Indian material, then in the weaving room of a model white home of the old Colonial period. Seemingly the heddle was copied by one or the other, and if so the Indian was certainly the imitator. Perhaps this weaving technique was brought from the east by the Iroquois bands migrating from New York, though it may have come earlier. This also applies to the making of splint basketry and the working of silver and German silver. An exhibit card in the museum named above says of this last:

> The art of silver-smithing was introduced among the Indians along the Atlantic coast by some of the very early European colonists and became so much a part of their culture that its true origin was lost and it was later supposed to be as much a native art as basket making and various others. In these earlier times the Indians obtained silver largely by hammering out coins. When the Stockbridge came from the Atlantic coast and settled in northern Wisconsin . . . they brought with them a knowledge of the art of silver-smithing. A few of the Menominee took to this work and became in due course expert workmen.

Just where this information was obtained is not known to the writer; from inquiries among the Menomini, however, it would seem that the craft of working silver was introduced among the tribe at least in part through Ottawa sources in times considerably earlier than this Iroquois movement. Unfortunately it can hardly be known to what extent the craft, and also the patterns of the artifacts produced may have been based upon a truly aboriginal craft such as cop-

per working. A critic might answer any hasty advocacy of
the latter by surmising that any extensive working of copper
among the lakes tribes was also a product of white stimulation. (Plate VI, p. 205.)

Not less puzzling is the problem of how far changes took
place in Menomini art and decoration. The period around
1830 appears to mark the commencement of a new phase in
Menomini art. Up to that time there had been certain
changes in decoration throughout the woodland area; the
Indian accepted freely such new materials as cloth, wool,
ribbons, beads, and thread in all colors, together with adornments such as metal spangles, thimbles, "rich armbands,
gorgets and nosebobs"; he apparently utilized new techniques of stitching and also appliqué (though this may have
had a pre-white forerunner);[9] he seems also to have taken
over or received the inspiration for new decorative forms,
such as the military shoulder epaulette and trouser stripe
and perhaps various geometric figures. Yet the old materials, skin, quills and dyes, and the old techniques and forms
were by no means disappearing as yet. Furthermore, whatever the whites contributed in the way of stimulation and
materials, the results were an expression of the Indian
spirit and genius.

The new phase of art was to be marked by an extreme
elaboration and efflorescence: by the almost complete re-
placement of skin and quill by cloth and bead, of old color
pigments by new, the development of increasingly elaborate
floral and realistic designs in place of older geometric motifs,
and a much greater use of highly ornate pouches, bands and
sashes.

One striking fact about this new art development is its
wide distribution through the tribes of the woodland area
and even some distance into the plains area. The writers
would not venture to state from what center or centers the
diffusion actually took place, or attempt to date its progress
in the various regions; to do so would need a much wider
range of study than was undertaken for the purpose of this

[9] As suggested in Champlain, ii, 127.

survey. There is some evidence to suggest, however, that among those launching the innovations were some of the Menomini and other Indian women married to the whites, indicating that the stimulus if not the actual art patterns came as a result of white influence—of this more later.

Considering now the social and political changes of these centuries the most significant development was the emergence of the "band" as a major unit of organization. This provides a particularly interesting example of social readjustment, for as pointed out in the first critical reconstruction of the ancient life the older village and clan (gens) system apparently broke down more or less completely as the bands emerged. A lack of knowledge of the dynamics involved caused both Hoffman and Skinner to consider the band system much older and more rigid than it really was (to their informants of course it had a hoary past) and hence their accounts tend to mix it with the pre-white system thus obscuring their analysis of both.

After the first dichotomy of the tribe, in which apparently the Bear people moved south,[10] the Menomini gradually sorted themselves into bands which about 1830 were nine in number. Obviously from the analysis of the fur-trade enterprise the cause was directly economic. As early as 1762, according to Gorrell's observations, the two Menomini "villages" were becoming merely summer headquarters for their occupants, since all the able-bodied tribesfolk would set out by canoe along the inland rivers for the fall and winter hunt. Naturally all could not keep together, hence the families ranged in congenial groups. As the nearer forests became denuded of game these groups had to go farther afield and each tended to assume customary rights over a given river path and hunting territory; furthermore because of the credit system, the traders sent agents along with the band. When they returned for the summer they camped at places convenient for fishing, making gardens, and gathering

10 The village on the Fox is said to have been the headquarters of the "Old King", head of the Bear people; furthermore, in Hoffman's version of the story of the tribal division (p. 37) it was the Bear group who migrated, the cause being a quarrel over sturgeon fishing.

maple syrup, berries, wild rice, and other natural foods—
not all together, as numbers were increasing, but rather at
suitable locations on their fall canoe routes. Such factors
tended to stabilize the band organization, and of course the
earlier villages lapsed, becoming rather the headquarters
for two of the bands.

Out of fragmentary evidence, much of it obtained by
the writer from very old people, it would seem that the
bands, while becoming geographically definite were anything
but rigid; they comprised loose aggregations of kinsfolk and
friends who had hived off "to try their luck hunting in some
new place", yet who could change their band affiliation or
at least would visit and move freely from one group to another. At first the bands tended to follow clan lines, as representing linked families congenial to one another, though
the old people say there was no necessary rule. The bands
were not bands because they were originally clans, but were
rather economic and friendship groups which naturally were
built along clan lines. Personal preferences gradually broke
up much of this distinctiveness. Nevertheless at least some
of the bands retained strong clan marks right up to reservation days; the Oconto river band for example is said to
have been mostly "Beavers" and the Calumet band east of
Winnebago lake were "Thunderers". No development of
any marriage rules relating to band members ever took
place, and in fact the emergence of these units was undoubtedly the main factor in rendering obsolete whatever rules
may have existed in the village and clan life. The degree
to which the older organization has disappeared even from
memory in modern times would certainly indicate that by
1830 it had already disintegrated, leaving only certain particularly tenacious elements, notably connected with death
and with other fear producing experiences, to be carried
down to later days. In the further study it will be seen
how the mobile band system in its turn passed quickly out of.
existence with the sedentary conditions of reservation life.

Amid these changes the more intimate unit of living, the
small family or household group, appears to have been rel-

atively little modified, as fitting just as well into the band as
the village. The most obvious shift was in the direction of
monogamy, resulting from a trend towards equalization in
the numbers of each sex coincident with lessened warrior
mortality; perhaps, too, the monogamous family was a less
unwieldy canoe-and-hunting-trip unit. Presumably the
household emerged as more of an entity and assumed
greater functional importance as the clan ties relaxed and
under the more loosely knit band system. Such individua-
ualism shows strongly in modern reservation days.

Many phases of intimate group living appear likewise to
have remained little touched by the changes. Evidence
from later days indicates that the kinship ties still operated
in general along traditional lines, and likewise the education
of youth, and birth, marriage, death and mourning customs.
True, the Menomini women married to whites had opportunity to become familiar with certain white practices; records
of a Catholic mission at Mackinac show that a number of the
French residents had their nuptials regularized by the
fathers there and their children registered and baptized.
But the French and British made little attempt to interfere
with Menomini social customs, as was to happen under
American control. Again, the code of the frontier was not
of such a kind as to provide any elaborate example of what
observances were usual among stable white groups, while
the "coutume de Paris" was seemingly nearer to Indian patterns than to those of the incoming Americans.

Coincident with the changing of the larger social structure a considerable modification came about in the tribal
leadership. A document of 1849 says that there were twenty-
six chiefs in the Menomini council. While in general the
administrative officials and traders respected and used the
chiefs, the circumstances under which the Menomini gave
recognition to this or that individual became rather altered.
Men apparently still acquired prestige through their hereditary status (the head chief of the Bear clan, for example),
likewise through dream revelations or personal valor. Yet
certain new standards of worth were introduced as regards

leadership: success in obtaining furs, in directing hunting and trading operations and in obtaining credit, in ability to orate, in the newer military strategy, and in getting on well generally with the whites and with other Indian tribes. The conditions of the time were such as to foster the development of a mercenary spirit and the emergence of "swashbuckling personalities" among the tribesfolk such as were found, say, in ancient Greece or the city states of Italy in the Middle Ages.

The warlike propensities of the Menomini were seen finding vigorous outlet in the services of the whites, even far from their own territories, and the war leader probably waxed in importance. The band organization brought into prominence leaders who showed economic abilities. The capacity of a band leader (*okemau*) was to be judged not only by his social and religious qualifications, (if these came into the picture at all), but also by his ability to handle the furtrade enterprise to the satisfaction both of his followers and of the white traders to whom he customarily made himself responsible for the delivery of the furs collected. Other opportunities for achieving prominence came from the new political dealings with the whites.

Among the most useful Indian institutions in the new order was the tribal council, and its importance undoubtedly was enhanced in post-white times. The extensive contacts between the tribes and the many formal consultations with whites called for frequent councilling, while such periodic inter-tribal councils as were held at Montreal, Detroit, Mackinac, and Green Bay were grandiose affairs. A Quaker vistor in 1849, describing a Menomini council meeting, remarks on the great courtesy observed among its members.

> Everyone allowed his fellow ample time to express an opinion, without interruption, and there was none of the vociferation and excitement (that might be expected) . . . all was conducted with decency, order, and, apparently, with forebearance of each other.—from articles in *The Friend*, vol. xxiii.

Where in the intimate intercourse of the small compact groups of pre-white days there would be no great place for formal oratory, this now came to the fore.   The major councils gave opportunities for the good orator to make his mark, particularly any one who might have a grasp of both Indian and white languages.   The "speaker" to be a chief became an important personage, likewise the interpreter, who was usually of mixed descent.   The council likewise had its ceremonial aspects enhanced.   The custom of presenting "porcelain collars", which corresponded to wampum, as the ritual accompaniment of a request or speech, was evidently taken over from the eastern tribes in post-white times.

It is only against this analysis of the changing functions attaching to leadership that the emergence of the mixed blood Carron family, offspring of an outsider married into the Menomini can be understood.   By 1821 the socio-political system had shifted to a point where a grandson of Old Carron was actually able to gain support from one faction of the tribe—perhaps mainly those who were likewise of mixed descent—for his nomination to the position of head chief in opposition to the hereditary claimant, Oshkosh of the Bear clan.   More than six years of controversy ensued and the matter had finally to be settled by representatives of the white government.

This incident not only reveals the extent to which the old polity had weakened but also indicates that in the new order the status of chieftainship had in general increased in importance.   The head chief was now a particularly responsible person, as the United States adopted a policy of negotiating with the tribes regarding land and other matters as though they were independent nations and their principal leaders were kings or presidents.   Of Oshkosh, victorious in the struggle for the post, the Quaker visitor of 1849 wrote: "His word was law."   Besides the widening functions pertaining to the tribal leadership, it was reinforced by distinguishing marks in the form of medals, uniforms, certificates, and such extra goods as were issued to the chiefs. This, indeed seems to have been the heyday of Indian chieftainship, with the gap between leader and follower far wider than in pre-white times, and the former basking in the reflected glory of their contacts with the white "chiefs". Later, it will be seen, the American policies were to be reversed, the Indian leadership being liquidated with the government dealing with the Indians as individuals rather than tribal wholes.

The whites in general interfered comparatively little over the first two centuries with the internal ordering of tribal affairs, or with the relations between tribes except where this was prejudicial to white interests. The Menomini of 1830 was still counted a "savage" in his behavior. But as white settlers moved into the region in greater numbers, bringing their codes and values and their legal machinery, the tribesmen were beginning to feel the pressure of adjusting their conduct more to white ideas. Chief Oshkosh himself was put on trial at one time for murder, and though he was not punished the event must have had profound repercussions in Menomini thinking. When the Catholic missionaries once more gained an influence among the tribe there came about drastic changes in the behavior of those who joined their following. A story is told among the Menomini of how a youthful Christian refused to avenge his uncle's death, much to the indignation of his relatives; finally one of his sisters retrieved the family honor by exacting "blood vengeance" herself. Concerning the code of blood vengeance there exists an interesting record of how adjustment may come in such a custom as a result of new circumstances:

It appeared that a young Menomini in a drunken fray had killed a Winnebago, and the culprit was demanded by the headmen of the Winnebago tribe. A council was held, and instead of the Menomini, the chiefs of the tribe offered them whiskey. The Winnebago could not resist the novel temptation, and it was agreed that ten gallons of whiskey should be produced by the Menomini, to be drunk by all parties over the grave of the deceased.—Captain Marryat, "Wisconsin in 1837," *Wis. Hist Colls.*, xiv, p. 153.

Many documents at this time refer to the effects of liquor upon the tribe, particularly after the establishment of a "Shantytown" at Green Bay. In 1820 the agent reported that: "no quarrels, disturbances, or murders, have been known among the Menominees, during the four years of my residence among them, except such as have their origin in whiskey.'' Indeed, during the period of the land sales the liquor made available by the traders is said to have brought them "to the lowest point of human degradation"; by 1844 it was reported that "there is no tribe upon all our borders so utterly abandoned to the vice of intoxication as the Menominees", and "drunken rows" were a recognized factor in depopulation.[11]

The influence of newly arriving Christian missions has been mentioned above. Already an analysis has been made of the impact of the Jesuits in the seventeenth century, and of how what appears on the surface to be of genuine antiquity in Menomini religion, may in some phases, notably the Mitawin lodge, represent changes of early post-white times (pp. 48–50). Apart from the possibilities of modifications there visualized, it can be said that the old "pagan" religion continued to dominate the minds of the tribesfolk except perhaps for some of the mixed bloods and Menomini women married to whites. When from 1827 on direct mission work was carried on once more among the tribe the great majority were found unresponsive over the first three decades; a few, however, were converted and it will be seen in quotations to be set out in the next chapter that they led the way in the economic and social readjustments of the nineteenth century.

The records show as one of the most significant adjustments of the day—this paralleled on many similar frontiers —the emergence of one of the local languages, the Chippewa, as a *lingua franca* among the Indian tribes and between them and the whites in the whole upper lakes area. The fact that the Chippewa became the common medium is hardly to be wondered at; the Chippewa region, at the outlets of lakes Michigan and Superior, was in a real sense the gateway to the upper country, and Mackinac in its center was a key trading, military and mission post. The missionaries reduced the Chippewa language to writing, and pro-

---

[11] Note, however, that liquor assumed something of a religious significance among the tribe (p. 55).

duced a religious literature which in the nineteenth century
was made the basis of mission efforts among the Menomini
and other tribes. Without doubt this common tongue was
the main medium by which whatever cultural exchanges
occurred among the tribes were made possible. However,
as mentioned already, the land treaties brought about a
segregation once more, and the need for such common means
of communication lessened. There was no tendency for the
Menomini tongue to die out during this period of linguistic
intercourse; somewhat enriched as will be seen by French
words (the greeting "bon jour", for example) and perhaps
by words from other tribal tongues, it was used for intra-
tribal purposes and continued tenaciously right to modern
days.

Summarizing now the results of these two hundred years
or so of contact with whites it is seen how the Menomini and
other tribes of the region had achieved a new integration of
their life and culture, mainly on the basis of the fur trade.
The first century had been primarily a time of reorganization in intertribal relationships and in the tribal modes of
living under the new commercial and political influences.
The second century, for the Menomini at least, was marked
by spatial and economic expansion, also by increasing political and military cooperation with the whites.

Though Menomini culture underwent great changes,
these mainly comprised voluntary modifications by the
tribesfolk themselves in accordance with their own wants and
preferences, hence there was a minimum of strain; whatever
new cultural elements were taken over were fitted into patterns of thought and living that remained essentially Indian.
Those few specialized types of whites with whom the Menomini had contact were not interested in forcing upon the
tribe radically new modes of life; it was essential to both the
French and the British that the Indian should continue to
live close to his old environment and remain a hunter; they
desired to use, not to refashion him. The exception to this
was the Jesuit, yet even he wanted little other than to create
a new spiritual loyalty. The white man, indeed, reorganized

his own ways along lines suited to life in the region, and adopted not a few cultural elements from the Indian. In both instances the new modes of living tended to become stabilized, so that there developed an equilibrium of economic, political and social relationships among Indians and whites in the upper country that had some permanence. In a sense it was a condition of mutual respect and of mutual exploitation, with of course from the viewpoint of the whites the Indian in the subservient position, a stage in the relationship of peoples that can be observed in many settings both geographically and historically.

But a new and very different era was beginning. The policy and program of the United States authorities for the Menomini from this time forward was foreshadowed in a conversation that commissioner Morse recorded in 1820 as taking place between himself and a group of Menomini warriors:

> I stated to them the design of the Government concerning the Indians viz. to teach them agriculture and the arts, to dress and live like the white people &c.

To which a Menomini chief replied:

> It will look droll . . . to see Indians in such a situation. We are willing . . . to receive these blessings, if others will.

From this point on the steps taken and the progress made in civilizing and assimilating the tribe will be reviewed; also the reaction of the Indian to the ''blessings'' of this ''droll'' situation.

VI. WHITE PRESSURE AND PASSING LANDS

In the two decades to 1852 the Menomini lands passed into the hands of incoming whites, and the tribesfolk were removed to a "reservation" in the stony swamp-lands of the northern wilderness, there to be subjected to the civilizing process. This experience was sharp and dramatic; not without reason it is a portion of Menomini history still much recalled and of great interest to them. All that has happened since to the tribe was only a further development of the situation created in these crucial years.

Between 1830 and 1850 the white population of the present Wisconsin grew from some four thousand to over three hundred thousand. At first such newcomers consisted mainly of miners and lumbermen, "prairie settlers" from the eastern states of America, and various business and professional pioneers. But after 1846 great numbers of farmers arrived, a large proportion of whom were immigrants from Europe, particularly from Germany, Ireland, England and Scandinavia; the Indian was indeed to have the experience of meeting with white culture in all its heterogeneous types.

In 1836 a territory of Wisconsin was created. The first legislative assembly met with the characteristic clamor of frontier politics centered on the question of a site for the new capital. Green Bay clearly had the strongest claims in terms of its historical background and of numbers. But it was passed over in favor of the future Madison, then a mere paper town, because of the central position of the latter between the Bay and its rival industrial center growing up around the lead mines. This choice of a capital well to the south of Green Bay is significant, too, because it implied that the water route of the upper lakes over which for two centuries the furtrader, soldier and Jesuit had travelled was now losing its importance. Communications and settlement were from henceforth mainly to come overland from the east, passing south of lake Michigan. For the Menomini this was a momentous decision, as their lands were thus left for the time being a frontier area rather than the focal point of new and rapid territorial development. For years the pressure of settlement was directed to south and west Wisconsin; in fact, right to the present day, northern Wisconsin has been comparatively isolated.

A short chronology of events in the Green Bay region will aid in appreciating the course of Menomini-white contacts up to the period of removal to the reservation. They can be summarized as follows:

1816, Indian agency formed; 1820, post office founded; 1822, Catholic church built; 1824, first road along the Fox river, first court session, school formed; 1825, newspaper published, "Durham" boats first used on Fox; 1827, Episcopal mission started, saw and grist mills built, outbreak among the Winnebago tribe; 1832, outbreak among the Sauk and Fox known as the Black Hawk war, land rights given to start a number of timber mills; 1834, Land Office opens at Green Bay, Bank of Wisconsin starts, rise of commercial lumbering; 1836, rapid settlement by the whites of lands south of the Fox and Wisconsin rivers; 1843–47, lumber mills started in the Fox valley; 1848, Wisconsin created a state, steady immigration from Europe; 1851, Fox river canal opened; 1852, the Menomini removed to their reservation.

From this outline some idea can be gained of the progressive American invasion of the Menomini region, in which all but the most energetic of the old French families were pushed aside, the Indian lands were alienated, and the wilderness gave place by way of the lumber mill to farms.

Ahead of the moving frontier of settlement went the United States officials seeking to quell Indian feuds and define tribal boundaries with a view to making "treaties" of purchase. Once these were completed, tribe after tribe was removed, by force if necessary, to new territories in areas not yet wanted for white occupation. The "Great Father at Washington" negotiated with the Indian "nations" first through the War Department, and after 1824 through a special Indian Bureau constituted within this department; it was to be many years before Indians were to become subjects and in time citizens of the country in which they lived.

A first difficult undertaking for the American officials in their dealings with the Menomini was to get them to break completely with their British loyalties.[1] Nominally this had been achieved by a treaty in 1817 according to which the chiefs made a pact of "peace and friendship" in terms of which the past would be "mutually forgiven and forgotten," and the tribe would from thenceforth be "under the protection of the United States and of no other nation." Apparently this was the treaty which, as being signed by unauthorized people, caused great indignation among the tribesfolk (p. 93). Still more ill-feeling, however, was aroused by the treaty of which Morse spoke (p. 97); this was concluded by the Indian agent "professedly in behalf of the Government," and purported to alienate a large area of land on the Fox river; as the rightful chiefs would not sign, it is told, the official proceeded to "create Chiefs to sign his Treaty." But the move was repudiated by the Washington authorities.

In 1825, a grand council of the tribes was called at Prairie du Chien to define inter-tribal boundaries. Representatives gathered from the Chippewa, Ottawa, Potawatomi, Sauk and Fox, Winnebago, Sioux, Illinois, Iowa, Yankton, and Oto, but the Menomini chiefs excused themselves and stayed away. As a result, an article in the treaty ruled that the matter of settling the Menomini boundaries be left over. This, it will be remembered, was the time when disputes were in progress within the tribe concerning the title of head

[1] William Powell, for many years official interpreter to the Menomini, and himself of part Menomini descent, tells how: "As late as 1830 quite a number of the Menominee . . . went to Drummond's Island and got British presents. . . . The American Indian agent . . . warned the chiefs that . . . their medals would be taken away from them, and they would no longer have any claim upon the American government. This firm action . . . had the desired effect." *Recollections*, in *Proc. Wis. Hist. Society*, 1912, p. 164. An amusing incident of the time is related by a trader; an old Menomini chief received a pension from the British for having killed an American officer in the wars; he would journey north for payment, returning in time to get his annuity from the United States government for land sales. "He finally carried the thing so far as to raise the British flag in front of his wigwam on the (American) payground," which action caused his arrest by a squad of troops; he was threatened with hanging if he repeated the performance. See *Wis. Hist. Colls.*, ix, p. 499.

chief, and when feeling was running high towards the incoming New York Indians over the special land agreements of 1821.

Nevertheless the Menomini consented to attend a council held at Butte des Morts two years later. Here a government commission decided upon the claims of Oshkosh to the position of head chief, and at the same time a treaty was made defining the boundaries of Menomini territory together with that of white settlers at Green Bay. An immediate distribution of goods to the value of $15,682 was made to expedite the proceedings, with a promise of $1,000 annually for three years, and $1,500 annually for the education of their children as long as Congress should approve.

Yet this council failed to reach anything like a satisfactory definition of the land titles of the incoming New York Indians, about which controversy had been raging:

> The New York Indians claim to have made bona fide purchases and the Menominee and Winnebagoes deny it, alleging, their intention to have been, only, to grant permission to their Brothers in New York to sit down among them.—Letter of Secretary of War, *Wis. Hist. Colls.*, xii, p. 173.

The agreement made in 1821 had provided the Menomini with their first real experience of the meaning of private ownership of land as against usehold, and they were indeed finding it bitter. The newcomers had paid in cash and goods some $2,000, and were seeking to establish rights to more than six million acres of land. Indeed, according to a protesting letter of the Indian agent, these comprised the best portion of Menomini territory from the viewpoints of fertility and access. The dispute was finally referred to the President of the United States for adjudication. In passing it may be noted that an outbreak occurred at this time among the Winnebago under the leadership of Chief Redbird, a reminder of the unsettled state of the tribes as they were pushed off the lands they had sold. The historian Thwaites refers to this as a period marked by "predatory expeditions and simmering opposition to the whites."

In 1830 a further council was held at Butte des Morts to go once more into the whole question of the New York Indian claims. The instructions to the government commissioners

draw an interesting comparison between the position of the
Wisconsin tribes and that of the Indians from the east:

> In regard to quantity (of land to be allotted) . . . it may be proper
> to remark that Justice to the Winnebagoes and Menomonees, and utillity to
> the New York Indians, require, that no more shall be taken from the first
> . . . than will subserve the interests, and promote the comfort and pros-
> perity of the last.   Indian Tribes in a hunter state . . . require large
> Tracts of country; whilst Tribes, whose condition is essentially agricul-
> tural . . . require a less extensive domain.—Letter of Secretary of War,
> *Wis. Hist. Colls.*, xii, p. 174.

One of the commissioners, from whose journal the above
quotation is taken, has left a vivid description of the gathering, at which the Menomini apparently arrived in force,
severely taxing the supplies of government rations in the
form of pork, flour and corn.   This council resulted in a new
treaty the final details of which were negotiated at Washington in the following year by a delegation of Menomini
chiefs.   "As evidence of their love and veneration for the
Great Father" the Menomini passed half a million acres
of their lands to the eastern tribesmen, and for this act of
loyalty they were to receive four annual payments of $5,000.
Adding to this the total amount obtained in 1821, the Menomini therefore received for this first of their land cessions
approximately four and a half cents an acre.

The Washington treaty of 1831 also defined further the
boundaries of land north and south of the Fox and Wisconsin rivers over which the Menomini had claims.   Of this
the whole of the southern portion, amounting to two and a
half million acres, was to be ceded to the government for a
total compensation approximating $125,000, or about five
cents an acre.   A special area was decided upon in the
treaty, with its center at the present Neenah, Wisconsin,
to be "set apart and designated for the future home of the
Menomini upon which their improvements as an agricultural people" were to be made.[2]   In order to "wean them

[2] The quotations are from the treaty; see *Compilation of All Treaties,*
1873, for the full text and amendments; also *Indian Land Cessions,* in *18th*
Annual Report, Bur. of Am. Ethnology, ii, pp. 710–12, 716, 726–30, 760 and map
64.   Diagram 3 which shows this and the land cessions which follow, is based on
this map.

from their wandering habits'' the compensation allowed was
to be spent as follows: support for five farmers and five
housekeepers to instruct the tribe, a miller with grist and
sawmill, blacksmith shops and materials, all for ten years;
houses to be erected ''as soon as the Indians agree to occupy
them''; issues of household articles, stock, implements, cloth-

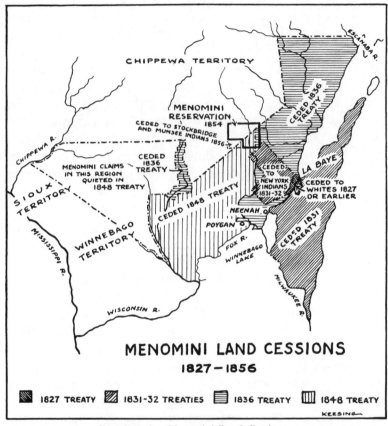

DIAGRAM 3.   Menomini Land Cessions.

ing, flour and provisions; payment for twelve years of a
$6,000 annuity; formation of a trust fund for education; a
house for the tribal interpreter; and gifts for the chiefs
then in Washington.   Peace and harmony were again emphasized, and the government reserved the right to buy more
of their lands should such be desired.   The general policy

of the government for the Menomini future, as indicated in the above compensations, is stated in the final part of the treaty:

> There shall be procured and given to the said tribe one thousand dollars' worth of good and wholesome provisions annually, for four years, by which time it is hoped their hunting habits may cease, and their attention be turned to the pursuits of agriculture.

When this treaty came before the United States senate for ratification, the terms relating to the New York Indian cession were disputed, hence amended. But the Menomini firmly refused to agree to new proposals which would have pushed them back upon the Wolf river "on lands of decidedly inferior quality"—the very area, it may be noted here, of their later reservation. A compromise was finally reached by which the Menomini ceded a more valuable area but of the original half million acre size, and this the Senate confirmed so as to end the "tedious, perplexing, and harassing controversy."

Government contractors now proceeded to build a mill at Neenah, and farmers were appointed to live among the Menomini, with their wives acting as the new instructors in housekeeping. An old trader comments on these improvements thus:

> All the efforts pledged to the Menos for their lands will not produce the least good. 5 good farmhouses have been erected on cleared land for farmers who are to receive 500$ and their wives 300$ and huts for the Indians in the woods which they say they will not live in. A saw mill is erected and a grist mill both of wh. it is feared will go to ruin for no timber is cut and the Menos have not yet learned and it is supposed they never will learn to plough.—from Kemper's diary, *Wis. Hist. Colls.*, xiv, p. 443.

The Indian agent of the time is also doubtful whether "all the mills and farmers in the Universe" would be as effective as putting aside an amount, the interest on which should be spent for "Corn, to be distributed at Midwinter, and early in the Spring of each year . . . forever."

In the documents of this period there are many references to the Menomini. When in 1832 a section of the Sauk and Fox under chief Black Hawk made a final stand against

the encroachment of whites upon their tribal hunting
grounds, even though legally sold, the Menomini came into
some prominence as fighting for the Americans.   Whether
this was due, however, to the development of a new loyalty
or to the long-standing feud that existed between them and
these traditional enemies must be a matter of opinion.[3]
Upwards of three hundred Menomini warriors took part in
the campaign under the leadership of local white officers,
American and French.

The records of this event are all the more interesting in
that several writers of the time speak of the pacific attitude
of the Menomini tribe.   Following their lead it has been
customary for modern writers to refer to the "quiet and
peaceful disposition" of the Menomini as an outstanding
trait of their character.   But this is by no means apparent
from the records of the 1832 campaign.   A missionary
observer writes of one of the warparties that assembled:

> Saw perhaps 50 of the Menominies who were on their way up the Fox
> r. on a war expedition to join the United States army against the hostile
> Sacs . . . Their painted faces, ornaments, drums, whistles, warclubs, spears,
> &c. made them appear indeed savage and warlike.   Their songs uttered from
> t. throat consisting in deep gutteral sounds and very loud . . . and t.
> occasional whoop was calculated to made one feel that darkness . . . still
> broods over this region.—Diary of Rev. Marsh, *Wis. Hist. Colls.*, xv, pp.
> 64–65.

Interpreter Powell, in his reminiscences, gives a vivid account of the fighting.[4]   He tells how, in addition to their
white officers, they were led by a war chief or "prophet"
who consulted the powers, gave the signal for attack with
a sacred whistle, and awarded a wampum belt to the warrior
bringing him the first scalp.   The Menomini refused to
desist from taking scalps when this was requested by their
officers.   An array of weapons ancient and modern, the
surprise attack, warwhoops, and the boasts and celebrations

---

[3] In 1830 and 1831 there had been hostilities between the Menomini and
the Sauk and Fox; in the latter year a party of Menomini were surprised near
Prairie du Chien and twenty-six killed. Some of the Menomini actually claim
today that the war against Black Hawk was a campaign in which the Americans
consented to act as their allies in securing vengeance!

[4] In *Proceedings Wis. Hist. Society*, 1912, pp. 164–68.

of victory there pictured show anything but a quiet spectacle.

Further glimpses of the Menomini in 1834 appear from the following:

Returning from Navarino (a section of Green Bay) saw a Men. woman drunk, a large boy with only a cloth on and others especially men nearly naked some with nothing but a dirty ragged blanket . . . We met with several Menomenee lodges at one a fellow nearly naked was climbing up the roof . . .

Mr. Grignon whose wife is a Meno . . . claims a great deal of land here and has a saw mill at the rapids (at Grand Kakalin, the last outpost of settlement along the Fox river) . . . In walking over the meadow from the mill to the landing passed an Indian burial place, 2 poles with white flags flying, a pale fence partly surrounding the place and thick sticks of wood covering graves . . . A short distance below a roman cath chapel built by Menos of logs . . .

Big Wave an old chief of Menomenees with a few other Menos . . . came to the house . . . Big Wave with a regimental coat and a large medal of Washington was the principal speaker . . . Many wild Menomenees fantastically dressed were about.—Rev. Kemper, *Tour to Green Bay, Wis. Hist. Colls.*, xiv, pp. 415 ff.

The Menominee Indians . . . (raised) a few patches of miserable corn, on the lower grounds . . . At the Great Kakalin, about twenty miles up the Fox river, a missionary establishment succeeded in bringing many of the Menominees to clear land, build comfortable cabins, and practice the art of husbandry. Some half-breeds occasionally preferred a hut to a wigwam, and raised a little corn, and a few potatoes. With these exceptions this interesting tribe existed in a state of worse than savage wretchedness . . . Their attachment to the United States, has not been exceeded by any Indian people. But . . . whiskey . . . (has brought them to) the lowest point of human degradation.—Whittlesey's *Recollections, Idem*, i, p. 68.

The reference to the mission station on the Fox river indicates how the Menomini were renewing their contact with the religion of the white man. Soon after the Catholic and Episcopal churches had started work among the whites at Green Bay, both turned their attention to mission activities among the Menomini. In 1827 the latter organized a boarding school for Indian children, and three years later a similar institution was started by the Catholics. Both schools apparently received government grants which were in fullfilment of the treaty stipulations concerning education. But their doors had to be closed for want of pupils after the land sale of 1831 which caused the tribe to move from the immediate vicinity of Green Bay settlement.[5] About 1834 father Van de Broek, a Dominican, started the small mission on the Fox river that is mentioned above.

> This tribe at that time was scattered over an extensive territory, "over two hundred miles around," as Rev. Van de Broek writes . . . the missionary found only four houses (at Grand Kakalin), to which he added a wigwam . . . This served as a church, school and dwelling. The Father taught the Indians to read the books of Bishop Baraga in the Chippewa tongue; instructed them in farming and even carpentering and a little later, with the help of some Canadians erected a church with steeple and a dwelling house.—*History of the Menominee Indians, Am. Cath. Hist. Researches,* 1887, p. 152.

The progress of this mission in its task of introducing Menomini families to the white religion and also to education and agriculture was interrupted by another land cession and the removal of the tribe still further back into the wilderness.

In 1835 a surveyor Featherstonhaugh passed along the Fox valley on his way to the "Minnay Sotor" river; he wrote:

> As we passed from this place (Butte des Morts), we met several canoes, with Menominey Indians in them, all the men having their faces entirely blackened over with charcoal, which is their mourning for the death of a relative . . . The Men had very good teeth, and the women wore their coarse hair in long, thick queues . . . wound around with strings of white beads.
>
> I climbed a lofty tree and . . . got an extensive inland view of the country, which was a perfect wilderness and nearly dead flat, without any vestige of man or his labors, for the few Indians who frequent the country are all fish or rice eaters, or both, and seldom stray from the streams . . . a more perfect wilderness could not be imagined . . . we came up about 4 pm. with two Menominey lodges, the people of which let us have six fish for some biscuit.—Featherstonhaugh, *Canoe Voyage,* pp. 175–80.

Catlin, the artist, was another visitor of this period. He wrote of the Menomini thus:

> The Menominies, like the Winnebagoes, are the remnant of a much more numerous and independent tribe, but have been reduced and enervated by the use of whiskey and the ravages of the smallpox, and number at this

---

[5] See Davis, *Mission review, Wis. Hist. Colls.,* v, p. 513; also Whitford, *Early History of Education, Wis. Hist. Colls.,* v, p. 328.

time, something like three thousand.—Catlin, *North American Indians*, ii, p. 147.

In speaking of small-pox he is referring mainly to a great epidemic said to have carried off approximately one quarter of the tribe about 1834, and still spoken of among the older Menomini.

In 1836, by the terms of a further treaty, negotiated at Cedar Point on the Fox river, another four million acres of Menomini land were ceded to the government for white settlement. This comprised the area east of the Wolf river, the purpose being to open up the northern pine forests and the rivers to white lumbermen. In addition there were sold eight townships, or 184,320 acres, along the Wisconsin river. Included in the cession was the land around Neenah on which all improvements under the 1831 treaty had been made. The tribe agreed to move within one year to a new center at lake Poygan. The compensations received for this cession totalled approximately $800,000, or in all about nineteen cents an acre; but as the new treaty cancelled all compensations unpaid or still to come by the terms of the 1831 treaty, this figure really was nearer seventeen cents. The main items were:

$20,000	annuity for twenty years.
$ 3,000	worth of provisions annually.
2,000	pounds of tobacco; 30 barrels of salt.
$500	for farming utensils, cattle or implements.
2	blacksmiths, together with shops and materials.
$80,000	for those of mixed blood not receiving the annuities.
$76,000	to be invested for tribal purposes for releasing the government from the terms of the 1831 treaty.
$99,710.50	claimed by traders, etc., as Menomini debts to be paid after investigation of their validity.

These need little comment. The final item indicates how profitable the Indian trade was at this period of the land treaties, and how the traders, after running the Indian into debt, would boldly demand payment from the government out of treaty allowances.

A contemporary writer, de Neven, was present as an eye witness at the first payment made to the Menomini under

the terms of this new treaty. The agent is described by him
as arriving at the payground with thirty boxes of coin;
already traders had been selling whiskey, and a large proportion of the Indians were drunk, so that the council was
postponed a day, while the agent destroyed all the liquor to
be found. Nevertheless, on his departure after the payment, there ensued another orgy of drunkenness: "sleep
... was impossible. Next morning the ground was literally
strewn with men and women plunged in complete intoxication." Another of these payments is reported in a contemporary newspaper as follows:

The annual payment of the Menominees took place week before last.
The pay-ground is situated in a dense forest, on the east shore of Pauway-
gun Lake, some 10 miles from the habitation of any white man . . . The
tribe number about 2,500 souls. In addition to cattle and farming utensils
. . . and . . . pork, flour, corn, salt, &c, they had $20,000 in specie equally
distributed . . .

As usual . . . we learn that a large number of traders, black-legs and
spectators were present in all some 300. For some days before the arrival
of the Indian agent, a brisk barter was carried on . . . for the furs and
skins . . . After the payment, a cash business was commenced with the
Indian, and continued until he was drained of his last dime. There is a law
prohibiting the sale of liquor at all payments . . . but it is virtually a dead
letter. Large quantities of it are annually sold under the very eyes, as
it were, of the government officers . . . at an enormous profit . . . 10
pounds of pork were made a legal tender for a pint of whiskey . . . a
barrel . . . for $147 . . . we are told that it was difficult to determine
which predominated, whiskey or Wolf river water! The Indians . . . got
drunk and sober on the same drink.—*Watertown Chronicle*, November 3,
1847.

In 1844, Colonel McKenny, a government officer who had
had considerable dealings with the Menomini, wrote of them
as follows:

Few of our tribes have fallen from their high estate more lamentably
than these Indians. They are, for the most part, a race of fine looking
men, and have sustained a high character among the tribes around them.
But the curse of ardent spirits has passed over them and withered them.
They have yielded . . . with an eagerness and a recklessness beyond the
ordinary career of even savages. There is, perhaps, no tribe upon all our
borders so utterly abandoned to the vice of intoxication as the Menominies;
nor any so degraded in their habits, and so improvident in all their
concerns . . .

He who . . . believes that all the misery of our aboriginal people is owing to the coming of the whites among them, may easily change these opinions by surveying their condition, starving and dying during the winter, because they are too lazy to stretch out their hands in autumn (for wild rice) . . .

They seem to be favorites with all the adjoining Indians, and hunt upon their own land, and upon that of others, without hesitation and without complaint. They are reduced to about four thousand two hundred persons.—McKenney, *Indian Tribes of North America.*

A more hopeful description of Menomini conditions was written three years later by Ellis:

Tribal strength	2500
With cattle and farms	300
Live by fishing and hunting	2200
Number of good loghouses	62

The Menomonies are a brave and patient people, the firm friends of the government . . . The greater share of them are hunters, living exclusively by the chase and the fisheries; for the last they resort to Green Bay, and the rivers falling into it, where they take at all seasons of the year, but especially in the winter, large quantities . . . of trout and sturgeon . . .

Some three hundred of the Menomonies are Christians and farmers: the number is increasing, and the tribe will ere long become civilized, and abandon the chase. On a late visit to their village (at Poygan), I counted sixty-two log houses, erected by themselves most of them comfortably furnished and occupied. They have cleared up from the heavy timbered lands small fields, which are well fenced, and fine crops of corn and potatoes occupy every foot of ground . . . The teams, farming utensils, &c, supplied them by the government, are in good order and highly prized: the quantity, annually, should be increased.—in Schoolcraft, *History of the Indian Tribes,* vi, pp. 691–92.

It is evident that the Catholic fathers were having some success in their efforts to induce the increasing number of families that were affiliating with their mission at Poygan to abandon hunting for agriculture.[6] Yet the main body of the tribe do not appear to have shown any keenness to become "civilized" in accordance with the official policies and mission hopes; their scattered bands still roamed over the wilderness, gathering foods in forest and stream according to the old seasonal cycle. Likewise they showed no desire for the white man's education; actually the tribal council

[6] See also a letter by Bishop Henni, in *Wis. Magazine of History,* x, p. 73.

refused a clause in the 1836 treaty providing an annual sum to be spent on the education of the Indian youth, declaring that "they were not desirous of applying that sum to the aforesaid purpose."

"The American never comes unless he wants something! Without a want he never takes us by the hand." Such was the remark of a Menomini chief when United States officials met representatives of the tribe in 1848 at lake Poygan to negotiate for the cession of their remaining lands. Meanwhile the native titles of the Chippewa, Ottawa, Potawatomi, Sauk and Fox, Winnebago and Sioux had been steadily quieted over the northwest territory. After the stern suppression of the Black Hawk outbreak, the "now pliant tribes" offered little resistance, and as fast as treaties could be made and the land surveyed they were removed to more isolated regions to make way for incoming settlers. Captain Marryat, in a description of Wisconsin in 1837, was led to remark:

> The Indians . . . are *compelled* to sell—the purchase money being a mere subterfuge, by which it may *appear* as if the lands were not being wrested from them, although, in fact, it is.—in *Wis. Hist. Colls.*, xiv, p. 139.

The frame of mind in which the Menomini chiefs met the white commissioners in 1848 is shown in an account given by one of the French habitans related to the tribe, in which he purports to set forth the conversation of a Menomini chief among a group of his tribesmen:

> You don't expect he has come to decorate your ears with silver ear bobs? No, he comes simply to get the balance of our country! . . . he proposed to remove us across the Mississippi . . . he says there is an abundance of all kinds of game there; that the lakes and rivers are full of fish and wild rice.
>
> (His listeners interrupt: "Why doesn't he go himself and live in such a fine country!")
>
> You know how the Kechemocoman (Great Knife, as they named the American) never gets rebuked at a refusal; but will persist, and try over and over again till he accomplish his purpose.—Porlier, in *Wis. Hist. Colls.*, viii, p. 228.

On the fourth day of negotiations one of the officials left "as angry as well could be, having lost all hopes the treaty could be made''. It is reported by a number of witnesses, including whites, that the Menomini were then threatened with forcible removal at the pleasure of the government if they refused to sign. Realizing that they were inevitably to be ''crowded off the seat'', most of the chiefs finally put their marks to the document.

This treaty, which was ratified in January, 1849, opened with the usual expression of ''peace and friendship''. The Menomini were to cede, sell, and relinquish forever all their lands remaining in Wisconsin, and in their place were to receive a tract of not less than 600,000 acres in Minnesota that had been ceded by the Chippewa. The compensations specified covered the costs of removal, a gift of $40,000 for ''half-breeds'' who might elect to stay behind and hence would not participate in further benefits, certain grants for farming, milling, and blacksmith equipment, and ten annual payments of $20,000, the last to start in 1857 on the expiry of the annuities allowed by the terms of the previous treaty. The government agreed to pay the costs of a delegation to examine the proposed new site.

When the delegates returned from this inspection the tribe immediately began to temporize, and representatives went to Washington to press for new terms. Powell, the Menomini interpreter, reports having translated a speech made by the head chief Oshkosh to the President:

> The Crow Wing country was not what it had been represented . . . The tribe did not like to move to that country because the Indians already there were continually engaged in intertribal war. He preferred, he said a home somewhere in Wisconsin, for the poorest region in Wisconsin was better than that of the Crow Wing. He said that the latter was a good country for the white man, for he was numerous, and could protect himself from those warlike tribes; but his own tribe was small, and he wished them to live in peace for the little time they had to live.—*Proc. Wis. Hist. Soc.,* 1912, p. 175.

Pending the settlement of these negotiations, official consent was given for the Menomini to occupy temporarily an area between the upper Wolf and the Oconto rivers; thither in 1852 they were removed from their improved area round Poygan lake under the supervision of government officers.

According to the records the two winters spent awaiting the government's decision as to the tribal destiny were a time of great want and starvation, in spite of official rationing.

In May, 1854, a treaty was finalized with the consent of the state legislature of Wisconsin by which the Menomini were allowed to retain as a permanent reservation the land thus temporarily occupied. This comprised in all twelve townships, or 276,480 acres. An additional compensation was allowed on account of the discrepancy between this and the promised area of 600,000 acres, this a further annuity of $242,686 to be paid in fifteen annual instalments commencing at the expiration of the other annuities. Certain alterations were also made in the compensations awarded in 1848, the main being:

> $15,000 for the establishment of a manual labor school, grist and saw mill, and other improvements.
> $ 9,000 for a miller for fifteen years.
> $11,000 for a blacksmith and equipment for twelve years from 1857.
> $40,000 as an improvement fund to replace the removal costs west of the Mississippi.

The price in this final cession amounted to about fifteen cents an acre, making therefore at a rough estimate, certain amounts and areas being doubtful, some thirteen cents an acre as an average price received for the millions of acres that comprised the tribal territories or in which they had a partial interest. The treaty was ratified by Congress in August of the same year, with a significant amendment requiring that it be binding only when "assented to by Oshkosh and Ke-she-nah, chiefs of said tribe". Actually up to that time the head chief and another of highest rank had refused to put their marks to the agreement.

The following documents relating to the treaty will reveal the hopes of the government and the attitudes of the Menomini at this time. The commissioner who negotiated the agreement wrote immediately after its completion:

> The consideration which had the most weight upon the minds of the Indians, was the large amount of means to be immediately expanded for their improvement . . . The Indians exhibit an earnest desire to improve

their condition by adopting agricultural and other pursuits and I flatter myself that if the funds are soon appropriated and properly expended the Indians will raise sufficient for their own support by the next season.—Supdt. Huebschmann, letter May 21, 1854, *Indian Office files.*[7]

The annual report of the Commissioner of Indian Affairs of that year gives the official viewpoint:

> The tract granted them . . . is deemed to be more than ample for their comfortable accomodation . . . (They receive) pecuniary and other beneficial provisions . . . Having thus been permanently and most liberally provided for, and all causes of discontent removed, it is hoped and believed that in a few years the Menomonees will exhibit some evidence of moral and social advancement.—from *R.I.A.*, 1854.

The Menomini attitude at the time and after can perhaps best be shown by quoting from a handwritten petition filed in the Indian Office some ten years later, this signed by all the "Chiefs and Headmen of the Menomonee tribe to their Great Father". It asserts that:

> The person . . . sent to treat with them . . . compelled them by threats of destruction to sign that treaty . . .
>
> That Article 4 of said treaty contains a clause cutting them off from all claims on the United States which clause was not known to the chiefs and headmen of our Nation when said treaty was signed . . .
>
> (They ask that their Father) would send to them an honest man to hear the truth from the lips of our white brothers who were present when the treaty was made and who signed the same as witnesses . . .
>
> (Interpreter Powell certifies that) they were very unwilling to hear the terms proposed but the Superintendent told them that unless they made the treaty they must go to the Crow Wing country. They had a great dread of this and many were willing to sign, many refused . . . (The head chief Oshkosh refused to sign, and after the amendment by Congress he did it only reluctantly saying:) "I do it without my consent, my tribe compel me to sign it." (Other witnesses to the treaty wrote confirming the assertion that article 4 was never read.)—Petition, Jan. 15, 1864, *I.O.F.*

In the disputed article 4, the United States agrees to pay the compensations mentioned in consideration of the surrender of the Menomini lands and "of the relinquishment by said tribe of all claims set up by or for them, for the

[7] Unpublished documents which the writers quote direct from the Indian Office Files in Washington will be indicated from this point forward by the abbreviation "*I.O.F.*" those from published annual reports of the Office, by "*R.I.A.*" (*Reports on Indian Affairs*).

difference in quantity of lands" given as their reservation under the two treaties. Apparently "all causes of discontent" were by no means removed by the treaty.

Only one other land transaction remains to be spoken of. Two years after the Menomini had been granted the twelve townships on the upper Wolf river, the government found it necessary to remove the Stockbridge and Brothertown (Munsee) tribes from the path of settlement, though the Oneida tribe were permitted to remain on a small reservation near the Fox river. The Menomini were asked by the government to cede two of their twelve townships for the use of these tribes. In a treaty of February, 1856, they agreed to this, receiving for the cession of their two southwesterly townships a compensation of sixty cents an acre. Thus these eastern tribes, after many movements from their original home along the Atlantic seaboard, finally found a permanent place alongside the Menomini in the forest fastnesses of Wisconsin; the relations between these neighbors in the years that followed will be seen in due course.

The records of the time immediately preceding the removal of the tribe to the reservation continue to present on the whole a melancholy picture of Menomini life. The superintendent at Green Bay wrote:

As far as I have been able to collect data in relation to the decrease of the number of Menomonees, it appears that the decrease since twenty years is to be accounted for by the ravages of the small-pox in 1838, of the cholera in 1847 which latter was superinduced by misery and starvation,— by men being killed in drunken rows, and by the fever, which, from time to time, commonly in the winter, has been raging among them, being clearly the consequence of want of provisions and other necessities; which was not alone their fault, as, since the first attempt was made to buy them out . . . until the present year their affairs have been such as not to encourage any improvements.—R.I.A., 1854.[8]

[8] An amusing incident connected with the cholera epidemic of 1847 is reported by Powell in his recollections. A white doctor was officially commissioned to attend a Menomini group stricken with the cholera: "The doctor left a quantity of mustard with the Indians, with directions to put a plaster . . . (on) anyone attacked with the disease. The next day on entering the wigwams, every Indian, old and young, was found spread flat on his back, covered with a mustard plaster. All had resorted to it as a protection."

Yet it is difficult to know just to what extent this "degradation" and the "pitiful conditions" pictured by the contemporary observers are judgments made on the basis of white
standards.   When in 1849 a commissioner was sent to Green
Bay to distribute the so-called "half-breed payment" of
$40,000 under the terms of the 1848 treaty he was given to
understand by local whites that the Menomini were "mere
children", quite incapable of transacting business, and abandoned to drink.   Himself a Quaker, he set out sympatheti-
cally to get to know the Menomini; as a result he records
exactly the opposite.   He found them to be for the most part
forest dwellers living well away from white settlements,
organized into bands and led by respected chiefs, orderly in
council, and, "Pagan" and Catholic alike, enjoying harmonious relations among themselves.   The troubles were
rather between the Indians and the whites, and the blame
for such he places upon the whites.   A few selections may
be given from his long and interesting series of articles in a
Quaker paper:

> They were scattered over a wild region, some hundred miles apart
> . . . 9 chiefs (are) living at (lake Poygan) . . . their number does not
> exceed 2300 according to a roll prepared at the fort a year ago . . . (the
> word of the headchief Oshkosh) was law . . . The Menomonies consist
> of nine bands . . . The chiefs numbered twenty-six . . . The courtesy
> observed by these people towards each other, when in council, was another
> agreeable circumstance . . . The chiefs were frequently offered spirits
> but they refused . . . In the matter of money they are much like leaky
> vessels . . . The poor creatures had so often been badly treated . . . (by)
> tricks and impositions . . . (He refers also to the threats used by the
> commissioner to make the Menomini sign the treaty of 1848.)—in *The
> Friend,* Vol. xxiii.

Anyone wishing to get a picture of Menomini life at the
time more detailed than the space of this survey can allow
would do well to refer to this document.   Its accuracy can
hardly be questioned, as the details given concerning the
names of chiefs, the location of their bands, and the like
were confirmed by inquiry from the old people of the tribe
today.
    The half-breed payment itself, described in this docu-
ment, is a very significant event in Menomini history.   The

period of the treaties has already been referred to as perhaps a time of the rebirth of distinct tribal entities, since each Indian was called upon to identify himself with this or that tribal unit removing to such and such a place. At this payment of 1849, all Menomini of part-white descent were given the opportunity to buy out their "rights" in a cash payment and so sever all official connections with the tribe. This option must be understood against the background of the times. The Menomini were to be removed to a wilderness in the northwest among tribes perhaps hostile; buying out rights meant staying in the familiar region, accepting citizenship with the whites and having the privilege of taking up land for settlement. In this test of loyalties, the last sifting of the Menomini tribe took place. Some three hundred mixed bloods accepted the payment, apparently all Catholics and already considerably advanced in farming. Once however it was decided that the Menomini were to stay in Wisconsin, some renewed informally their relations with the tribesfolk, even going to live on the reservation; they and their descendants came to play quite an important rôle in Menomini affairs, even though not on the official tribal roster.

Such is the story of white pressure and passing lands. Increasingly the Menomini were made subject to the will and manipulation of the government; having come earlier to feel the force of white political control, they were beginning to feel the pressure of control in more fundamental aspects of their lives, the civilizing and assimilating process which was to mark their reservation experience. The period was characterized not only by physical disease and population decline but also by considerable social and psychological disorganization, the accompaniment of the sudden accession of wealth obtained from the land sales without any corresponding instruction in its value and use. When, minus their lands and with most of the proceeds in the hands of white traders, the main body of the tribe were removed under official supervision from their homes at Poygan lake and in the Fox and Wolf valleys to the forest fastnesses of the upper Wolf, there to be joined by other Menomini bands from along the shores of Green Bay, the opinion of everyone as to the tribal destiny seems to have been that voiced by one of the government officials:

The Menomonees . . . are reduced to a mere fraction of their former numbers . . . We may assume . . . in a few years hence, nothing will be left of these people, but their name.—Baird, in *Wis. Hist. Colls.*, iv, p. 218.

VII. THE FIRST RESERVATION EXPERIMENTS

The migration of the main body of the Menomini in 1852 to the area on the upper Wolf, confirmed to them two years later as a permanent "reservation", is still vivid in the minds of the people today: the birchbark canoes laden with households and household goods, the grim old chiefs, the bustle of the camps, and the final disembarkation at the bend of the river where the present Indian settlement of Keshena stands.

Some eight miles to the south, at the site of the present city of Shawano, the Menomini canoes had passed the last outpost of white penetration into the wilderness, a sawmill built in 1843 and worked by a handful of whites. The spot chosen for the first settlement was just below a waterfall, the first break in the Wolf river passage necessitating a portage. Already it was well known to the tribe, for bands of Menomini had been hunting and perhaps living for years in the region. The river at this point was celebrated as a breeding place for the sturgeon, and to the east numerous small lakes offered good fishing. The area was for the most part densely forested, with fairly plentiful game; yet there were clearings here and there on either side of the river which gave promise of easy agriculture. At Shawano lake not far to the southeast was an abundance of wild rice.

In physical terms, therefore, this setting was like what the Menomini had known in the past; the tribe, just beginning to have the opportunity, for better or worse, of more intensive contact with whites, were thrust back into the setting of their earlier existence. There was an important difference, however, in that the area was now small and defined, and pressure was being brought to bear to wean them from their old economy. True, the tribesfolk were not at first closely restricted to their own lands. Some decades were to pass before white settlement advanced up to and around the reservation line. Nevertheless their isolation from white centers meant that for long practically all their contact with whites and white ways was to continue to be specialized and selective. The new culture tended to come in carefully supervised and controlled forms, brought by government officials, traders and missionaries. Even what informal contacts took place on or off the reservation were with special types of whites: frontier adventurers, lumbermen, liquor runners and the like.

According to the report of the government agent supervising the tribal migration, 2,002 men, women and children came north from Poygan in the fall of 1852. These inland bands were soon joined by the majority of members from coastal bands whose headquarters had been at the Menominee, Peshtigo, Oconto and other river mouths. Actually, however, a few of the latter did not come permanently on the reservation until much later. As already noted, some of the mixed bloods accompanied the tribesfolk, and even a few of the French habitans of the Bay region preferred to throw in their lot with them. The reservation group, therefore, did not correspond exactly to the "Menomini tribe", meaning those whose names were now placed on the tribal roll as being entitled to annuity benefits, nor has it done so since. Throughout the study from this time onwards two Menomini groupings must be distinguished: first, those having political rights; second, those participating in the reservation life. In general the official statistics refer to the first, but otherwise the materials except where specifically stated deal with the second—the Menomini community.

It was not long before the majority of the bands and families moved out from their first camp at the new Menomini "payground", now the settlement at Keshena. A map of the reservation today shows many of the sites— lakes, streams and springs—where they settled, as such places usually came to have their names associated with the spot: for example, Oshkosh and Chickeney creeks, Watahsah and Moshawquit lakes. The geography of the tribal dispersion was gathered in considerable detail by the writer from the oldest people on the reservation. Most of this however must perforce be passed over;[1] there will merely be shown the trends of settlement and their effects upon the tribal life.

The various leaders, it is told, chose locations that appealed to them, and the members of their bands either grouped themselves near-by or selected other areas where they and their families might live:

> Some bands lived together; others broke up because individuals chose to build in different parts.   Only when annuity time came, or the issue of a ration from the warehouse, would the bands come together in their groups.   Then each group would come to its *okemau* (leader).   The money or the ration would be put down in heaps here or there; the leader would then divide it, and the families would go their ways with their share.   The bands broke up mostly within a few years of being on the reservation.[2]

This pictures a steady disintegration of the band system almost from the first days of the reservation period.   Just as it emerged as an adjustment to the roving life of fur-trade days, so now it broke up with geographical confinement and the commencement of a more sedentary life.   Yet the band organization did not entirely disappear, even when the older bands were dispersed.   As Menomini families gradually moved over the reservation area they usually settled in congenial cooperative groups under different leaders and were called bands.   In some instances these leaders were of no high rank, and their following in no way corresponded to the membership of the pre-reservation bands; when such new bands became settled and less isolated from other groups, they in turn tended to lose their unity.

Interestingly enough the old totemic dualism, and especially the division of the tribe into "Christians" and "Pagans", largely determined the location of the various families.   The Christian chiefs such as Aia'miqta, Käron

---

[1] The writer lodged with the Wisconsin Historical Society a manuscript giving notes about Menomini groups and families as told by the oldest people on the reservation.

[2] From here on such quotations, given without an indication of their source, represent oral statements made to the writer by Menomini on the reservation today.   It has been felt unnecessary to give the actual names of informants in the study, particularly since some of the material to be quoted later is controversial or personal.

(Carron), Lamotte, Akine'bui (Kinepoway), Osh'kiqhĭ-
nä'nĭŭᵛ and Wa'ta'sau, together with their followers, made
their homes on the east bank of the Wolf round the payground, though later one of them, Akine'bui, moved northwest to what is now known as the West Branch settlement.[3]
Those following the Indian religion divided into two groups

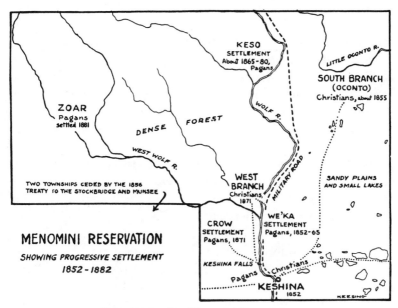

DIAGRAM 4. The Menomini Reservation.

more or less based on the old division of Bear and Thunder.
The Bear people, headed by Oshkosh, together with such
other chiefs as the one eyed Shu'nu'ni'ŭᵛ (Souligny), Mä'-
tshikine'ŭᵛ (Chickeney), and Sha'wano, settled along the west
bank of the Wolf, an area now growing over with forest,
but even yet remembered as once open country. Most of
the Thunder people settled further up the Wolf at a place
known as We''ke (Wayka) creek, led there by a chief of that

---

[3] The phonetic form of these names has been used rather than the Anglicized
spelling given in the records. Many such personal names were adopted later
as family names when these became customary. It may be noted that there is
considerable divergence in the phonetic rendering of Menomini names given by
Hoffman, Skinner, and the others; indeed, sometimes the same ethnologist gives
two or three different spellings of a name in different places.

name, otherwise Powahe'kûna (Poegonah), also such chiefs as Keso and Ni'aqtawâ'pomi. It is told how "every spring this Oshkosh and this We''ke (meaning the respective peoples) would assemble on either side of Keshena falls to fish for sturgeon".

When, following on the treaty of 1854, the Menominee river band arrived on the reservation, they mostly made their homes at the original payground, to which place the important young chief of the band, Keshi'niu' (Keshena) gave his name; some, however, moved to the northeast, including a group under Tshitshikwo'nûwau. The Peshtigo band, led by Äsha'wûnĭ'pĭnas made their headquarters in this direction also, near a lake now called Peshtigo. The Oconto band under Pikwû'kûnao went east to the reservation line, but "having bad luck the first year" moved away north to found the settlement known as South Branch on the Little Oconto river. Practically all this early settlement was near the waterways, for the canoe was still the essential mode of Indian travel and transport.[4]

The central fact in any study of the changing Menomini life from this time forward is the presence among the tribe of white officials, whose activities were directed from Washington. In 1854 the Superintendent of Indian Affairs for the Bay region, under whose jurisdiction the Menomini were placed, wrote:

> After much reflection as to the probability of success of the attempt to civilize them, which is now being commenced, I have come to the conclusion that, if it fails, it will not fail because these Indians are not capable of improvement, but because the government will not succeed during the series of years which will be required to educate the next generation, in finding the proper persons to carry out its benevolent objects.—*R.I.A.* (Report Indian Affairs), 1854.

In 1855, government agency buildings were erected at Keshena settlement itself, and an "agent" took up residence. His duties were to disburse annuity payments and other treaty benefits, direct the employees authorized under the treaties, regulate trading operations, and supervise In-

[4] For a map of these early distributions, see Diagram 4.

dian interests generally. In addition to his work among the Menomini he controlled the affairs of the neighboring Stockbridge and Munsee, also of the Oneida tribe near the Fox river. It may be mentioned here that of the first six agents (that is, up to 1870), the affairs of four were investigated and they were replaced as a result of complaints and charges brought against them by the Menomini leaders. Numerous periods of tension between the officials and the Indians are shown in the records, especially in the correspondence files of the Indian Office: troubles between agents and the tribal council, sometimes marked by divisions within the tribe itself, and fairly frequent delegations representing the whole or part of the tribe visiting or attempting to visit the "Great Father" in Washington in order to get redress. Yet amid these political difficulties marked economic, social and educational changes were taking place as a result of official activities.

A word may be said concerning the relations of the Menomini with whites other than federal officials. On the whole they were particularly unfortunate. Almost immediately after 1854 Wisconsin state surveyors attempted to operate on the reservation, and before long the state put in claims for large areas of Menomini reservation land as "school" and "swamp" reserves; timber interests were soon trying to obtain control of rich pine forests found to lie within the formerly unwanted area of the reservation, and lumber stealers made great depredations; and certain lawyers and traders did their best to harvest the annuity payments and to obtain large sums of the tribal money held in trust by the government. The Menomini council was even led to complain about the seducing of their women by whites. As early as 1856 it was reported that:

> Obstacles have been thrown in the way of these Indians, and the vicious and unscrupulous have endeavored to thwart all the efforts made for their improvement; and the grasping avarice of unprincipled white men in seeking to obtain their property . . . has rendered them somewhat restless and uneasy.—*R.I.A.*, 1856.

Obviously, in spite of good intentions, the government was unable to prevent entirely the abuses that seem to have been the lot of such groups on the frontiers of white settlement the world over.

The records of the time, backed by vivid memories, describe the tribe during their first two winters in the new area as being "almost in a condition of starvation". Awaiting the pleasure of the whites concerning their further removal, out of touch with the resources of their old areas and of the trader's store, living "wretchedly" upon pork and flour doled out by the government agent, they were indeed in a state of disorganization. But once their stay in the region was assured and the official program for their future amelioration commenced, the Menomini took heart and began "settling in".

It seems doubtful whether, even if the Menomini had been able to revert completely to their old foods, the reservation area would have provided sufficient to have sustained over two thousand people for any length of time. Either some would have had to migrate, or famine would have reduced their numbers. Still less could such an area supply enough furs for them to carry on the type of economic life developed over the preceding two centuries. The government aim, however, was to get the Menomini to cease roving and settle in agricultural pursuits. But this meant not only training them in the arts of farming, but also providing food to support the families during the immediate period before crops could be ready, and to obviate any need for leaving their new farming pursuits in search of Indian foods. The government, therefore, besides supplying under the terms of the treaty a farmer and a "manual labor farm", likewise tools, implements, seeds and stock, had to continue a system of rationing.

By the fall of 1854 some "corn and potatoes, some wheat, oats, and peas, and a large supply of vegetables" had been raised. Nevertheless the agent writes that, but for the official rations, the tribe would have been "driven as usual, to their hunting grounds". A contract advertisement of the time lists the following articles as being supplied for the Menomini: wheat flour, mess pork, salt, tobacco, three yoke of oxen and equipment, four plows, and five milch-cows. Already a white blacksmith had been appointed in accordance with the terms of the treaties, and three Menomini assistants were taken into his shop for training. Saw and grist mills were built, the first to cut timber for new and permanent houses, barns and fences, the second to grind the expected tribal grain; these were supervised by a white miller employing Menomini labor. Under the management of the tribal farmer, the model farm came into being. In 1856 this official reports good crops, also that nearly one hundred Menomini were employed on the farm, in the mill and in the shops.

> Indian laborers have been exclusively employed to do the work of the tribe. The agent, farmer, miller, teacher, and one blacksmith are the only white persons located on the reservation . . . The different bands have carpenters among them, who are erecting houses for the various families . . . One hundred who one year ago lived by the chase . . . are clearing and cultivating land and building houses.—Report of agent, *R.I.A.*, 1856.

The following year the Menomini chiefs requested additional rations, as game was becoming very scarce and those who were farming could not yet be self-supporting. At this time agricultural progress received a setback from a new quarter:

> The wheat crop was destroyed by the smut and rust . . . and the frost of the 24th of August was equally fatal to their corn, potatoes, etc.—*R.I.A.*, 1856.

Immediate provisioning had to be resorted to by the agent to prevent the whole tribe from "returning to the chase." No better success was achieved the following summer, owing to late and early frosts, and the tribe was definitely thrown back on the old economy of "fishing and hunting", supplemented by maple sugar, rice, and roots; indeed, much of the seed grain distributed officially in the following spring was eaten to ward off starvation. The report of the farmer for 1859 said:

> The majority of them are willing and inclined to work and enlarge their farms, and follow the habits of the whites; but they are no economists,

and have but little calculation. Their annuity is small, their debts large; therefore they are poor, and not able to go on any faster . . . They have to spend a great part of the time in fishing and hunting for subsistence.

Another natural factor now began to effect the farming operations. The light sandy soil round Keshena on which, because of the ease of clearing and cultivation, most of this first farming had been done, became worked out. Those wanting to continue farming were faced with the necessity of moving to heavily timbered ridges where lay the better class land. The visitor to the reservation today can judge how difficult and costly would be the clearing of such land because of trees and stones, needing oxen and heavy plows, also very hard work. Such farming, too, involved still another dispersal and rebuilding of houses. It says a lot for the spirit of the Menomini that some at least of the families made this new venture.

In the later decades, it will be seen, little success attended government efforts to make agriculturalists of the Menomini. Nevertheless there seems to have been no lack of enthusiasm in these early years. At "a full and open Council of the Menominee Tribe" in 1859, a request was sent to Washington as follows:

That the department might consent they should appropriate for cattle, farming implements &c for each individual family . . . They also want a part of their reservation surveyed into 80 & 40 acre lots and allotted to every head of a Family and to Individuals . . . As it is the desire of the Government to have them till the soil instead of the Chase, that they have got the will to cultivate the soil, but not the means within their reach.—Letter, *I.O.F.*, Sept. 25, 1859.

In this document is the first of many requests that the government should subdivide Menomini lands; yet even to the present day the reservation has not been individualized, for reasons that will become apparent. The following year the Menomini council wrote further letters asking that an amount be appropriated from their funds for farming equipment, listing the following: 30 yoke of cattle, 40 plows, wagons and gear, seed, axes, nails, glass, cowbells, carpenters' tools, harrows for each band, shovels, spades, pitchforks, also some provisions. "They want to see what they can do in the way of farming . . . to imitate the white man. They also want one Cow to each family and two Bulls for their tribe''.

These expressions of the tribal wishes are remarkable as coming at a time of great political disruption both among the Menomini themselves and between the Menomini and the whites. In 1858 the head chief Oshkosh died as the result of a drunken brawl. The problem arose of who should be the succeeding head chief. The "Pagan" or Mitawin people wanted Ä'kwine'mi, the eldest son of Oshkosh; the Christians, who were by that time in the majority, asked that "the second son—a Christian—should be made head chief"; likewise some of the eleven other band leaders asked that the government should appoint one from among their number instead of either candidate. The eldest son, Ä'kwine'mi, was finally chosen to succeed the father, and held the position until deposed for killing one of the mixed blood traders in 1871.

At this time, too, trouble was being created by a lawyer and a group of traders who since 1854 had been trying to get the consent of the tribal council to the payment out of their trust funds of an enormous sum as "debts" due to them. According to the records, they had, by attempted bribery and by threats that they would get the government to remove the tribe west of the Mississippi, finally forced the council to support their claim. But a most significant event occurred to forestall this. The young men of the tribe asserted their rights in a way apparent from the following document:

> The resolution and memorial which the chiefs had unanimously signed . . . (conceded) to the young men an equal voice with themselves in all questions in relation to the granting to any claimants their annuities or any part of them. This arrangement had been made at the time to allay the excitement among the young men against the chiefs, who had a short time previous signed a paper in favor of paying . . . (It) must appear the more proper, as integrity and intelligence is found as much or more among the young men, than among the hereditary chiefs of the tribe.—*I.O.F.*, 1860.

This adjustment in the council and in the relations of old and young is an interesting symptom of the social changes of the time; henceforth all petitions concerning finance were signed by "the Menominee chiefs and young men". It need hardly be said that the claim mentioned above was quickly repudiated.

Another disturbing influence at this period came from a number of the mixed bloods who, having settled on the reservation after disposing of their shares of the payment of 1849, formed a nucleus of agitation and according to official reports, "excited a turbulent and rebellious feeling". The main grievance played up by them was a shortage in the annuity amounts. This trouble culminated in the departure for Washington of a delegation from the tribe, in spite of opposition from the agent. The latter even went so far as to depose one of the band leaders, Karon (Carron). The agitation resulted in a full investigation of the affairs of the Keshena agency, and the removal of the agent. Apparently this proved satisfactory to the tribe for the time, for in 1861 the chiefs, warriors and members of the Menomini tribe in full and open council disclaimed all relations with the mixed bloods.

From 1860 on the practical interest in farming found expression in increased effort, in spite of the natural handicaps. In 1861, the farmer reports some 400 acres as cultivated and mostly fenced, the miller ground 3,650 bushels of grain, a workman was hired to repair farming equipment, and more stock and implements were distributed. The blacksmithing operations included, in addition to the usual metal repairs, the manufacture for the tribe of numerous bark and buckskin awls, crooked knives, hoes, rat and fish spears, hunting knives, fire steels, and axes, also repairing of guns, traps, kettles and sugar boilers. In the next few years new saw and grist mills, also barns and fences, were erected, a bridge constructed over the Wolf river, and hundreds of tons of wild marsh hay cut and stacked for the wintering of stock. Nevertheless, in 1863

the Commissioner of Indian Affairs drew a dismal picture
of the "almost hopeless poverty" of the Menomini:

> Upon the Menomonee reserve there are thousands of acres of wet and
> worthless marsh, and of the remainder a very large proportion is nothing
> but sand . . . the climate is another source of discouragement . . . It is
> difficult to conceive of locations more illy adapted to the support and wants
> of a people but little acquainted with the arts of civilization, and it needs
> no argument to show their almost worthlessness as locations designed to
> encourage Indians to abandon their former modes of life, and engage in
> the cultivation of the soil.—*R.I.A.*, 1863.

When after this a severe winter caused much stock to die,
and a summer followed in which the crops were destroyed
by drought, even the enthusiastic agent was moved to write
that the Menomini:

> would soon become good farmers if they had any good farming lands to
> till; but the entire reservation is almost utterly worthless.

Once more the tribe was forced back upon "other resources" besides farming to maintain themselves, that is,
they had to return to their old economy of forest and stream
so far as government rations were not available.

The printed Indian Office reports of the time, which give
very full accounts of Menomini affairs, tell how in the
spring great quantities of maple sugar were manufactured,
mostly for sale to the traders. "Large numbers . . . removed to different localities to hunt and fish, and allowing
their families to gather their wild fruits for winter use."
In the fall the people travelled to Lake Shawano to harvest
wild rice. Those few who continued to farm found "little
encouragement to do so . . . (being) compelled to depend
on the issue of provisions made from time to time" to avoid
starvation. Such was the economic position after nearly
two decades of farming experiment.

Up to the reservation period the Menomini showed no
inclination to adopt white forms of dress and housing,
though the missions were beginning to effect changes among
the Christian Indians. In 1860 the resolutions of the tribal
council included a request that the government purchase
"some cheap and durable clothing to clothe ourselves and

families during the winter''.   Even four years earlier than
this an agent reports that ''One hundred, who one year ago
lived by the chase and wore their blankets, now dress like
the whites''.   Further documents indicate something of the
revolution in clothing that now took place:

> 1863: Within the last year many of the younger members of the tribe
> have thrown off the blanket, and other apparel which pretty distinctly mark
> pagan life, and have adopted the dress of the whites.—*R.I.A.*, 1863.

> 1865: Four years ago one-half of them were Blanket Indians, now less
> than one-fourth retain their original dress.—*Report on Condition of Indian
> Tribes,* 1867, p. 461.

The reasons for this change seem clear; first, there was an
increasing opportunity for contact with whites, hence for
becoming familiar with the new types of garment; second,
the government supplied much material year by year, as can
be known from the contemporary contract advertisements
for fabrics, wool, yarn, threads, beads and the like; third,
and doubtless most important, garment-making in the white
styles was taught from 1853, or probably even before, as
part of the newly launched educational program.   A sewing
school was established with a special teacher, and women as
well as girls attended.[5]

The reservation sawmill provided a plentiful supply of
lumber for house construction, while tools were supplied
through the government.   It is not surprising therefore that
many of the Menomini, knowing they were settling permanently, decided to give up their old-style lodges at least for
general use and to occupy houses of white pattern.   The
Christian Indians were again the most amenable to the new
influences.   By 1862 there were reported to be 112 frame
houses, 75 log houses, and 150 wigwams, and six years later
the number of log structures had risen to 200.   Such early

---

[5] A typical extract may be given from the annual report of this school:
''Those attending have in every instance abandoned their native costume. . . .
Garments made by women and girls since my last report (are) . . . pants for
men, 109 pairs; for boys, 140 pairs.   Shirts for men, 79; for boys, 82; skirts
for women, 178.   Gowns for women, 40.   Dresses for girls, 77; skirts for girls,
120.   Gowns for girls, 130. . . . Shrouds and sheets for the dead, 28.   Sun-
bonnets for girls, 20.''—*R.I.A.*, 1861.

houses were comparatively small, usually with only one room, much, indeed, like a log built version of the rectangular summer dwelling of bark. The new homes had the advantage of being warmer and of not needing to be repaired or renewed frequently; on the other hand they tended to become unsanitary and "filthy" as a result of the Indian mode of living, adapted to more temporary residence. Most homes had fenced in gardens, and usually some form of outhouse or barn for goods and livestock. Yet the older types of lodges by no means disappeared this early; the Menomini family had many occasions away from the home base when such structures were essential to its needs.

As the whites began to introduce teams of oxen, wagons, farming implements and sleighs among the Menomini, the waterways and foot trails had to be supplemented by roads. Three main trails out of Keshena, northeast to South Branch, northwest to West Branch, and west to the Stockbridge and Munsee reservation, together with several smaller ones were widened, the Menomini supplying the labor and the cost being met out of the tribal funds held by the government. Horses and oxen now assumed importance in Menomini life at the expense of the canoe, and hence the expenditure of energy in reaping great annual harvests of wild marsh hay for fodder. Settlement began to move from the vicinity of streams to locations accessible to the roads.

In the 'sixties an elaborate military road was constructed from Green Bay north to the shores of lake Superior—a vast project for those times. Made ostensibly as a defense measure against the British in Canada, it is interpreted by some historians as having been really fostered by influential lumber interests who wanted to have the region opened up. For the Menomini this highway through the wilderness was of great importance, as it passed north from Shawano across the reservation by way of Keshena and the east bank of the Wolf river (the present highway 55).[6] Soldiers, lumber-

6 See Diagram 4.

men, adventurers of various kinds, and later settlers and
tourists used it, and all such folk left their mark upon the
tribal life; indeed it served as a main channel through which
the exploitation of the northern wilderness proceeded.

From 1853 the task of education was taken over directly
by the government, though financed with Menomini money.
The records indicate that until 1869 such schooling, while
far-reaching in its effects, was more a matter of personalities than of equipment and curricula. Immediately after
the shift to the reservation a Mrs. Dousman, who had conducted a small Catholic school for girls at lake Poygan, was
appointed with her two daughters to teach the women and
girls on the reservation. Several men teachers were tried
for the boys but none proved at all successful. In 1862
separate schooling was abolished, and two departments,
primary and secondary, were formed, along with the special
sewing school—these wholly in charge of the Dousmans.
The contemporary accounts pay warm tributes to these
teachers, "to whose untiring zeal . . . may be ascribed
much of the progress of the tribe". Indeed some of the old
people on the reservation still speak of them with affection.
According to official accounts most Menomini at this time
were manifesting "a strong desire to have their children
instructed . . . to wean them from their former savage
enjoyments, and to make them proficient in transacting the
ordinary affairs of civilized life". Both Christian and
Pagan families sent their children to the schools; attendance
was punctual; the roll steadily increased; and the teachers
reported that "with but little solicitation (they) abandon
their native habits to assume those of civilized life". The
work of the schools, the books used, and the progress made
from year to year are set out in detail in the annual Reports
on Indian Affairs.

Certain problems arose out of Menomini economic and
social life, however, to complicate schooling. The maintenance of the old food cycle conflicted with the time periods
normal to the white school. Work had to cease entirely
when the families moved to the sugar camps in the spring,

PLATE III

MODERN LOG HOUSES

BUILDING A LOG HOUSE

A HOME IN A FOREST CLEARING

Note the three used automobiles, two of them already out of commission.
Nearly all Menomini yards today have such "antiques."

PLATE IV

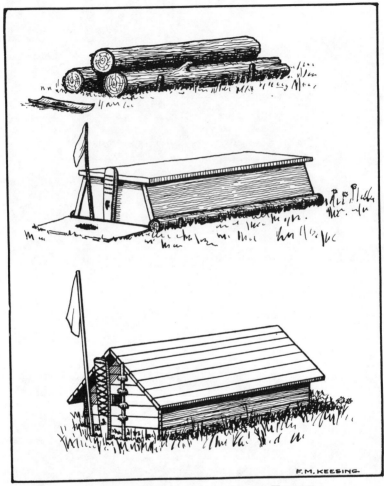

MENOMINI GHOSTS CHANGE TO MODERN HOUSING

Top: An old form of log grave covering.

Middle: A board gravebox in use during the late 19th century, with white flag and totem-stick marked with "coups" and totem.

Bottom: One of several forms of modern grave "houses," first used by Christians but now by "Pagans." Offerings are put through the front hole. The totem, a chicken, represents a clan formed in post-white days.

while in the summer and fall attendances would be bad as a result of berry picking and the harvesting of the wild rice. Other factors interfering with school progress were bad health and epidemics; the pressure of home duties; early marriage in the case of girls; also destitution and lack of clothing.

This early schooling had a profound influence upon the younger generation in breaking down traditional ways of thought and behavior. Yet the results in terms of formal learning were not great, judged from the white standard:

> Though the Menomonee have had schools established among them for more than twenty years past, very few can boast even a limited acquaintance with the English language, and still fewer can read or write it. In early youth they spend perhaps a portion of the year attending school, the effect of which is soon obliterated on their return to and mingling with their savage and uneducated associates.—*R.I.A.*, 1867.

This points to the basic difficulty of teaching the Indian, the language problem. From the first English was adopted in the government schools and the Chippewa discarded. Yet there was little stimulus for the Menomini to learn the new language, their own tongue being sufficient for all ordinary purposes; such acquaintance as they might gain with English was almost entirely academic and hence forgotten after school days. No attempt appears to have been made to frame a system of education based on the use of the tribal vernacular, though not until some years later was the use of Menomini in the schools officially forbidden.

These first experiments in schooling practically came to an end with the death of two of the teachers and the departure of the third about 1869. In reality, however, influences had been at work earlier to disrupt the schools. The dispersal of Menomini families from the Keshena area made a central school increasingly impossible except as a boarding establishment. Furthermore, a serious conflict developed between the government and the missionaries, in the course of attempts by the latter to gain back control of the education of Catholic children.

When the bands removed from Poygan there also came north a Catholic priest, father Bonduel, who had been working among them.[7] In due course a chapel was built at Keshena among the Christian families. But Bonduel soon left the reservation, and until 1880 there were only irregular visits by priests of various Catholic orders. In the year mentioned, the Franciscan fathers established a permanent mission once more. They reported that:

> The Menomonees to the greater part of their number had been Christianized by Catholic missionaries, but never learned their religion so thoroughly as to have their lives regulated according to its precepts; nor could this be, since they had none to stay with them permanently giving them the instruction so much needed. The temporary visits of the former missionaries only served to keep alive the Christian belief in those that had been converted, and prevent their lapse into paganism . . . It cannot be wondered at that they really were found by the Franciscan fathers in such a degraded moral condition.—*Report of Mission*, in *R.I.A.*, 1886.

Yet whatever lack of depth there may have been in the Menomini appreciation of the new religion during these earlier years, at least it provided some real outward marks of distinction; the Christians were seen as grouping themselves apart from the "Pagans", and generally being more responsive to the new influences. By 1858 it was reported that the majority of the tribe were Catholic, and from 1862 on, official estimates place "about two-thirds" as adherents of the new faith. In 1863 a period of strained relations commenced between the officials and various missionary visitors, which reached a crisis two years later.[8] From a mass of correspondence in the Indian Office files, it appears that during May of 1865, when all the crops were due to be

---

[7] This father had continued at Poygan the work begun by Van de Broek at Little Chute. It is interesting to find that the Catholic fathers now on the reservation consider that "he obtained this reservation for the Indians—went to Madison and to Washington on their behalf".

[8] According to the official records (this being the only version available), a priest who left the reservation in 1863 was "dissipated and licentious"; in 1864 another arrived, and immediately commenced to interfere with the schools. The agent also reported that priests at this time sought to claim money direct from the annuities of their flock before distribution; he alleges extortion by them from the Catholic Indians, especially for saying masses on behalf of dead relatives.

planted, a priest "held meetings every day during the month . . . all day" among the Catholic Indians. During this period of alleged obstruction to the official farming operations, an epidemic of small-pox broke out. The conservatives hastily "left for the wilderness" and were practically unaffected, but there was great mortality among the Catholic families. The priest continued to hold meetings of Catholics and also public burial services in defiance of repeated government orders, and only when the missionary was forcibly arrested and removed was the epidemic stayed.

A test of Menomini loyalty to the Great Father in Washington came when the Civil War broke out in 1862. Disaffected groups of Winnebago and Potawatomi did their best to get the tribe to join a "secret union" of western tribes against the Federal government. Apparently some individuals were persuaded, but the Menomini council pledged unanimously its allegiance to the North. This resolution was backed up in practical fashion, for one hundred and twenty-five Menomini warriors enlisted in Wisconsin regiments, and of them about one-third were killed. According to the tribal memories this "war-party" left amid ceremonies approximating to the war rituals of earlier times

About 1863 the area round the Menomini reservation, and even the reservation community itself was being troubled by straggling bands of Winnebago and Potawatomi. Some of the Menomini chiefs wrote to Washington about the matter:

We are becoming alarmed to see so many strange Indians coming on our reservation within a few weeks . . . we wish to assure the whites through our Agent that we detest them as bad as the white men do . . . we do not like the Winnibagos and Potawatomas because they are some of his (the Great Father's) bad Red children and do not listen to his good advice. . . . We do not wish them to come on our reservation . . . If (they are sent off) . . . we know that we will be happy and never have any trouble with our neighbors the whites . . . and that as there is a few of our Tribe that have not turned their attention to Farming, we the chiefs would be able to prevail upon them to do away with the chase and become Farmers and put away the Blanket, but as long as there is other Tribes amongst them I fear we shall not be able to prevail upon some of our young men

as they still retain our old Indian costume and as those Potawatomas and
Winnibagos that comes on our reservation have all the vices of all uncivilized Indians and induces good many of our people to be like themselves
therefore we hope that our Great Father will cause those that are not of
our Tribe . . . to be sent off our reservation.—Letter, *I.O.F.*, Aug. 12,
1863.

The great majority of the Menomini were seemingly at this
time arrayed, at least in intention, on the side of the civilizing process. Doubtless, too, the younger men who returned
from the war exercised a potent influence toward the changing of the old ways.

In these first years, according to the annual government
estimates of the Menomini population, the tribe was decreasing in number. Yet the movement of families and individuals must have made these figures rather approximate. A
"report on the condition of Indian tribes" published in
1867 said:

The Menomonee Indians have decreased about 100 in four years. In
1861 they numbered about 1,900. Now they number about 1,800. The
cause of this decrease is attributable to epidemics of dysentery and ery-
sipelas, to the smallpox and loss of soldiers in the military service . . . The
most common disease among the tribes of this agency (Menomini, Oneida,
Stockbridge and Munsee) is pneumonia . . . but there is very little tuber-
cular disease among them . . . There is considerable intoxication . . .
(and) scarcely a crime committed by an Indian . . . is not directly attributable to the use of intoxicating liquor.—*Report*, pp. 461–62.

This is a rather typical quotation from the records describing the health conditions of the time. Apart from occasional distribution of medicine, also the isolating and vac-
cination of many of the Menomini during the epidemic of
1865 referred to above, no medical work was done in this
early period, nor was there any resident physician. It was
said that "a large proportion of them have more faith in
their own 'medicine men,' and a 'medicine dance' than in a
white physician. Hence . . . a large per cent of the sick
die". The officials appear to have done their best to enforce
government regulations against supplying drink to Indians.
But in this they received no encouragement from the local
courts; actually in one case of the arrest of whites for running liquor on to the reservation:

the district judge . . . in the presence of the indicted parties, and from the bench, censured those who were responsible for bringing such cases into court. He said it was no use to stop the traffic.—*Report*, 1867, p. 463.

The period of the sixties, and particularly from 1868 to 1870, was marked by serious disorganization among the Menomini. Already something of this has been glimpsed from the records: the failure of the early farming experiments, the lessened effectiveness of school and mission work, and the scattering of population away from the area of first settlement. From 1864 on, agitation against the government had been increasing, apparently again headed by mixed bloods, and particularly directed against the terms of the land treaties. The special occasion for this was the beginning of payments in terms of the 1854 treaty, now that annuities and benefits under the previous treaties had expired. A letter from the head chiefs to the Indian Office, one of a number in the same vein, claimed:

We were forced to sign the treaty under threats of being removed west of the Mississippi river. We signed the treaty under protest . . . We, a short time since, received our first installment of money under that treaty, and received it under protest, from the fact that we have a larger claim upon the government . . . If you will compare the payroll of 1854 with that of 1868 you will find that we are rapidly passing away from earth . . . for the want of proper food to sustain nature, and which we are unable to procure under that treaty. We are not sufficiently advanced in civilization, agriculture, &c., to procure the necessaries of life.

At this time, too, the Menomini preferred charges against three successive agents, all of whom were investigated and replaced. The sentiments of one of these officials concerning tribal affairs is worth quoting:

The distinction of *chiefs* and herding in *bands* should be destroyed. Annuities should be withheld or paid in useful and necessary articles distributed to such as need and make good use of them. The idle and vicious should be treated with no favor, and distinctions among them only the reward of merit. Land should be given to them in severalty . . . and they should be taught to depend each upon his own unaided efforts to procure the necessaries of life . . .

The most demoralizing influence with any band of Indians is the possession of a common fund to be paid to or distributed among them. It attracts the most vicious and unprincipled whites around them; they lean upon it as their sole means of supplying their daily wants. They refrain from individual enterprise or exertion, spend their time in indolence and dissipation, and neglect to make provision by their labor for themselves and families. The more educated they become, the greater is the mischief to them of those payments, for they are naturally brought more readily into association with a class of whites who engage in no reputable employment . . . and whose only resource is to beg, borrow, or steal.—in *R.I.A.*, 1869.

Such is an evaluation of the new dependence relation being developed under paternalism, and which was to become a main feature of the later economy of the tribe. While the distinctions of chiefs and bands did disappear in due course, the further remarks are almost identical with many that were heard by the writer some sixty years later.

Still another cause of trouble resulted from the existence on the reservation of a resource henceforth to be intimately bound up with Menomini affairs, timber. The lumbering interests soon coveted the great areas of pine on Menomini lands, particularly in the northwest townships yet practically unoccupied. By 1863 inquiries appear in the official records from the Menomini chiefs as to the prospect of selling the lumber cut in the tribal mill. Shortly after this a number of contracts were let by the Indian Office to lumbermen to cut "dead and down" timber on the reservation. The Menomini council, already aware from past experience of timber stealing by whites and beginning to see the possibilities that lay in this tribal resource, organized a committee to supervise on behalf of the tribe the activities of these lumbermen. As early as 1866 complaints were reaching the department that green standing timber was being cut instead of the authorized "dead and down". In 1868 great fires raged over the reservation among the standing timber, and it was alleged that these were intentionally started to increase the amount available for white exploitation. In that year the agent writes:

The whole Reservation was not many years back a dense forest of pine timber. The winds and fires, from year to year, have made havoc with it and the Reserve today presents to view extensive pine plains with scarcely any vegetation among them, comprising nearly one-half its whole extent. A few years more will in like manner destroy what is left.—Letter, *I.O.F.,* June 30, 1868.

In December of the same year a petition was sent by the heads of eight Menomini bands protesting against the activities of the "Pine Ring", as an association of certain lumber interests was called. They also asked the department to disregard the wishes of two other headmen, alleging that they had been "bought over with bribes". This serious split in the tribal leadership was augmented by another split on the question as to whether a certain lawyer should be hired as an attorney to oust the agent and get satisfaction concerning treaty compensations. The correspondence of the time has two dominant subjects, treaties and timber.

The first experiments in reservation life which started with some measure of hope had thus reached a very uncertain stage as the end of the second decade neared. In 1870 a lieutenant of the United States army was appointed as temporary agent, and a thorough inquiry held. He sums up the position of the Menomini tribe in blunt language:

The superintendent who located this tribe selected a poor sandy barren, and obliged them to live on it . . . and pretend to make farms. The money squandered in this manner would have been sufficient to clear and improve at least a thousand acres of good land that would have benefited them. The tribe is disgusted with their home and discouraged with farming. Some of the better class have moved into the hardwood timber, and are making good homes . . . if persisted in (it) will be of great advantage to the tribe. The usefulness of an agent is impaired by the vagabonds who surround the tribe. Some of the band chiefs are dissatisfied with the head chief and do all in their power to create a disturbance. They are encouraged in this by parties who know any change will work for their immediate benefit.

VIII. PROGRESS IN WARDSHIP

In assuming responsibility for Menomini maintenance during what was hoped would be a brief interval necessary to wean them from hunting to agriculture, the United States authorities met the expenses involved out of tribal funds accumulated from the land sales. Now, as the end of "treaty benefits" loomed in view, both the government officials and the Menomini leaders very naturally looked to commercial lumbering as a means of supporting the tribe. While no attempt will be made here to cover the full history of lumber production on the reservation, those aspects which bear upon the economic and social changes of the time must be reviewed.

The climax of efforts made by the lumbering interests to get control of the Menomini reservation pineries came when Congress passed an act in February, 1871, providing for the sale of a portion of the tribal lands, provided the consent of the council was obtained. This crisis in Menomini affairs effectively ended internal dissensions among the tribesfolk. Faced with the loss of what they were beginning to see were valuable resources, the Menomini leaders stood firm against such sale:

> They unanimously express their unwillingness to part with any portion of the lands ceded to them as their Reservation . . . The Council was fully attended and very united in action . . . They look upon any move to deprive them of a portion of their lands with a jealous eye.—Agent's letter, *I.O.F.*, March 30, 1871.

Never since then has there been any disposition on the part of the tribe to take advantage of this authorization by Congress, so that the lumbermen, whose immediate and anxious inquiries as to the availability of the land are recorded in official correspondence, were disappointed. It was written some years later of the Menomini that "they mourn the loss of the large tract of land they once occupied, and are afraid they will eventually be driven from their present location".

What might be called the first phase of economic experiment was seen to end with the migration of bands and families away from Keshena as the soil became worked out. In 1871 the chiefs, in requesting some provisions from their Great Father, told how:

Many families of this tribe have been changing their homes the past year moving from the poor sandy soil on which they have been living, to the timber lands . . . This change has involved much labor on their part in building new houses and roads.—Letter, I.O.F., Dec. 15, 1871.

Some of these folk moved to South Branch, which the members of the Oconto band had settled earlier (Diagram 4). Apparently all were Christians and they proceeded to break the area into farms. The Crow and West Branch (Kinepoway) settlements were also founded at this time, the former being occupied by "Pagan" (Mitawin) families,[1] the latter by Catholics. An old Menomini recalled to the writer the beginnings of the Crow settlement as follows:

Where the Crow settlement now is, that was a good place for making sugar. All the Pagans went up every year for this. One time Old Man Crow decided to stay. He started to cut the forest and make a farm. The produce was good so he had his big family brought up. Two or three other families joined him; so the agent named the place Crow after him.

Apparently these people were of the Bear section (moiety). The agent of the time speaks of "Old Man Crow":

Little Crow . . . is about 50 years old and has been considered one of the best hunters of the tribe for many years. Some five years since he commenced to clear a small piece of land and make himself a farm, with no help but his axe. He now has 15 acres under cultivation, with comfortable house and barn, owns 5 horses, 1 yoke of oxen, 1 cow, 14 swine, has raised the past year 70 bushels of oats, 60 of corn, 60 of wheat, 200 of potatoes, 8 of beans, besides garden vegetables and the cutting of 15 tons of hay.—R.I.A., 1872.

Of the West Branch community it was said:

The first man at West Branch was To"kwini'ko. He farmed two seasons there in the hardwood, and got much farm produce. On the plains

[1] Everyone right to the present continues to refer to those maintaining the old religion as "Pagans." But as this word tends to have an unfortunate stigma the writer has decided to use in referring to them the name of their central institution, the Mitawin lodge.

they couldn't raise anything. The third season Akine'bui and his band moved up: because he was a chief they named the place after him.

Those of the Bear families who did not actually go so far northwest as the Crow settlement moved in that direction, making their center first near Keshena falls and later beside what is known as Chickeny creek on the present highway 47. In 1872 the agent wrote of "the great moving of nearly the whole tribe within two years . . . the larger portion . . . settling in the vicinity of the West Branch of the Wolf river, from four to six miles west of Keshena." Apparently the one group not much affected by these happenings was the Thunder people, for they had abandoned their settlement at We'ka creek (p. 151) some years earlier, probably at the time of the 1865 epidemic, and had moved in their canoes up the Wolf river nearly to the northern boundary of the reservation.

This transfer to the better lands gave something of an impetus to farming. The officials did their best to encourage agriculture by securing and distributing seeds, stock and implements. By 1876 it was reported that "with the exception of 12 to 15 families they all have permanent homes and cultivate their patch of ground". Two years later a competition was held for the best "cultivated farm", "yoke of oxen", and the like, the prizes being paid for, at the request of the chiefs, out of the tribal funds. But farming on any extensive scale was confined to a very few. Concerning Menomini work effort at this time an enthusiastic agent writes:

Will Indians work? As proof, I will state that the members of this tribe have earned the past year in cash labor, at the government farm and mill, and in lumbering in the reserve, $6,600; and they have also cut and sold over $1,000 worth of hay besides providing for their own stock. I also estimate they have received for labor outside the reservation on railroads and at lumbering work $12,000; making at least $19,000 that they have received for labor, besides building, clearing lands, raising crops, making sugar, gathering rice and cranberries, hunting for furs, etc. There is no doubt but the Indian will work much like other men if he receives the same help and inducements.

Along with the new opportunities shown here as opening out through which the Menomini could earn money, the old cycle of gathering the natural products was still being maintained by most if not all families. But much of the produce was now disposed of to the traders for goods. In the spring great quantities of maple sugar were manufactured, in one year the amount being estimated at seventy tons. Berries were picked in the summer, and wild rice in the autumn, though, according to Powell in 1877, "not . . . to the same extent as formerly". Fall and winter hunting produced many furs—indeed, game tended for a time to become more plentiful on the reservation as the forests outside were cleared or milled and it became a refuge for wild life. The use of wild marsh hay eliminated to a large extent the need for cropping to provide winter feed for stock. The frequent moving about required by these pursuits, however, continued to be a constant drawback to settled farming; an agent remarks for example, that sugar is made only "at a fearful cost of health and to the utter abandonment of homes, farms, stock, and everything for the time being."

Until 1872 the only timber cut by the Menomini on their reservation was that needed for housing and other improvements, or incidental to the clearing of forest areas for cultivation. Commercial lumbering on the reservation was engaged in only by whites, either under contracts supervised by the Indian department, or else illegally. The proceeds from the contracts, or from compensations exacted where convictions of trespass could be obtained, were lodged in the Menomini trust funds. But in the year mentioned a tribal lumber camp was organized, operated under supervision of the Indian agent, and using Menomini labor exclusively. During the first season some twelve million feet of pine were cut and driven to mills down the river; as a result the Indian workers received over $3,000, and the tribal funds benefited to the extent of some $5 per thousand feet. In the next five years such lumbering tended increasingly to stabilize the work effort of the tribe; being a winter occupation it apparently took a place more or less corresponding to the old fur hunting. The Menomini both from this experience within the reservation and from working for white lumbermen outside soon learned the work very thoroughly. Tales are related today of the skill acquired by many in felling trees, damming streams, and especially in the dangerous work of driving logs down the treacherous falls and rapids of the Wolf river.

The period from 1878 to 1880 was marked by very hard times for the Menomini and exceeding strained relations with the government. The Indian department gave orders for logging to cease, while in addition agriculture received a setback through floods and other causes, so that the tribe was thrown back almost entirely on the old economy. Shortly afterward the annuities and benefits specified in the treaties expired. A fresh outburst of agitation followed, both in view of the Menomini grievances over the treaty terms, and because such annuity payments, the distributions of goods, and the special services had continued for so many years that they had come to be regarded as normal and permanent features of Menomini life and of relationships with the government. The result was another investigation of the affairs of the tribe, and certain shifts in official policy. Before discussing these the history of this decade in matters other than economic can be summarized.

In 1872 the Keshena schools, barely maintained after the passing of the Dousmans, were closed for lack of pupils. Instead, small schools were started at South Branch and West Branch settlements, the first under a mixed blood Menomini teacher, the second with white teachers. A report says of them:

> (They) are teaching those they can induce to attend, sometimes forty and sometimes two. The boys prefer playing ball outside the schoolhouse to studying inside, and (the teachers') unusual enthusiasm has failed to excite in them any great desire for learning.—Agent's report, *R.I.A.*, 1873.

A scheme was now proposed for establishing a central boarding school at Keshena, making attendance compulsory. By 1875 the Menomini council were persuaded to support the idea. The local schools were abolished. Opposition to the central institution was voiced by a priest then visiting on the reservation, but this was overcome by threats of his removal. In the first year the attendance at the new boarding establishment was 76, and the numbers grew rapidly.

The removal of Menomini children for most of the year from their home setting to one under full time control by whites was perhaps the most potent move made up to this time by the government in its attempt to "civilize" the tribe. Numbers of the people speak of the boarding school as contributing the really destructive blow to old beliefs and customs.

In 1874, members of the tribe, presumably under official urging, requested the government to send them a white doctor. At first several medical men made temporary visits, but from 1876 on a resident physician was appointed. His detailed accounts of Menomini health may be found in the annual reports of the Indian Office for the years that follow. Anticipating further discussion of health work on the reservation it may be noted that from this time on mortality among the tribe was lowered and not only was depopulation gradually arrested but in the new century the tribal numbers began to increase.

In 1871 the head chief, Ä'kwine'mi, was arrested and tried for murder. Found guilty, he was deposed from his position and imprisoned for a period.[2] Another son of Oshkosh, Ni'uopêt (Neopit), was appointed chief. This marks an important step in the contact of the Menomini with the legal and judicial system of the whites, and indeed the first elaborate move toward replacing the authority of chiefs and councils, also of Indian customary law, by white authority and social control. It produced a profound impression, in no way forgotten to the present. From this time forward the Menomini became increasingly acquainted with the machinery of white law enforcement both within and out-

[2] On his release he returned to the reservation but never attained again to any authority.

side the reservation. One of the chief agencies in this education appears to have been the court and jail of the near-by town of Shawano, with which, according to the columns of local newspapers published at the time, many a Menomini, chief and youth alike, was familiar, mainly as a result of the effects of Shawano "cider".

In 1880 the Indian department organized a special Indian police service on the Menomini and other reservations, employing Indians chosen for their special fitness. Shortly after this a "Court of Indian Offenses" was established at Keshena, with three chiefs as judges. These moves were inspired partly by a manifest decay in the authority of Indian chiefs and a lessening effectiveness of old customs, partly by an increasing need for the enforcement of codes within the reservations corresponding more or less to those in the near-by white communities. It was considered essential for the assimilation of the Indian that he should come to know the rules of American living, complex as they were, and difficult as it might be to break down conservatism.

An interesting symptom of the changes taking place during this period is the appearance in the records, in 1874 and 1875, of requests from groups of Menomini to be made United States "citizens".[3] Just what they understood by citizenship and its privileges and duties is hard to say; from the documents it would seem that they thought of it as carrying mostly privileges. When a poll of the tribal council was taken on the matter, 166 expressed a desire to become citizens, 18 wished to "remain as Indians", while 8 were "not decided". But no official move was made; not until 1924 was citizenship granted to all Indians.

The year 1880 can be said to mark the commencement of a modern cultural revolution among the Menomini in which the results of these preliminary efforts at "civilizing" the tribe became really apparent. It will be well to pause at this point for a glimpse at happenings around the reserva-

[3] In 1871 the old status of the tribes as "nations" was abolished by Congress, and all Indians became "subjects" of the United States.

tion, as the impulse to change came largely through increasing contact with the larger world.

The early maps of Wisconsin show a number of scattered white settlements appearing in the northern wilderness. These were founded as a result of four main urges: first as "taverns" and stop-over places on important trails; second as postal points on early mail routes; third as milling centers; and fourth as railroad depots. In 1863 the area in which the Menomini lands were situated was constituted a "county", with headquarters at the milling settlement of Shawano. Twenty-eight years later the area was redivided, and three counties, Shawano, Oconto and Langlade, were formed, the reservation lying mostly in the first, partly in the second, and being bordered by the third; apart from boundary adjustments unimportant for the Menomini region these counties have remained the same right to the present. The period of the tavern settlements covered from about 1855 to 1885. Those affecting the Menomini were for the most part built along the military road. North of the reservation boundary appeared such stopping places as the Log Cabin and Langlade, while within it were built the Boyd, Corn, Beauprey, and Mag. Lawe taverns, owned by mixed blood Menomini. On other trails such towns as Antigo, Polar and Hollister had like origins.

(These) were typical of the western mining town, where the frontier elements held full sway. Hotels and travelers' rests would spring into existence in a day . . . (with) saloons and dance houses . . . the river driver, the woodsman, the teamster, the Indian, all gathered there.— Dessureau, *History of Langlade Country*, pp. 24–25.

Most of these places adjacent to the Menomini reservation developed into lumbering centers. Other sawmilling communities such as Lily, White Lake and Mattoon came into existence as the forests were progressively cut away. Besides the military road, the Menomini reservation had passing across it another great artery of traffic for whites north of the area, the Wolf river; every year great logging drives were conducted upon it through the tribal territory.

On the main postal routes such as the lake Superior and Oconto trails, centers like Leopolis, Gresham, Gillet and Pulcifer were founded and formed the nuclei for later settlements. During the 'seventies the first railroad was pushed steadily north through Shawano, and by 1881 it reached as far as Antigo. This line passed a short distance west of the reservation. In the records of the time there appear several applications to run tracks across the reservation itself; but this scheme did not materialize until 1906. The main center of white influence upon the Menomini at this time, as it has been since, was the town of Shawano, which in 1874 became incorporated as a city and by the following year could boast some 6,500 inhabitants.

So attractive was life in the lumber centers that numbers of the Menomini, especially persons of mixed descent, settled rather permanently off the reservation. This, however, gave offense to more conservative members of the tribe, and was frowned upon by the officials. An agent reports:

I learned soon after last payment that a number of families belonging to the tribe had for some time been living away from the reservation among the whites . . . After consulting with the chiefs . . . I gave notice that all such families should be stricken from the pay-roll if they did not return . . . by the time of next payment.—*R.I.A.*, 1871.

The records show that some of the families returned, but others actually preferred to make their own way and were for the time being eliminated from the roll.

The timber boom could not last, any more than could fur trading, as intensive exploitation steadily exhausted the available supply. True, milling operations have continued north of the reservation right to the present day. By the 'eighties, however, farm clearings approached to the southern boundary. In place of the rugged woodsmen came permanent settlers, many of them immigrants from Europe, bringing their families and a tradition of frugality and industry. Their long hours of steady labor, the working of their women in the fields, and the intense competition they offered in local markets was probably to serve more as a deterrent than as a stimulus to the Menomini as regards farming.

The Keshena Indian Agency controlled not only Menomini affairs but also those of the Oneida, living near the Fox river, and of the Stockbridge and Munsee on two townships southwest of the Menomini reservation. The annual reports consistently refer to the Menomini as the "least civilized" of the three groups. In 1881 the Oneida were considered sufficiently advanced in farming to have their reservation allotted "in severalty", that is, in individual holdings, and some years later the same was done with Stockbridge and Munsee lands. The most important contact between them and the Menomini came about with the opening of the Keshena boarding schools, for all children in the Keshena agency attended. Before this, apparently, the Menomini had had little intercourse with these peoples. The Oneidas lived some distance to the south. The Stockbridge and Munsee, while geographically adjacent, were Lutherans, hence under suspicion by both the Catholic and Mitawin sections of the tribe; furthermore, boundary disputes had aroused ill feeling between the two peoples.

The relations of the Menomini with their ancient Indian neighbors of the upper lakes area, Winnebago, Chippewa and Potawatomi, varied according to religious affiliation. The Christians were more or less completely out of touch with these peoples, looking down particularly on bands of Winnebago (who had returned to Wisconsin from the western reservation where they had been removed at the time of the land treaties) as "uncivilized". The Mitawin Menomini, in contrast to this, maintained close affiliations with the "Pagans" among these tribes, especially the Chippewa and Potawatomi, among whom as will be seen the old religion and ceremonial life were far more vitally preserved.

Out of this association came an outstanding crisis in the modern Menomini history. About 1880 an Indian religious cult known to white observers as the "dream dance", or in Menomini terminology the "peace dance", made its appearance among Wisconsin tribes.[4] This cult, claimed as a "new revelation" from the sacred Powers, had as its central feature an old-time Indian symbol, the medicine drum. Though incorporating elements obviously adapted from white religion, its theology and elaborate ceremonial of dancing and chanting followed patterns essentially old. Some Potawatomi approached the leaders of the conservative Menomini to accept initiation, and received their consent. In the summer of 1881 representatives of the Chippewa and Potawatomi arrived on the reservation, with their "Grandfather", the drum, to teach the tenets and rituals. Their meetings and dances soon began to interfere with farming operations. According to eye witnesses still living, even "a good many Catholics dropped their religion and went dancing".

The agent of the time, a newcomer, also the Franciscan fathers who were then establishing a permanent mission on the reservation, opposed the new cult strenuously. The tribesmen from outside were ordered to leave, but they refused. The newly constituted Menomini police were powerless to remove them. A party of Catholic Indians was then organized, and broke up the meetings. The agent, fearing serious trouble, sent for a detachment of United States troops, which took up quarters on the reservation for some weeks. Certain informants say that he also took the sacred drum, and as a result the agency was stoned, but others deny this—"there was more wind than trouble". At least these events had profound effects. For one thing, the presence of soldiers afforded the Menomini a significant demonstration of the power that lay behind the official word. Still more important, the tribe was split far more definitely on the basis of religion than had ever been the case before. Where to this time the Mitawin and the Catholic groups

[4] Apparently this "prophet" religion was distantly connected with the well-known "ghost dance" of the plains tribes. Such spontaneous religious cults are a well-known phenomenon, not only among the American Indians but also among peoples in similar situations of pressure and transition the world over. See Barrett, *The Dream Dance of the Chippewa and Menomini Indians*.

had been on the whole friendly and cooperative in matters outside the religious sphere, relations now became exceedingly strained. Each group kept strictly apart from the other; the Mitawin people retreated into their conservative shell, while most Catholics broke very consciously with the old ways, hence became more amenable to white influences.

Actually the Mitawin group itself seems to have been split into two factions by this cult of "Dreamers". Some claimed that it should wholly supersede the older religious system, including the Mitawin lodge. Others, particularly members of the lodge itself, regarded it merely as a "peace dance", an additional ceremony symbolic of a new unity among Indian peoples. Numbers of the former group, who incidentally were also of the old Thunder clans, moved away northwest to the dense forest area of the reservation now known as Zoar; there, cut off by distance and lack of communications, they associated themselves rather with the wandering bands of Chippewa, Potawatomi and Winnebago than with their own tribesfolk.[5] Though this split among the conservatives became mellowed by time, and intercourse was fully resumed together with common participation in both the dream dance and the Mitawin ceremonies, it was found by Hoffman and Skinner to be quite bitter at the period of their visits, and has by no means yet been forgotten.

In reports of succeeding years there are many references to the distinction that now arose between Christians and conservatives. The following are examples:

Many of the . . . Pagan party clothe themselves entirely in buckskin and subsist principally upon the chase.

The Pagans . . . are that portion of the tribe not connected with the church. They are peaceful and temperate and the most law-abiding class in the tribe, the head chief being one of this class. They are making slow progress in civilization, however, . . . and shun the ways of the white man, including the greater number of his vices.

[5] This was the only clear account obtained from informants as to the motive for the settlement of conservative families at Zoar. Yet it is possible that some families were there more or less permanently at an earlier date than 1881.

That portion of the tribe known as pagans still continue to hold their old time dances. They are sometimes visited by roving bands of Pottawatomis, Winnebagoes, and Chippewas, who join them in dancing. The pagans are the least industrious members of the tribe, and will only cultivate, with a few exceptions, small patches of corn, beans, and potatoes. They are the berry pickers, sugar makers, and hunters of the tribe, by which they eke out a scanty subsistence. Within the past two years a few . . . have been induced to clear land, raise more crops, and to cut a few logs.—from *R.I.A.*, 1883, 1885, 1888.

Of course the Mitawin people were in various phases of their life subject to pressure from the authorities; their children were compelled to go to school, health services were insisted upon in times of serious illness, while white forms of social and moral control reached out increasingly to affect their lives. Yet the dead weight of passive opposition to change, especially in matters relating to religion, was constantly manifest.

Taking up once more the economic story it was seen that about 1880 the tribe was in a very uncertain position; lumbering had been officially banned, while annuity payments and other recurring benefits from the land treaties came to an end. In the year mentioned another official investigation of Menomini affairs took place. On the financial side it was found that there remained only a special trust fund created by the 1836 treaty, together with some money from lumbering, the whole totalling $153,039.38. By act of Congress this residue was lodged in the United States treasury, the interest at five per cent to be used yearly for tribal purposes.

1881 came with the Menomini still dependent on their own immediate efforts at food getting, except for a small per capita payment from this interest. Meantime officials on the reservation pressed the Indian department to allow the tribe to sell or utilize their timber resources; the agent of the time writes:

The Menomonees have repeatedly asked the United States to sell (their timber), and invest the proceeds in United States bonds, the interest to be used annually for their benefit and support . . . Under existing laws, it must remain to decay and waste (when burnt or blown down). This is very discouraging to the Menomonees, who are continually asking permission to cut the dead and down timber going to waste on their land, thus giving them employment during the winter season, and means wherewith to . . . farm in spring and summer . . . Their urgent request at every council, besides the sale of their pine, is the allotment of their land in severalty that they may have a home of their own . . .

At present they have nothing to do for a large portion of the year except to engage in their old-custom dances, hold council, or go outside to look for work . . . (hence their) morbid condition. They are not allowed, under existing laws, to cut a load of wood from the dead timber wasting on the reserve, and sell it to the nearest market. Nor can they legally cut a few hoop-poles from the dense undergrowth . . . and sell them to buy the necessaries of life for their hungry children. Is this not a national disgrace? . . . laws that are intended to elevate and civilize . . . practically hold (the Indian) down hand and foot . . .

It is not money that elevates the Indian; he does not, generally speaking, know the value of it; but it is employment in some kind of honest industry.—*R. I. A.,* 1881.

It would appear that the official prohibition of lumbering in these years was a direct result of the activities of the "Pine Ring" among Washington legislators. They still had hopes that the Menomini would sell the northwestern townships on which the best timber stood. But the attitude of the tribe is expressed emphatically in a letter dictated by head chief Neopit himself to the local paper:

I desire to make the following statement . . . Shortly after the passage by the great council at Washington (Congress) of the act of February 13, 1871 . . . a general council of the Menominees . . . fully and unanimously disapproved, and in the strongest terms protested against . . . the sale of all our pine and agricultural lands, leaving us for homes and farms four townships of barren sand plains. We want to sell our timber for a fair price, and we will give the purchasers four or five years to take it away in, and then we want our lands allotted to us . . . But we will not consent to the sale of any more land. We want it for our children and grandchildren. We accepted our present reservation when it was considered of no value by our white friends. And all we ask is to be permitted to keep it as a home . . . Neopit, his mark.—in *Shawano County Advocate,* Mar. 16, 1882.

The Indian department now proposed that the Menomini be given permission annually to cut "dead and down" timber, and this was confirmed by a special act of Congress in 1882. Such permission was granted for the next six winters, in the hope that it might "open a way to better times". The venture was on the whole most successful, in spite of low prices received in certain seasons because, it was alleged, of "collusion amongst buyers". Ten per cent of each year's proceeds were put aside on account of "stumpage", and this was used for the tribal hospital and as a poor fund.

As the lumbering enterprise expanded, farming operations slumped more or less proportionately. A report of 1884 says:

> Two years ago the farming pursuit was almost wholly abandoned. The Indians having become distracted by the glittering prizes they fancied they saw in the lumbering enterprise, turned disgusted from the plow and field . . . The farms of those who pretend to farm will not exceed 4 acres . . . on the average.
>
> The condition of this tribe at the present time will not compare favorably in an agricultural point of view with its status twenty-five years ago . . . Potatoes, beans, and seed-oats . . . distributed (were) in many cases . . . eaten by those who received the same, and the oats fed to their stock, and in some cases the fields were abandoned after being planted or sowed.— *R.I.A.*, 1884.

Two years later a new agent, apparently unfamiliar with the records which have been sketched here, was led to remark: "Apparently but little effort has been made to induce this tribe to endeavor to obtain their living by cultivating the soil"!

This incoming official initiated a unique scheme to stimulate Menomini agriculture. He decreed that only those Indians who farmed in summer could log in winter, and that those breaking in timbered lands for cultivation could sell for their personal benefit the green timber felled. Between 1886 and 1891 about 1600 acres of new forest land were broken in, with correspondingly better results in farming, and this new agricultural impetus lasted nearly to the end of the century.[6] With further development of lumbering, however, the farming operations of the great majority of the tribe gradually declined again to what might be termed a garden patch economy. Nevertheless the records show

[6] See particularly *R.I.A.*, 1886, 1887, 1889, 1895.

very tangible material improvements, such as the digging of water wells, planting of fruit trees, and buying of equipment with proceeds from the sale of surplus produce in the better years. The position of farming by the beginning of the new century was thus described:

> Farming is carried on to some extent, but as a rule in a very indifferent manner . . . The issue of seed grain has been discontinued at this reservation, and as the Indians have not acquired the habit of looking forward . . . and making provision for the coming season, they often find themselves not only without the necessary seed, but in many instances the means with which to procure it.—*R.I.A.*, 1903.

The report tells that "lumbering is the most important industry and the main source of revenue for the Indians":

> Every able-bodied Indian who so desires, can find employment during eight months of the year at good wages cutting and banking logs and driving them to their destination; therefore the necessity to cultivate their land has not been forced upon them . . . There is also considerable work in the woods adjacent to the reservation peeling hemlock bark. During the berry season the women and children earn considerable money picking berries. Hunting, fishing, and trapping also yield them some revenue.

In 1888 the Menomini logging operations were once more stopped. A ruling was handed down by the Attorney-General of the United States that as "the right of Indians on an Indian reservation is one of occupancy only" and the "title to the timber is absolute in the United States", the Menomini lumbering was illegal. The Indian department succeeded, however, in getting a special act through Congress the following year allowing the enterprise to continue.[7] Complaints were then lodged by white lumbermen that the Menomini were refusing to pay their debts to merchants, were spending their money foolishly, and were starting fires to increase the amount of dead and down timber. An agent's report states: "As pine timber is becoming scarce, the lumbermen are clamoring to have this pine sold (i.e., the green standing pine)"; but he adds that "the Indians are almost unanimously opposed. They want to log the timber for themselves". This indicates a reversal of the earlier desire to sell, apparently a result of growing experience in lumber-

[7] *R.I.A.*, 1888, 1889, 1890.

ing and a consequent realization of the value of their timber resources. An official inquiry revealed "some truth" in the lumbermen's claims. Because of this an entirely new policy was initiated by which the temptation to fire green timber was removed.

In 1890 an act was passed authorizing the cutting of standing timber under the supervision of white logging superintendents. Contracts were to be let annually to individual Menomini for amounts in specified areas up to a maximum number of feet, while the proceeds of each year's sale were to be divided, after payment of contractors and of operating expenses, one-fifth to go to the stumpage fund for hospital and poor relief, and the remaining four-fifths to tribal trust funds. The Menomini in council at first rejected this, but on being informed that on no other terms could they log at all, they of necessity agreed. The system after a short trial proved most successful, and was continued apparently to everybody's satisfaction into the new century. Nearly every year the full amount allowed, varying from fifteen to twenty million feet, was cut and banked on the Wolf and Little Oconto rivers ready for sale by tender; each fall a sum of $75,000 would be advanced as credit to finance the workers, who through their chiefs of squads would contract to log specific areas; and in the spring those willing to drive the logs to the mill would usually be hired for the task by those who purchased the lumber.[8] By 1905 the "Menominee Log Fund" in the United States treasury, comprising four-fifths of the net profits, amounted to more than two million dollars, and the tribe had become one of the wealthiest in the country.

Menomini economic effort, first directed by the government towards farming, thus became increasingly stabilized in lumbering. As an occupation of the late fall, winter, and early spring it was particularly congenial, and as already noted not unlike the fur hunting of earlier days. In the summer months the people did what they pleased, knowing

[8] A description of this method of Menomini logging is given in *R.I.A.*, 1895, p. 325.

for sure that they would have credit with the traders for the winter. They gathered berries and other forest products, also manufactured sugar in spring and harvested wild rice in the fall. From the interest on their trust fund small per capita payments were distributed from time to time; indeed, by 1906, the amount of logging profit was so large that the government increased such allowances. During all this period educational and health work, also most of the costs of administration, continued to be met from Menomini money, and since the timber on the reservation showed no signs of any immediate exhaustion the economic prosperity of the tribe seemed fairly assured.

In 1906 an important change in the Menomini lumbering business was mooted. Instead of cutting and running logs to the mills of the whites down-river, the Menomini proposed that the lumber be milled on the reservation itself to their own profit. This was agreed to, and in 1908 a tribally owned mill started operations in the northwest townships, and a milling town, Neopit, sprang into being: but of this more later.

When in 1880 the Franciscan order, assisted shortly after by Sisters of St. Joseph, took over the Menomini mission (p. 164), they quickly won both the loyalty of the Catholic Menomini and the respect of officials. Branches of the main Keshena church were organized among the Catholic communities at South Branch and West Branch. In 1886 it was reported that ninety families were served by the Keshena church, sixty-five by that at South Branch (Little Oconto), and thirty-five at West Branch (Kinepoway), this giving an idea of the relative size of these settlements and of the distribution of Christian families at that date. A report of the fathers states:

Immorality (formerly) had full sway among them. Special incentives thereto are, above all, two vices viz, dances and drunkenness . . . A great change for the better has been brought about. Dances on the reservation become more seldom every year, and if there be any there are not so many partake as formerly, nor are the excesses so great and numerous as they used to be . . . To limit drunkenness a temperance society was founded

. . . opening with 15 members . . . The present number (is) 95. This society has proved to be the most effective means to break up intoxication. A women's society was started . . . principally . . . for the moral improvement of the members themselves, which so far has had a very good success.   Another society of a very similar character was formed . . . for young girls, numbering . . . about 100.   The least could be done with the young men in general, a few excepted that belonged to the temperance society.—*R.I.A.*, 1886.

Besides giving religious and ethical training, the mission undertook educational and health work.

In 1883 the fathers started a small school at Keshena which developed in due course into a boarding school for Catholic children similar to the government school founded earlier.   The control of this enterprise was largely assumed by the Sisters of St. Joseph.   Financial support was received out of Menomini funds, this in the form of "contracts", or so much per head for the support of a certain number of children, provided sufficient signatures of tribesfolk consenting to the subsidy were obtained each year. Naturally most Catholic families sent their children to the parochial school.

Practically the whole educational enterprise in these years was centered in the two Keshena boarding establishments.[9]   They grew steadily, particularly after school attendance was made compulsory for all Indian children between the ages of six and eighteen.   The curricula as defined by the government had from the first a strong practical bias:

The pupils of both schools are taught the common branches of education, (the boys) farming, carpentering, shoemaking, blacksmithing, and other industrial branches.   The girls are taught housework, sewing, baking, and knitting, and many of both sexes take a keen interest in their work.— *R.I.A.*, 1886.

At an early date an order had been put into effect prohibiting the use of the vernacular in Indian schools, so that all children had to learn English; furthermore, apart from

[9] Several smaller day schools were organized from time to time in the more distant settlements, but except in the new town of Neopit all these had merely a temporary existence.

English, the children of different tribes in the same school had no common medium of communication.

Those pupils whose parents consented were sent, after completing the fourth grade, to one or other of the great Indian concentration schools, Carlisle in Pennsylvania and Haskell in Kansas. Many sons and daughters of leading Menomini families, including those of Chief Neopit, went away for a four year period, or even longer under a preliminary "outing system" organized by the Quakers in Pennsylvania. The effect upon Menomini youth was profound; a Carlisle graduate said:

> Until then we did not know anything about the world outside. We didn't even know that other tribes than the few around here existed. After we had finished our years of school and of working out in white families during the holidays we came back to the reservation. The principal used to tell us that we had to be "missionaries" of civilization to the people at home.

A son of one of the chiefs told the writers how his father, in sending him off to school, said:

> You have learnt from me the ways of the Indian; I cannot teach you the ways of the white man, for they are unknown to me. But this is a new time, and you must learn those ways. Go!

This willing acceptance of the school as a necessary institution in Menomini life is seen also in official reports:

> Parents now voluntarily bring their children to the school, which is in strong contrast to a few years back, when the police had to be sent out to bring in the children. The most of the Menominies are now as anxious that their children should receive an education . . . as they were a few years ago that they should not be educated and trained to lead a different life than they had led.—*R.I.A.,* 1897.

The chief dissenters to education were naturally the Mitawin group. In 1903 the Lutherans from the Stockbridge Indian settlement of Red Springs tried to found a school at the Zoar settlement, but failing to receive support, abandoned the project. Even in 1929 the writer saw the police busy trying to catch truant Zoar children in the woods at school opening time.

In 1882 the new educational opportunities being opened to the Menomini were discussed in an editorial in a Shawano newspaper as follows:

> If the idea of really becoming like civilized people should enter the Indian mind through the medium of the children . . . no power in the country can keep up the robbery and rascality which have characterized our dealings with Indians through many administrations. Nevertheless the young Indian should be educated for his own sake, his family's sake and that of the nation, particularly as it costs a hundred times less to educate him than to kill him, which is the only alternative that has ever been discovered.—*Shawano County Advocate,* June 8, 1882.

The reference to killing the Indian is a reminder that to the west of Menomini country the United States had at this time been facing the expensive and difficult task of breaking in the plains tribes to official control by force of arms. The Menomini experiment in schooling, therefore, may be seen as part of a new development in Indian policy aiming toward education and assimilation instead of merely segregation and protection.

In 1886 the first Menomini hospital was opened, the reservation doctor cooperating with three Catholic Sisters who acted as nurses. There the sick, the orphaned and the aged were cared for at the expense of the tribe.

> When the hospital was first established it was quite difficult to persuade patients to go . . . for treatment, but lately many are asking to be taken in. In many cases it was the patient's first contact with civilization, as many of the pagan Indians pride themselves in living as Indians and rigidly reject the white man's ways . . . the medicine men do all in their power to prevent the Indians from going.
>
> While our wild Indians still maintain their medicine men and their medicine dances it frequently happens that the Agency physician is called in for advice and medicine when the medicine man himself falls sick or is ailing.
>
> As child births are still looked after by the "old women" the agency physician finds himself relieved of that exacting and sleep-destroying element of medical practice.—from physicians' reports, *R.I.A.,* 1887, 1893.

Here for the first time serious competition developed between the Indian and white medicines, and between those possessed of their respective secrets. A steady improvement in conditions of hygiene is reported from year to year.

Liquor is mentioned as still one of the worst enemies to health, while tuberculosis, apparently not at all prevalent earlier, accounted for the greatest mortality.   The aged and indigent folk of the tribe were issued "rations" every two weeks, comprising usually twenty pounds of flour and ten of pork, the number of recipients ranging from seventy to one hundred.   In all of this the expenses were borne by the tribe rather than by families and individuals.

The Indian police force organized in 1880 for the tribes of the Keshena agency consisted of eleven Indian men, of whom six were detailed to the Menomini.   The "Court of Indian Offenses" organized in 1883 had its duties defined by an "Indian Code".   According to this:

> The Sun-dance, the scalp-dance, the war-dance—and all other so-called feasts assimilating thereto; plural marriages; the practice of the medicine man; the destruction or theft of property; the payment of or offer to pay . . . the friends or relatives of any Indian girl or woman (when taken as a wife), are declared to be Indian offences.

In addition the court was given jurisdiction over "misdemeanors" committed by Indians, civil suits where Indians were the parties, and violation of the liquor regulations. The government very wisely appointed as judges three outstanding chiefs of the tribe, Neopit, Ni'aqtawâ'pomi and "Chickeny" (Mä'tshikine'ŭ^v).   The first two, interestingly enough, were leaders of the Mitawin lodge, so that necessarily there had to be a rather liberal interpretation of some of the above offenses.   Indeed the Indian Code had from the outset to be elastic, and among the Menomini the official policy was adopted of leaving alone certain of the older practices so long as they did not result in direct trouble. The Indian Commissioner himself in 1889 described the whole court system as "a tentative and somewhat crude attempt" to break up the old ways.

The deliberations and decisions of the three chiefs were treated with every respect by those Menomini brought before the court.   The most prevalent misdemeanors of the time, as shown by the annual reports, were drunkenness and breaking of liquor regulations.   The court also had the task

of adjusting marital difficulties, such as wife beating or unfaithfulness. The usual punishment was to impose a fine,
or a certain number of days' work on the roads, or both; not
until 1904 was a permanent jail built and the keep of prisoners arranged for.

Such arrests of whites as were made from year to year
were little deterrent to the liquor runners and saloon keepers
who operated round the edges of the reservation and reaped
a rich harvest, especially at per capita payment times. As
for the regulation of family matters, not only the court and
the mission, but also some of the officials took a direct hand
in attempting to refashion Indian conduct to white patterns:

> Intemperance and lack of respect for marriage relations are the two
> great drawbacks . . . The utter disregard and lack of respect for the mar-
> riage relations, whether civil, religious, or by Indian custom, is simply
> shocking . . . The agent is kept busy adjusting their (marital) differences.
>
> Stringent measures are being taken to compel them to resume their
> lawful marriage relations and take out marriage licenses and to be legally
> married.—*R.I.A.*, 1904, 1905.

Quotations like this, together with the contemporary reports
of the missionaries, indicate that there had come about a
considerable social disorganization as the Indian had his old
standards of conduct disrupted first by association with the
lumbermen and other frontier whites, then by the superimposition of church tenets and the statute law.

Soon after the establishment of the Indian court system
the traditional authority of chieftainship was officially abolished. Already the prestige of the old tribal leaders was
waning in the new order. That they themselves had moved
far in their ideas is indicated by the fact that as early as
1880 a letter in the Indian office files contains a request from
the chiefs that they be paid for their services "when same
are required for the benefit of the tribe". In 1890 the
authorities called Neopit and his fellow chiefs to Washington, and there persuaded them to surrender formally their
titles of leadership. So long as these same people were
used by the government as judges in the Indian court and
taken cognizance of in the council and on similar occasions,

this surrender did not mean much. But later, when their authority passed with old age or death, their normal successors had little other than a sentimental and nominal prestige, and the officials were able to appoint anyone they wished as judges or to positions of authority in the conduct of tribal business. More and more the traditional leadership was undermined and the function of the council circumscribed. In their place the government built up a system of direct and paternalistic relationships between itself and the individual Menomini, with results that will be seen in due course.

Such then was the position of the tribe at the turn of the century. It has been seen how, after the first decades during which economic experiment was predominant, various patterns of wardship emerged, these designed to "civilize" the Menomini and to prepare them for participation in the general life of white America, rapidly approaching in the persons of white settlers. However, the task was being found by no means so easy as the first white administrators had hoped. Thus one agent, offering his resignation at this time, wrote:

Unfortunately the Indian question is far from being solved, as the Indians are slow to accept reforms, and this with their extremely suspicious natures makes work among them very difficult.

No doubt the Menomini by this time had reason to be constantly suspicious of things white. Just how far the cultural revolution of which the beginnings have been glimpsed was to allay these suspicions and bring about progress in assimilation will be seen in the survey of the tribal experience in the twentieth century.

IX. ETHNOLOGICAL AND MUSEUM DATA

The material presented thus far concerning the reservation period has been taken almost entirely from official records. As such, it has one extreme of emphasis, the progress of the Indian in white ways and especially the response to government policies. Any references to the maintenance of old ways are incidental and often derogatory. At this point a body of data may be reviewed, the records of ethnologists and the gleanings of museum collectors, that have exactly the opposite emphasis, stressing the degree to which elements of the old culture have been retained.

Hoffman, the first ethnologist to visit the Menomini, worked on the reservation in the years 1890 to 1893 under the auspices of the Bureau of American Ethnology. Of later workers, listed in the bibliography, the most important was Skinner who identified himself closely with the Menomini from 1910 until his death in 1926. Such students were primarily concerned with trying to reconstruct the pre-white life. Nevertheless their writings reflect, largely unintentionally, the status of Menomini culture at the period of their visits, together with changes taking place during the memory of their informants.

Some of these ethnologists, along with other visitors, were also interested in collecting artifacts for museums, either by going direct to Menomini families or by employing certain Indians and mixed bloods as buying agents. Actually the tribesfolk were stripped fairly completely of objects of Indian workmanship that had any respectable antiquity, or even looked "Indian."[1]

The outstanding impression of any observant person who stands alongside the many white visitors peering curiously nowadays at all these Menomini artifacts through the glass

[1] Incidentally these were by no means always of Menomini manufacture, as the artifacts had not infrequently been acquired by them from Chippewa, Potawatomi and other groups. For the locality of important Menomini collections see p. 3.

194

windows of museum show cases is that such objects do not belong at all exclusively to the pre-white culture of the Indian, but represent in large measure products of post-white times. Materials, forms, techniques of workmanship, and decorations from white culture will be incorporated with those genuinely old. The marks of the trader will be seen, here a thimble, there some cloth or ribbon, elsewhere a glass mirror. A cross or text will show the influence of the missionary. Medals, shoulder epaulettes, and trouser braids indicate the contribution of the soldier.

On further inquiry it will be found that many of these artifacts can be dated as either of old or of comparatively modern workmanship. Some can even be traced to an exact time and place of manufacture. In the Green Bay museum there are various objects known to have been made by the Menomini wives of the first French settlers. Others, while they cannot be placed so definitely, can be judged as relatively old because of their sacred character and the remembered lore pertaining to them, or on account of their worn appearance; many, because of their perishable nature, can be known as modern. It seemed to the writer that such material from the Menomini past might contribute something quite significant to an understanding of the changing culture, hence it was given close study.

Two impressions quickly emerge from an examination of the ethnological writings and museum data: first, that some elements of old Menomini culture were retained in practice or at least in memory to an extraordinary degree even after some two and a half centuries of white contact; and second, that at the very time the recording and collecting was going on they were starting to disappear rapidly. Crafts were becoming obsolete; memories were getting dim as the older generation passed away; and objects evidently treasured for long periods were being disposed of, for a financial consideration, to outsiders.

ECONOMICS AND MATERIAL CULTURE

The writings of ethnologists, particularly of Skinner, give very full accounts of Menomini foods and food techniques. The museum collections are less helpful. Their displays of equipment for preparing maple sugar or wild rice, of fishing tackle, horns for attracting deer, and baskets such as are made for sale, hardly give any balanced view of the Indian economy old or new. Such an essential activity as picking berries, for instance, would hardly offer a very unique display for white America to look upon. It is from the written material, therefore, that the main information concerning the modern economic life must come.

Hoffman tells that "hunting is still engaged in" but not to such an extent as formerly; that wild rice was gathered; that sturgeon fishing on the reservation had come to a sudden end with the erection of power dams lower down the Wolf river; and that the maple sugar industry was becoming obsolete because of "the ease with which cane sugar came to be obtained". A new industry had thrived awhile, the gathering of "Senega snakeroot" for sale to whites, but as the plant had become scarce it was of necessity practically abandoned. He writes:

> The food of the Menomini Indians consists of such scant supplies of vegetables as they may raise, pork obtained from the Government and by purchase at the stores, meat and fish obtained by hunting, berries and wild fruits in season, and such dishes as the women have been taught or have learned to make by contact with civilization.

Lard was noted as a favorite dish, evidently a substitute for animal fats obtained from the hunt, while maple sugar was used in cooking instead of salt.[2] In 1901 Jenks reported that the wild rice crop was becoming uncertain, as "the whites who own the land adjoining Shawano lake—their harvest ground—frequently forbid them to camp there".[3] Skinner writing in 1921 tells that the last deer drive was held in 1870, but that deer were still hunted with dogs on their runways, also they were attracted by artificial salt licks, evidently modern; fishing was poor, though winter fishing through the ice was still engaged in; and wild rice was used only occasionally. He says of hunting, presumably speaking mainly of the conservatives:

[2] Hoffman, pp. 272–92.
[3] *Wild Rice Gatherers*, p. 1077.

To the present day, no hunter, however skilled, believes for a moment that he could be successful without the aid of sacred charms and incantations.[4]

In Bloomfield's "Menomini Texts" a literal translation is offered of an account given by an old woman of Zoar concerning the economic cycle of the Mitawin families at about 1921:

> The Indians go about gathering ginseng,[5] these Indians of hereabouts, trying to obtain something to eat and to make a living. When they have all come back, that is when they will hold a big (Dream) dance to pray that they may have success in earning things to sustain life. Every summer they gather ginseng and pick berries . . . to sell, eating porcupines as they go about, and woodchucks, skunks, quail, rabbits, fish, and raccoons . . .
>
> If I were not farming (as an Indian woman does in her little garden patch) I should make mats and quilts and beadwork, and I should go to Neopit to do washing, so as to earn money. . . . Baskets too I should make. . . . I should always gather raspberries and sell them.

This quotation reveals how far even among the most conservative families the commercial patterns of the new age have been taken over.

Both Hoffman and Skinner discuss in detail Menomini clothing, earlier and recent, and numerous articles of clothing and adornment are lodged in museums. Yet perhaps the best guides to the dress are various drawings and photographs published as illustrations in ethnological works.

A clear distinction existed between everyday dress and ceremonial dress. For ordinary wear the garments usual to whites of the frontier had been taken over by Hoffman's time except that in some cases the moccasin was retained, and the women's dress consisting of full gathered skirt and waist (p. 112) tended to persist after it had passed out of fashion among the whites. Skinner found all memory gone

[4] *Material Culture*, pp. 2–3, 173, 183–88, 198, 173; also in *Wisconsin Archeologist*, April, 1921, p. 73. By 1929 wild rice was still used ceremonially but had to be purchased; none bothered to harvest the rice on the few patches growing within the reservation.

[5] "Ginseng" is a root which was sold to agents, being exported to China for medicinal purposes. It has become very scarce on the reservation. By 1929 another industry had grown up—picking fern leaves in the fall for sale to agents of the florist business.

of the pre-white types of women's dress.   It may be noted
in view of Father André's apparent embarrassment when
first among the Menomini (p. 60) that standards of modesty
had evidently changed greatly, for Skinner wrote that the
tribe "count it shameful to appear at any sort of ceremony
with the body exposed".   Yet he noted certain sartorial
habits as persisting: Menomini men still pulled out their
beard hair, and the more conservative cut their hair at the
shoulder and retained the scalplock.[6]

On ceremonial and gala occasions "Indian costumes"
were worn by both men and women of the Mitawin group.
The museum collections have naturally concentrated on this
phase of Menomini dress as being the more spectacular.   In
the men's costume the earlier patterns of moccasin were retained, together with the breechcloth and legging, at least
in modified form, but a shirt-like upper garment was
obviously a product of white influence.   The women wore
moccasins and, in some old costumes, leggings of skin or
more usually cloth, but otherwise the foundation garment
was the cloth skirt and waist, usually gaily colored.   These
ceremonial garments of both sexes had a profusion of
adornment in the form of beads, ribbons, ear-rings, combs
and bells, obviously modern, and were supplemented by
headdresses of fur, eaglefeather roaches, pouches, bands,
garters, masses of necklace and other ornaments, some of
which are certainly of doubtful antiquity among the
Menomini.   At the same time some of the older forms of
adornment had become obsolete or lost something of their
earlier meaning.   Hoffman tells how:

> Emblems of personal valor or of exploits are seldom seen. . . . The
> custom of wearing specially marked feathers, to indicate some particular
> action or achievement, has long fallen into desuetude.[7]

A new stimulus to the use of "Indian dress" and ornament has come since Skinner's time, namely the employment
of the Mitawin folk to dance and otherwise entertain the
tourists who now flock to the reservation during the summer.

[6] *Mat. Cult.*, pp. 109, 130, 131, 133.

[7] *Meno. Indians*, p. 268.

Though such clothing takes on something of the nature of theatrical "props," and is very heterogeneous (partly the remnants not collected by museums, partly obtained from other tribes, and for the rest of modern manufacture, often quite poor), its use gives a new lease of life to this phase of culture. The rise of a neo-Indian art under the stimulus of such showmanship will be discussed shortly. (See Plate VIII, p. 231.)

A study of Menomini dress during the nineteenth century could be made in much greater detail than will be attempted here. Garments of the early years can be seen, especially in the Green Bay Museum, these primarily Indian. There are Catlin's paintings in 1830–36 (Plate I). Two drawings of the Menomini Chief Oshkosh in 1845 and 1850 show the first stages in the transition to modern clothing, with a mingling of old and new garments and ornaments. In the Wisconsin Historical Society there are portraits of Oshkosh and two fellow chiefs, Aia'miqta and Shu'nu'ni'ŭᵛ (Souligny), all dressed in formal dress clothes including top hats, but with some Indian ornamentation suspended about their persons. Other materials such as the reports of the reservation sewing schools lead up to the modern period. In general dress shows interesting characteristics of both change and conservatism, with utility the main guiding force as regards everyday wear, and the older and more decorative forms tending to be preserved for religious and ceremonial occasions—much as whites make, or used to make their main wardrobe display on Sundays and gala days. A comparison of Menomini clothing in museums with that of other Indian tribes at this time indicates that the modern elaboration of dress was merely one local example of a widespread development in the region, part indeed of a general efflorescence of art and craft that will be discussed in more detail shortly.

The ethnological records show the Menomini to be occupying log or frame houses as reported in the official documents, but reveal too that the older forms of housing had not disappeared entirely from use. Hoffman noted frequently alongside the more permanent home "a summer residence made of saplings and covered with mats or bark", while for temporary camps shelters of bark were sometimes used, though by then giving place to the less troublesome canvas tent.[8] Skinner found specimens of bark houses of both the semiglobular and ridged types, also the long ceremonial medicine lodge structure. He also noted an occasional conical plains tipi among the Menomini, these "very recent imitations".[9] Mosquito netting, stoves and other modern conveniences were widely used, even by Hoffman's time.

The transport and travel adjustments, formerly so tenacious, and represented in museum collections by numerous snowshoes, burden straps, cradleboards for carrying babies, and a few canoes of birchbark and wood, were noted as having changed radically in the new era of roads, horses, buckboards, and automobiles. Hoffman (pp. 32, 282–93) says:

> The Indians removed to their present home . . . . (by) . . . ascending Wolf River in canoes; yet today a canoe is looked upon by them with as much interest and curiosity as it would be in an eastern city, so rarely is one found . . . . even among the old men but few are now recognized as having, in their day, been experts in this industrial art. . . . Their more advanced mode of life does not demand extensive travel by such means.

Skinner found the log canoe occasionally used, but he himself collected for museum purposes the last birchbark canoe. The cradle-board was by then passing, though snowshoes were still made.[10] The Menomini, as noted earlier, found less practical use for the horse than most other Central Algonquian peoples. Yet the horse motif appears frequently on their artifacts of a religious and ceremonial nature, as it does among other tribes of the region. (See Plate VI, p. 205.)

Menomini weapons represented in museum collections

[8] *Meno. Inds.*, pp. 253–56, 292.

[9] *Mat. Cult.*, pp. 88, 99. In 1929 the writer found the tipi only as part of the "show" in tourist entertainment centers.

[10] *Idem*, pp. 216, 35, 212–13.

comprise war clubs and bows and arrows. They are of two kinds: some of normal size for practical use, some representations in miniature having ritual or magical significance. A few stone and bone implements are also shown, as for example axes and needles. But the very rarity of such weapons and tools are an index to how complete has been the transition to the forms brought by the whites. The influence of early traders is seen in the museum collections, as witness hatchets, knives, spikes for insertion in clubs, and arrow heads, all of metal. Some objects such as curved knives, awls, and firesteels were no doubt made by the white blacksmiths of the early reservation period. Hoffman (pp. 275, 276, 281) found in his day that stone arrow heads were used as "amulets", while the bow and arrow was employed only by "the younger members of the tribe" for killing birds and in target shooting, the iron points being procured from traders and manufactured in the East.

The museums display numerous other products of Menomini manufacture: tanned skin work, woven reed and bark mats, cord and string of vegetal fibre and thread of animal sinew, bags of buffalo hair and fibre, baskets and receptacles of bark, wood, pottery and shell for both ordinary and sacred use, spoons and utensils, drums, whistles, and flutes. Many of these appear to be old in form and ornament. With these are objects showing direct white influence, such as silverwork (p. 116) and metal pots, or influence from other tribes in post-white times, as for example splint basketry. Naturally the museum collections in themselves give little clue to how far they still had a place in Menomini life or were obsolete—this must be looked for in the ethnological records.

Hoffman notes that bark mats were rare in his day, though reed mats were still manufactured; that "some of the oldest women" claimed to remember when pottery was made (i.e., it had disappeared long before); and that apart from occasional use the old utensils had given place to those of white pattern.[11] By Skinner's time the techniques of skin tanning were still in use; buffalo hair work had long been obsolete and the making of string bags was rapidly becoming so; wooden bowls were rare; "clam-shell spoons" were still occasionally employed, but only for ceremonial purposes; and, while bone and antler horn were used occasionally in the manufacture of implements, stone and clay, other than for pipes, had passed, together with copper working. Only one man on the reservation still worked in silver. By contrast, splint basketry, "brought to the tribe by the Oneida and Stockbridges", was assuming the form of a considerable industry, the output as with that of other tribes being sold commercially to whites. Skinner describes a "huge and elaborately decorated drum" of modern manufacture which was used in the Dream dance ceremonies, and made of a "galvanized iron washtub", with cowbells, beadwork, and perforated silver coins among its embellishments.[12] Huron Smith in 1923 noted that native fibres were no longer being used and tells how "the hum of the sewing machine may be heard in many a Menomini home" (*Ethnobotany*, p. 73).

Obviously these decades marked the passing of most elements of the old material culture. The Menomini joined with other dwellers of America in utilizing the flood of major and minor inventions of the new machine age, so far as their means allowed, just as in earlier days their ancestors accepted from the trader's pack those articles which were useful or appealing. A certain conservatism is manifest, especially among the Mitawin families; even where an article may have been long since dropped from everyday use it was often retained for religious or ceremonial purposes. In general, however, it might be expected that the Indian of a generation or two hence would stare through museum case windows at most of the objects to be found there with about as much wonder as the white man.

[11] *Meno. Indians*, pp. 256, 257, 259.
[12] *Mat. Cult.*, pp. 231, 287, 293, 376, 360, 280, 293, 347–48.

Art and Decoration

The study of museum collections undoubtedly yields its most fruitful results in the aspects of culture concerned with artistic expression. Persons gathering specimens were inevitably attracted by the ornamental, the elaborate, and the colorful in Indian workmanship, whether of old or more modern manufacture, so that these are represented by a great number of objects. The student finds porcupine quill and animal hair work alongside bead, ribbon and metal work; geometric or stylized designs which have traditional significance are grouped together with floral and other patterns obviously recent; some old weaving or binding technique will adjoin the work of a sewing machine or a white man's paint brush. The writer subjected all this material to close analysis, and the main findings can be summarized here.

The older Menomini art specimens appear to have primarily religious and ceremonial motifs. Certain highly conventionalized designs such as representations of thunderers and other sacred beings presumably go back to pre-white times. The more recent specimens tend to be secular and purely decorative.

In most artifacts the materials brought by whites, so far as they were accessible, have been adopted freely, apparently as being more mobile (as beads and cloth), giving more variation (as colors), or having more aesthetic appeal (as silver buckles, metal jinglers and ribbons). There were also lessened technical difficulties, as for instance in working on fabric instead of skin. Thus Skinner wrote of the adoption of beads: "This is owing to the ease with which they may be manipulated, and to the fact that they require no preliminary tedious processes of gathering, sorting, dyeing, and softening (as did the porcupine quill)." Similarly new techniques of manufacture were taken over freely: sewing, metal working, painting, and etching. Questions emerge here, already mentioned, as to the antiquity of the use of the heddle, of appliqué work, and of the inlaying of pipes with metal. How far the forms and designs of art work are genuinely pre-white is not always clear. Certain artifacts having evidently a long religious history, such as doll charms, an owl carved on a pole, a fish effigy, and a unique skin wrapping from a warbundle with painted thunderers upon it, may well go back to antiquity. Yet as they are to be found in company with artifacts obviously post-white, such as a carved horse's head, or an etching of a thunderer with a gun in one hand, there is at least an element of doubt. (Plates V, VI.)

It is possible to observe in some degree a sequence in the objects, indicating the trends of development. Certain artifacts of stone, bone, pottery, and perhaps skin are obviously old and show no signs of influence from white culture. These have no decoration other than simple geometric markings and, in the case of skin artifacts, quillwork of highly stylized design. Next there are objects, also old, where trade beads —apparently then a precious commodity—are introduced sparsely, hammered one by one into a wooden warclub, or combined with skin and quill. Thimbles, bells and the rest of the trader's stock then appear on artifacts, as for example hung on medicine bags of the Mitawin lodge or on sacred lacrosse sticks. Gradually the quill is superseded entirely by the bead, and white materials and techniques are used by the Indian worker to produce a remarkable array of highly decorative art forms. Finally there are to be seen a few examples of modern workmanship, usually inferior in quality and designed purely for commercial sale as Indian curios.

In making mats, bags, pouches and the like, the technical limitations of the weaving process have seemingly tended to preserve ancient designs, even where new materials such as yarn, string, and commercial dyes have replaced the older bark, rush, fibre, or hair. The patterns still remain dominantly geometric, with the occasional introduction in the older work of conventionalized mythical beings.

Where materials and techniques permit, there has developed in recent times a great efflorescence of design and ornamentation. The student has merely to compare the

PLATE V

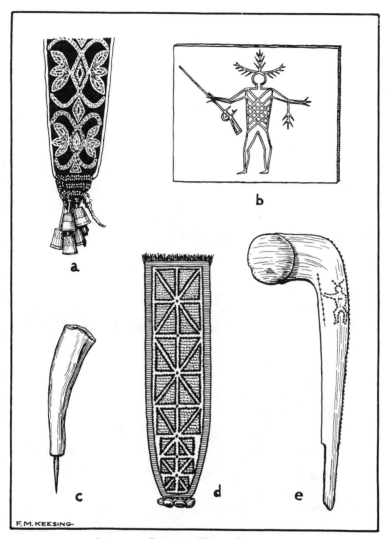

ARTIFACTS SHOWING WHITE INFLUENCE

    a. Tail of otterskin medicine bag with quillwork, also beads and thimble jinglers.

    b. Thunderer with gun, incised on a small block of wood carried in a medicine bundle.

    c. Awl, with metal point set in a bone handle.

    d. Tail of medicine bag, with bead design based on the British flag, also bells as jinglers.

    e. Warclub, with beads hammered into the handle to make a design.

PLATE VI

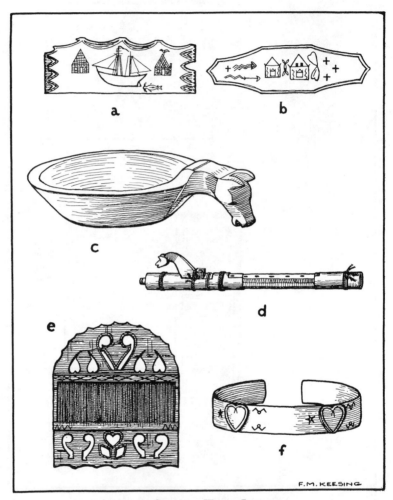

F.M.KEESING

ARTIFACTS SHOWING WHITE INFLUENCE

a, b. Moccasin cutting boards, with incised designs including ship, houses, etc.
c, d. Catlinite sacrificial bowl, and flute, with horse's head design.
  e. Heddle used for weaving beadwork.
  f. Silver bracelets, with heart design.

earlier and later objects in the Neville Museum at Green Bay, or the older collections in the Eastern museums with newer material at Oshkosh, Wisconsin, to gain a clear impression of this. Yet the tendency seems to be always for old *forms* and *meanings* of objects to persist even where *materials, techniques* and *designs* are changing; the artifacts are still essentially Indian. This applies also to other tribes in the region. Among the Menomini such efflorescence shows few marks of direct influence from white design, such as are to be found among certain other tribes. Interestingly enough the objects in which such white influences appeared most obviously were those in the oldest collection, at Green Bay. But as these artifacts mostly have a known history, it is not difficult to trace this to the impact of the early white settlers; the makers in practically every instance were their Menomini wives. It indicates that La Baye and other settlements were important diffusion centers of artistic influence, or at least of stimulation. In the newer collections there are few indications of borrowed design, though on three or four artifacts there are realistic pictures: houses, a church, a sailing boat, and flowers in a pot; there is also a popular beadwork design that seems directly based on the British flag, the Union Jack. (Pls. V, VI.)

Perhaps the most fascinating problem concerning design is the antiquity of the floral motif. During the whole examination of collections this question was kept in view. Probably the best material existing in any one place by which to test it may be found in the American Museum of Natural History, where a number of medicine bags both of ancient and of comparative recent make are displayed. The following sequence of design can be noted:

1. Certain very old bags ornamented only with colored quill have designs essentially geometric, with no hint of a floral motif.
2. Other old bags with quill have on them a scattering of bead and thimbles; some of these have designs with what appeared to be a conventionalized floral motif.
3. As bead and cloth become more extensively used, displacing the quill, floral designs appear in a variety of patterns, becoming more elaborate and free in those apparently most recent.

A set of medicine bags examined in the collection of Mr. Robinson showed the same sequence, likewise material found in other collections. The writer was forced to the conclusion that the floral motif is therefore a comparatively recent development among the Menomini, and that the earlier and pre-white art was predominantly geometric. This thesis was strengthened rather than weakened by the discovery of several exceptions, for in every instance of such floral design the artifact was directly traceable to Menomini women associated with whites.

As for dating the emergence of this efflorescence in design, it would appear from historical evidence such as Catlin's drawings and the descriptions given by the commissioner of 1849, that while some elaboration may have taken place earlier, the real burst of new creativity did not take place until about the middle of the nineteenth century, perhaps after the beginning of the reservation period. The museum collections may afford some clue to this, in that the different tribes cultivated certain distinctive styles of bead, floral and realistic work, which could be interpreted as the product of isolation in their various reservation areas after the land treaties.[13] It can be said here that the evolution in design among such tribes as the Winnebago and Chippewa has by no means ceased up to the present. However the Menomini creative urge appears to have been waning at just about the time that Skinner was among the tribe, for he found their own special types of art and decoration being replaced by Chippewa types from 1909 on; he says:

Old pieces of Menomini handicraft may be distinguished from modern degenerate, or, properly, more realistic designs introduced by the Ojibwa, for the old designs are highly conventionalized and the component units are smaller and broken . . . graceful openwork, without a filled-in background . . . At present the Menomini . . . are turning their attention more and more to realistic Ojibwa designs.[14]

[13] Possibly, too, a main factor in this art development was the sudden accession of luxury wealth from the land sales, also the greater leisure of the women as a result of the sedentary life and changing economic conditions.

[14] See *Mat. Cult.*, pp. 119, 257, 267, 269, 278.

The writer found the tribal artists of today also coming under Winnebago and Potawatomi influence. This, together with the commercialization spoken of above, seems to be the latest phase of change. The decorations that appear today on performers in tourist "pow-wows" or for sale on tourist stands in the reservation, where indeed they are products of Menomini craftsmen rather than brought in from outside, tend to be of a generalized neo-Indian character. At first poor, they seem to be improving in quality as the Indian, under the stimulus of white interest and admiration, begins to feel pride in them as well as sensing their commercial appeal. Furthermore the Menomini of today sees no incongruity in such "dress-up" affairs about putting on his head an eagle-feather warbonnet from the plains or wrapping himself in a Navaho blanket.

The evidence thus indicates a long process of change in Menomini art, during which its character was almost transformed. Much was taken over from the whites, especially new media and techniques; yet this did not mean that there was any extensive direct borrowing from white art. Rather, the modifications were made voluntarily by the Indian artists themselves and the results are essentially Indian. Especially noteworthy is the secularization of art, which appears to have gradually transformed its functions in Menomini life.

A brief survey of comparative museum materials from other tribes in the region suggested to the writer that what has been said concerning Menomini art also applies fairly generally throughout. The main impression gained is that in comparatively modern times a wave of artistic enrichment and creativity swept over the tribes from the eastern seaboard right out into the plains area, though as one passes west the great elaboration of floral designs and the profusion of bandoliers, garters, sashes and pouches give place to art work of predominantly geometric design, also realistic painting on skins, the decorative use of feathers, and greater emphasis upon the horse motif. The total picture suggested by comparative study would be somewhat as follows:

(1) in early trader days new materials were adopted freely by the tribes, but the meanings associated with art work, and usually its forms and designs, remained essentially Indian; (2) as a result of extensive tribal intercourse certain aboriginal arts were diffused more or less far and wide from the limited areas where they were practised in pre-white times, perhaps bark work from the northeast Algonquins and wood work from the Iroquoians, while such introduced arts as metal working and probably types of weaving passed westward from the eastern seaboard; (3) the early French and British settlements were centers of special stimulation; (4) with the period of the land treaties there came a great artistic efflorescence coincident with new resources and new leisure, this sweeping through the woodland tribes, transcending political differences and the local variations of Indian-white contact, and passing west even into the plains area; and (5) after a period of decay, commercialism is now giving a new stimulus to the Indian artist, with results transcending the mere economic sphere: a free and very generalized art is developing that might be called neo-Indian, and that draws its inspiration from regions sometimes far from the local area.

Social and Political Organization

Here the museum collections can help very little, for social and political institutions can hardly be ranged or exhibited on shelves. Such few artifacts as ceremonial pipes or the insignia worn by the "peace officer" of the Menomini tribe,[15] only hint at these aspects of life. The material for analysis therefore must come from the ethnological writings, though on the whole it, too, is scanty.

The pre-white social organization was seen to have become largely disintegrated by Hoffman's time, so that neither he nor Skinner received a coherent account. None of Hoffman's informants could give a clear picture of the totemic clan(gens) system, though it was remembered that

[15] Now lodged in the American Museum of Natural History; see Skinner, *Soc. Life*, note, 22.

some totems had become extinct and others had been adopted from neighboring tribes or even invented in modern times (p. 38). Skinner found only one man on the reservation who claimed to be an authority on the system, all others, "even those who were generally well informed on matters concerning the past," being able to give only "a garbled, unsatisfactory account." Skinner, being unfamiliar with the wider sweep of Menomini history, attributes the passing of the old organization to the coming of Christianity and the "changed social and economic conditions of reservation life under white control."[16] But as his only satisfactory informant was in 1911 eighty-four years old, and none of his fellow veterans knew the system, its breakdown must obviously be dated back of both the coming of the missions and the start of reservation life, as has been seen.

Hoffman found the band organization still fairly much remembered, though no longer an active force in reservation life, and recorded the names of eleven bands. He also noted that the prestige of chieftainship was in measure recognized by the tribesfolk, particularly that of the head chief Neopit, both in view of his hereditary right and in respect of his new authority as presiding judge of the Indian court. Twenty years later, however, Skinner found the memory of the bands vague, and the old leadership, including that of the heads of bands, practically ended.[17]

Regarding the Menomini family the ethnologists noted that plurality of wives had ceased, yet the old patterns of intimate group living were still in large measure retained, especially among the Mitawin people: the division of labor between the sexes, rights and duties among kinsfolk, and the traditional etiquette.[18] Most children of the conservative families passed through the ancient cycle of birth, naming and puberty ceremonial;[19] in Catholic families, however, baptism and other church customs had been adopted. Mar-

---

[16] *Soc. Life*, pp. 15, 16, 19.

[17] Hoffman, *Meno. Inds.*, pp. 44, 60; Skinner, *Mat. Cult.*, pp. 379–82.

[18] Hoffman, p. 43; Skinner, *Mat. Cult.*, p. 55, *Soc. Life*, pp. 20, 226.

[19] *Mat. Cult.*, p. 53, *Soc. Life*, p. 43.

riage was by then under strict civil or religious supervision, so that "Indian custom" marriages were passing; divorce also called for the services of the white man. Skinner says of sex matters that "the Indians are probably not more immoral than their white neighbors in Wisconsin, but certainly more openly so." As regards the individualistic spirit he writes:

> Among themselves, the rights of the individual were paramount. This regard for the individual carried itself from private to public affairs, so that the sanctity of a promise was often disregarded when the maker felt his obligation inconvenient. This is especially true nowadays when the old time strength of character of the Menomini has largely degenerated. It is this peculiarity which has caused the white man to condemn the Indian as utterly irresponsible and unreliable. It is, however, only fair to state that . . . there are many individuals whose sense of . . . honor is as high as the loftiest concepts of our own race.[20]

It would be interesting to know exactly how far this extreme of individualism found by Skinner really represents the persistence of the old assertion noted in the early records (pp. 40, 41), and seemingly disciplined to some extent in trader days, or is a product of the new commercialism, and still more of anti-social tendencies resulting from the passing of older community controls and the modern attempt to press Indian tribesfolk into the mould of individual Americans.

RELIGION AND CEREMONIAL

As regards this aspect of Menomini life a great amount of written information is available, including the works not only of Hoffman and Skinner but also of Barrett, Huron Smith and Bloomfield. Collectors have also been busy, and a great deal of the objective paraphernalia which at one time played essential roles in Menomini religion and ceremonial is now, bereft of its prestige and attendant lore, lodged in the museums of the white man.

"The present Menomini religion," Skinner wrote, "is a complex of ancient and modern beliefs, many of which seem

[20] *Soc. Life*, p. 7.

confused and contradictory.''[21]   On the whole the essentials
of belief and ritual had been preserved into modern times:
the Powers that governed life were those known to the
Algonquins of older days; ''the beliefs chronicled by Father
André'' were ''still in full blast among the tribe''; tobacco
was the necessary mediator; offerings were made; taboos
relating to women were observed; and personal privileges
and obligations received from supernatural sources through
dreams were largely adhered to.   Nevertheless there had
been much adjustment in detail, some unconscious, some
realized consciously.   An apparently new concept, the
''Great Spirit,'' often spoken of as ''our Father'' by the
Indian, had come into the picture, while the culture hero
Mä'näbus was referred to as ''the Christ of the Indian,''
and the lore had assumed here and there a Biblical flavor.
The ''blessing of the spirits'' was now rarely sought by the
old method of fasting, rather by other disciplines; faces
were not ceremonially blackened after Hoffman's time; and
the ritual tobacco would be bought from the trader's store.[22]
Again, with the passing of the old people who had led ceremonially ''pure'' lives, the ''mystic power'' granted to mankind by the spirits was considered to be vanishing, and by
Skinner's time almost gone.   A leader of the Mitawin group,
himself a practising medicine man, said to Bloomfield:

> That mystic power, he himself it was, this mortal man, who made it
> wane, that mystic power of his.   And now, for want of better, this is the
> way he knows of it; to take serious heed in all things that he may live a
> righteous life, that never at any time he do aught of wrong.   If he succeeds
> in doing only what is good, he will be helped by that Spirit who created
> all things . . . This is the knowledge of men; here on earth let us try, then,
> to live righteously, that our Father may give us mystic power.[23]

It will of course be realized that such goodness and right-
eousness, while they had come to incorporate certain values

[21] *Mat. Cult.*, p. 28.   He was of course referring to the conservative portion
of the tribe; the ethnologists were concerned little with the Catholics, hence the
great part of what is presented here must be taken to refer to the Mitawin folk.

[22] See Hoffman, pp. 38–39, 249; Skinner, *Mat. Cult.*, pp. 34–35, *Soc. Life*,
note 37, also pp. 38, 52, 84–85, 120, 205; Bloomfield, *Meno. Texts*, p. 5.

[23] *Op. Cit.*. p. 69.

and concepts of behavior from white religion, refer essentially to Indian morality, involving the practice of old Indian customs, submission to the traditional ideas, and the correct use of sacred charms and medicines.

The museum collections contain numerous Menomini "bundles," with their assortment of sacred materials, ceremonial apparatus for performing tricks, drums, bone tubes and similar artifacts of religious significance. Evidently the rituals associated with them had become sufficiently obsolete to allow their owners to sell without fear of supernatural retribution; in themselves they are mute evidence of transition. Skinner reported:

> The old people say that . . . there are no living Indians sufficiently pure in life (*i.e.*, ceremonially pure) to obtain the great bundles, and very few able to get the personal charms . . . The bundles proper have many songs, but nowadays many of these have been forgotten . . . The semi-annual ceremonies (of the bundles) are still held in the form of feasts, but in these degenerate days there is no attendant scalp-dance . . .
>
> In recent years the war bundle has ceased to be such an object of reverence as it once was. It is true that a number of these palladiums were carried in the Civil War by Menomini volunteers . . . . but it is so long since any of the Indians have seen any fighting that the younger generation has all but discarded them, and the faith of the old people is also tottering.[24]

It must not be thought however that this passing of many ceremonial observances meant a sweeping disappearance of religious conservatism. Skinner tells of a great number of "carefully guarded" charms in use in his day, while Huron Smith says of the medicines:

> Superstition is not dead among the Menomini and . . . many of their number still believe in their aboriginal remedies . . . Even some of the Christians, failing to get relief from the white doctor, will steal away to the medicine man or woman, sing the old pagan songs, dig the Indian remedies, and offer tobacco in the old pagan way.[25]

Again the burial ceremonies of the Mitawin people were essentially of the old pattern and were being retained with great tenacity. Yet Skinner notes how "force of circum-

[24] *Soc. Life*, pp. 94, 119, 125, 127. For a discussion of the songs see Densmore, *Menominee Music*.

[25] Skinner, *Op. cit.*, p. 158; Huron Smith, *Op. cit.*, p. 20. The writer found even white people resorting to the Indian practitioners.

stances,'' for example the lack of warriors who had killed an enemy in battle, was causing modifications in the ritual, and, while known to be incorrect, many of these were being sanctioned by the group. The Catholics, of course, buried their dead according to church rituals. Nevertheless the missionaries did not attempt to force changes too drastically, allowing certain concessions to Indian usage, especially where the deceased was an important person. In Hoffman's day the Christians used a wooden grave box such as had become customary earlier but of a different shape from those of the Mitawin people; offerings such as sugar or rice were left at the grave, and ''sometimes even on the grave-boxes of Christianized Indians, the totem of the clan . . . is drawn.'' Skinner notes that periods of ceremonial mourning and uncleanness were being observed by the Mitawin people, but that the length of time had been ''considerably reduced.''[26]

Hoffman found the Mitawin lodge still very powerful, but at a transition stage. On the one hand it was strongly under the influence of the related Chippewa lodge; on the other there was taking place ''a gradual degeneration and abbreviation of the dramatic rendering of the ritual''. The former system of four degrees and the wearing of distinguishing colors for each had become obsolete; meetings were shorter and took place over a weekend instead of at any period of the week, a concession to the fact that some members working according to white time rhythms. The ceremony, he says, was receiving less attention among the Menomini each year, because of

a variety of causes, chief among which are (1) the fact that many of the Indians are adopting the Christian religion . . . ; (2) because many of the younger men are attending school, and begin to observe the futility and uselessness of the various dances; and (3) the old men and women . . . are slowly dying off, which makes it difficult to find candidates to fill their places. It is evident, therefore, that the life of the society is a question of only a few years more.

26 Hoffman, p. 241; Skinner, *Soc. Life*, pp. 63–70. Even the stone monuments in Christian cemeteries occasionally have the totem animal incised upon them. For changing grave forms see Pl. IV, p. 163.

Hoffman cites an interesting instance of the meeting of the old and new religions in the same family. One initiate was a little girl, and while she was going through the ceremonies of the lodge "the mother, a mixed blood, . . . a staunch church member, . . . sat outside . . . eagerly watching her child". Skinner in his time found that Hoffman's prophecy was indeed coming true, and that the lodge was getting still more depleted in numbers and in ritual. Nevertheless the remaining members held to it firmly, and jealously guarded its secrets:

> Their revelation by a member, no matter how great his influence and authority, would inevitably result in an attempt at his murder, either through violence or by magic, by his fellows in the society.[27]

Hoffman also tells how the Wabano and Je'sako cults were reduced in both importance and numbers, though in his day several "juggleries" or special lodges of the latter still existed. Skinner tells of two practicing Wabano on the reservation, both of them being "sun dreamers", and wearing round their necks "huge brass or copper rings representing the sun's rays"; he speaks also of a Je'sako ceremony:

> In the evening, just about sundown, the performer's clients appear, bringing liquor for him to use; partly to pour libations to the gods and partly to drink in order that he may acquire the proper frenzy. In former times, before the introduction of ardent spirits, it is said to have been harder for a man to place himself *en rapport* with the mysteries.[28]

The function of liquor in such ceremonials has already received mention. Since early times the whites have assumed that it had the same connotation to the Indian as to them, that is a luxury drink, and, when indulged in to excess, a vice. Actually liquor acquired an important role in Indian religion, perhaps even from the first days when those who experimented with it "saw pleasing visions" (p. 55). This fact must be always taken into consideration when

---

[27] Hoffman, pp. 60, 76, 109, 72, 137, 38; Skinner, *Medicine Ceremony*, pp. 17ff. The writer found the lodge virtually "on its last legs" in 1929 with the dying off of its older members. The minimum number to carry on the ritual is eight; a ceremony witnessed by him had twenty-six Menomini present, of whom nearly half were too old for very active participation.

[28] Hoffman, pp. 155, 147, 48; Skinner, *Soc. Life*, pp. 191, 193, 94.

reading the later white comments on liquor and the Indian, especially concerning overindulgence.

According to Skinner "the belief in witchcraft is deeply rooted among the Menomini", and "it is the constant effort of the shamans and the members of the Mitawin to combat their activities":

> As far as our information goes, there are eight sorcerers in the tribe . . . divided into two companies of four each, using the owl and bear medicines respectively . . . It is known to the tribe at large that the associations exist, but so carefully is this intelligence concealed that a well known member of the Mitawin, or even a convert to Christianity, may (be one) in secret.[29]

Hoffman gives a fairly full description of the newer "Society of Dreamers" which came to the Menomini in 1881, and two decades later Barrett made a comparative study of the Chippewa and Menomini observances. From both descriptions it is clear that the Dream dance, while containing certain modern elements, was essentially Indian in its pattern. Its followers told how the Great Spirit:

> became angered at the Indians because the old customs and ceremonials of the Mitawin became corrupted, and that, desiring to give to the Indians a purer ritual and religious observance . . . (he) gave to them the "dance".

Hoffman notes the "remote" resemblance of the new ceremonial to the well known Ghost Dance of the plains tribes; he also writes

> Some Menomini Indians more communicative than others have intimated that a time would surely come when the whole country would be restored to the Indians as it once was, when the heads of all the whites would be severed from their bodies as a scythe cuts wheat. This belief has always had a greater or less number of believers who were in a state of expectancy.[30]

The Menomini and other tribes of the region were thus manifesting prophetic "compensations" in religion compar-

[29] *Op. cit.,* pp. 69, 182. The belief in ''witches'' (male and female) is profound even among the Christians, and numbers of them use ''holy water'' or carry sacred objects as a protection. This is one of the most persistent aspects of the old culture, and has been integrated thoroughly with the new theology.

[30] *Op. cit.,* pp. 157–58, 63.

able with those known the world over in situations of group oppression and frustration.

Skinner reports how in his time the society was still in high favor, being second only to the Mitawin, and that "although there are no rules to that effect, many Indians do not care to belong to both". Since Hoffman's time "a considerable change in the organization had taken place . . . much of the former formality had been lost, and it had fallen into the loose pattern of all Menomini societies, save the medicine lodge".[31] Bloomfield, by quoting a member, enables us to see something of the later attitudes of those taking part in the ceremonies; evidently they had mellowed since Hoffman's time:

> The reason the dream-drum exists is that this brown skinned Indian was given it by the Great Spirit. The reason they all frequent this dream-dance ceremony is that they may deal kindly with each other, that they may never fight each other, that they may never kill each other, that they may there treat each other as brothers and sisters, that there at the ceremony of the dream-dance they may feel pity and sympathy for each other, exchanging things by way of reciprocal gifts.[32]

Two other religious manifestations of modern days may be referred to. According to Skinner:

> Some years ago a number of those Menomini who had dreamed of the thunderers, "pooled" their rites, procured a drum, and began to worship together. Lightning struck the drum before they had long kept up the ceremony and broke up the association. This group or cult was shortlived, but it shows how such things start.

The drum here spoken of now reposes in one of the museums, a mute testimony to the disapproval of the Powers at such unorthodox innovation. The second cult was not of Menomini origin, being the Peyote religion which developed in special form among the Winnebago.[33] Skinner notes its appearance on the Menomini reservation in 1914 in spite of opposition from officials; he wrote later that should its influence increase this might mean the "deathblow to all the ancient customs of the tribe, already decadent" since:

[31] *Soc. Life*, pp. 173, 74.

[32] *Op. cit.*, p. 107.

[33] See Radin, *The Winnebago Tribe*. Compare, too, Petrullo, V., *The Diabolic Root*, Philadelphia, 1934.

membership in the order precludes any in all other societies, and demands the abandonment of all ancient practices, with the destruction of their paraphernalia.

He deemed this improbable, however, and it can be said that he was correct, as the new cult soon waned among the conservatives on the reservation except at the Neconish settlement at the northwest corner, mainly because of opposition from the Mitawin lodge.[34]

Both Hoffman and Skinner reported that the ceremonial dances and games were rapidly becoming obsolete to the extent that they were not already so. Yet the latter tells how in 1910 "a severe drought caused the Menomini to become very much worried lest they had done something to anger the great powers", so that a "rain dance" was performed. At the very time, however, that such peculiarly Menomini ceremonies were passing, various new "pleasure dances" were being introduced through other tribes, notably the Shawano and the Woman's dances from the Winnebago; also new games were adopted either from other tribes or as direct imitations of white games.[35]

The religious and ceremonial life of the Menomini, therefore, tenacious as it had proved over the centuries, was now for the most part passing or becoming modified. The old beliefs were giving way before Christianity, and even being altered subtly among the conservative Mitawin group, though magical and fear elements remained especially vital; the ritual life was becoming very attenuated; objects with religious meaning were passing into the hands of collectors.

LANGUAGE AND FOLKLORE

The ethnologists found the Menomini tongue still spoken, but the former *lingua franca*, Chippewa, had largely passed from use. The mnemonic system associated with the Chip-

[34] *Soc. Life*, p. 47; *Mat. Cult.*, pp. 42–43.

[35] Hoffman, pp. 241–44; Skinner, *Mat. Cult.*, pp. 74, 75, 53, *Soc. Life*, p. 209. Naturally the exhibitions for tourists consist of the secular dances, though sometimes the ritual game of lacrosse is played for show. Until recently Catholic Indians have been strictly forbidden to dance Indian fashion or to play the drum—a source of considerable conflict to many converts.

pewa was gone, while the Indian "sign language" was rarely used other than as a graphic aid in story-telling.[36]

The Menomini speech never became a written language as did the Chippewa. Hoffman says (pp. 60, 294):

> Two printed works, a vocabulary of about four hundred words . . . and the Lord's prayer . . . comprise all the published material in the Menomini language. The two works mentioned are a Catholic prayer-book and a Catechism . . . the editions of which are exhausted. A few hymns were also printed . . . on a small hand-press.

The appearance of Bloomfield's *Menomini Texts* in 1929 marks the first real attempt to standardize the spelling of Menomini sounds and to make available written material in the language.

A problem of great interest is to know how far the Menomini tongue has been modified through white contact and in order to meet the new conceptual needs of the changing times. No records relative to this are extant, but the writer was able to get from Dr. Bloomfield personally a list of "loan words" found by him in the Menomini speech. He says that they "were probably borrowed by other Indians (especially Iroquoian tribes) and through them came to the Menomini; it seems impossible to say whether any are direct loans". His tabulation includes nineteen French words made up as follows: the greeting "bon jour", in Menomini *posoh;* five French names for playing-cards; seven personal names, as Jean Baptiste (*Sapatis*), Marie (*Manih*); the French names for Englishman, Spaniard and German, also for pig, bull, cucumber, and coffee. A number of English words, too, were subsequently adopted, as for instance "telephone" and "automobile". Besides such direct borrowings the Menomini used the resources of their own language to label many of the new cultural elements and experiences. This is illustrated by the following English words, which have after them literal translations of the corresponding Menomini terms as used today:

| salt | material for producing strong taste. |
| plough | implement for doing the work of breaking up. |

[36] Skinner and Satterlee, *Folklore*, p. 235.

scissors	tool for hair cutting.
wheel	thing that moves by turning.
money	bright metal, silver.
flour	thing from which pieces are cut.
stockings	leggings that can be turned inside out.
glass bottle	transparent earthenware vessel.
boat	wooden canoe.

These fall into three general categories: the first three names are translated into Menomini in terms of their use, the second three in descriptive terms, and the last three by their resemblance to some known object in Menomini culture. This seems fairly typical of the process by which languages are adjusted internally to meet new needs.

Together with the language a store of lore was transmitted from generation to generation into modern times. In Menomini story and legend there are certain marks of influence both from other tribes, especially the Chippewa, and from white lore; also there have been added in post-white times accounts of outstanding incidents and persons, such as the warfare against the Sauk and Fox and the fame of a certain "buffalo medicine" possessed by Chief Oshkosh. Especially frequent is the mention of guns and objects of metal, while as noted earlier the tales relating to hunting appear to magnify this activity on account of the importance of the fur trade. Least touched by such changes was undoubtedly the ancient sacred mythology. The folklore as recorded by ethnologists is a source well worth analyzing for data on cultural change. On the other hand, there is little indication as to how far the Menomini maintained interest in such ancestral tales into modern times, or were taking over stories from the white lore, or indeed had a fund of tales that, because of their obviously recent origin and modern setting, were not of interest to such recorders.

Summary

The records of ethnological workers and the evidence of museum collections here viewed obviously have limited usefulness, for the primary aim of scientific writers and collectors was to show the old rather than the contemporary culture, hence the latter has been revealed only incidentally. Nevertheless when placed alongside the data from official documents concerning progress in the new ways a fairly rounded story of the Menomini experience is produced.

A special interest of the writer was to test how far museum materials could be used in a study of the processes of culture change, and some comments may therefore be made on the results. First there are several obvious limitations, arising from the special nature of such materials: they include only the tangible, hence give little help in understanding such aspects of culture as social organization or language; then there is a bias not only to the antique but also to the spectacular and the exceptional; again, museum exhibits are necessarily static and rigid, with objects isolated rather than in their working cultural context. Even where innovations are apparent, there is little indication of the circumstances stimulating such changes, or of the social and personal factors involved. However, the ethnological records fill in these gaps to a considerable extent. With these limitations in mind the positive contributions of the museum approach can be summarized.

An interesting fact to be observed from the Menomini artifacts is that seemingly the form, the material, the technique of manufacture, and the use and meaning of any object are capable of being modified more or less independently, and show different degrees of tenacity or responsiveness to innovation. A lacrosse stick keeps its form, material, and some techniques of manufacture, but its significance is modified. Beads and bells appear on a medicine bag without altering its sacred value and use. On the whole materials and techniques show a greater mobility or modifiability in this sense than have forms, meanings and uses. This was especially illustrated by the displays of ornamentation and art: here even forms and especially designs showed considerable flexibility. A complex set of factors connected with ideas of utility, with tastes and values, and with beliefs and interpretations, were seen to be back of such change and resistance to change.

Incorporating now the rest of the findings from the museum collections with an analysis of the ethnological writings it can be said that in the main the patterns of the earlier Indian life had proved surprisingly tenacious over the three centuries of contact with whites, especially so among the Mitawin group. Those aspects least affected seem to have been the foods and food-getting techniques, certain other elements of material culture mainly associated with religion, the primary group relationships, the meanings and interpretations of life behind changing religious forms, and the traditional language. These appear closely connected either with the immediate environment or with deep-seated mental and emotional patterns. Certain other elements, notably the old forms of housing and transportation, and the political organization of the tribe, showed great tenacity, but passed with the vast changes of reservation life. On the other hand, rapid changes took place from the first in such aspects of culture as dress, weapons, tools, art, the larger social institutions, and relationships with other groups.

In general, however, the dominant impression to be gained from this chapter is of a rapid disintegration of the old culture by the opening of the twentieth century, even of many elements that had proved most tenacious up to that time. As for the opinions of scientific workers concerning the tribal future, the following may be quoted. Skinner writes:

Conservative as were the Menomini, two events in recent years have acted to make a sudden end of the old-time culture. The influenza epidemic of 1919–20 swept away many . . . (of) those elders in whose memories reposed the rituals . . . The war with Germany also had a powerful effect . . . The Government accepted their young men as soldiers on equal terms with their white neighbors . . . The Menomini have definitely turned from the old road, and while many will persist in continuing their ancient customs for some years to come . . . the old way is doomed.

Bloomfield comments thus:

The Menomini are rapidly being made over into the cultural type of the uneducated white American; of that European-American culture which, with its art and science, is worthy to stand beside their own and perhaps above it, they know nothing. They are suffering, therefore, what can be regarded only as a cultural loss.

X. RECENT TIMES

The early twentieth century is marked above all by a steady penetration of the Menomini community by whites and white influences, with consequent ecological, economic, and social changes on the reservation. As communications improved and the forest gave place to farms up to and around the reservation boundary, the Menomini became increasingly acquainted, too, with the world outside, especially with the new urban life now growing up at a number of points accessible to the area.

In 1906 a railroad track was constructed through Menomini territory with a depot at Neopit, the new milling settlement, and extending telephone and postal services came to affect the more progressive families and individuals. About 1901 the first automobile owned by an Indian appeared on the reservation, but as at the time the tribal roads were described as "mere trails winding through the most accessible parts" it could have had little scope. From this time on, however, a great deal of labor went annually into road construction work. In 1923 the reservation was linked into the state roading system by the building of two main highways across it.

In this period, too, there took place an important shifting of the Menomini population. The founding of Neopit drew families from all the older settled portions of the reservation into the northwest townships hitherto occupied only by the Mitawin group at Zoar and further north at what is now called Neconish; from a town of tents during the first year in which the mill was established, Neopit assumed permanent form as the main residential center on the reservation. This modern redistribution is summarized in Diagram 5. Again, by 1910, statistics show that, besides children away at schools, a number of tribal members were living outside the reservation not only in districts of Wisconsin but also fairly widely distributed over the United States. The federal census of that year shows 34 Menomini as in Michigan, 13

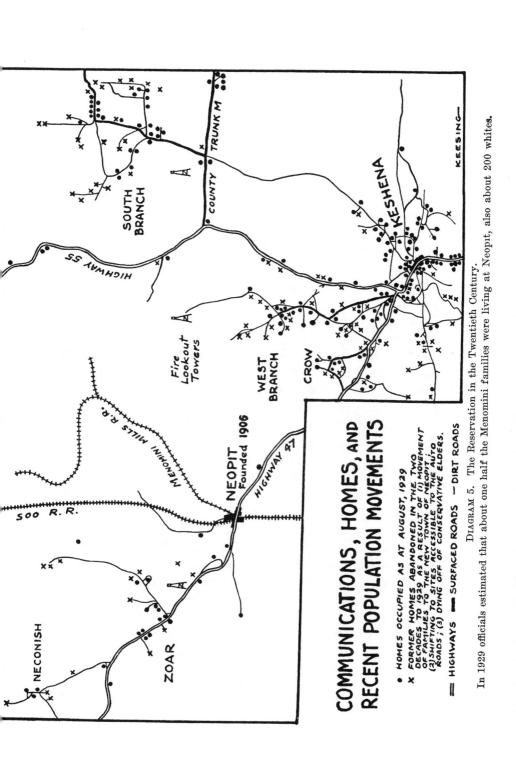

COMMUNICATIONS, HOMES, AND RECENT POPULATION MOVEMENTS

NECONISH

ZOAR

SOO R. R.

MENOMINI MILLS R.R.

NEOPIT
Founded 1906

HIGHWAY 47

NEOPIT

HIGHWAY 55

SOUTH BRANCH

COUNTY TRUNK M

Fire Lookout Towers

WEST BRANCH

CROW

KESHENA

KEESING

• HOMES OCCUPIED AS AT AUGUST, 1929

✕ FORMER HOMES ABANDONED IN THE TWO DECADES TO 1929 AS A RESULT OF (1) MOVEMENT OF FAMILIES TO THE NEW TOWN OF NEOPIT (2) SHIFTING TO SITES ACCESSIBLE TO THE AUTO ROADS; (3) DYING OFF OF CONSERVATIVE ELDERS.

══ HIGHWAYS ▬▬ SURFACED ROADS — DIRT ROADS

DIAGRAM 5. The Reservation in the Twentieth Century.

In 1929 officials estimated that about one half the Menomini families were living at Neopit, also about 200 whites.

in Minnesota, 9 in Pennsylvania, 7 in Oklahoma, 4 in Kansas, 3 in South Dakota, and one each in Nebraska and Oregon.[1]

Where during the early reservation period the Menomini numbers decreased, the main cause being reported as "the high mortality caused by tuberculosis", the yearly official estimates now indicate a very sharp increase. In the years 1902–05 the total Menomini numbers are given officially as under 1,300, but by 1917 the figure is 1,745 and twelve years later it is 1,939.[2]

This may be accounted for in two ways: first, a large natural increase occurred, corresponding with a declining deathrate and maintenance of a high birthrate; second, the tribal numbers were augmented by the admission of new members to the tribal roll. As early as 1902 a mixed blood Menomini family claimed rights with the tribe, and was admitted by vote of the tribal council. Because of the success of lumbering and the consequent per capita payments and other benefits accruing to those officially counted as tribal members, others were soon pressing for recognition. These were apparently all families or individuals who, though non-members, had been associated for long with the Menomini community or were married to members. Between 1907 and 1911 many were thus given rights, practically all mixed bloods claiming not to be descendants of those who had accepted the "half-breed" payment of 1849, and the rest women of other tribes and even white women married to Menomini men.

After 1911, however, the tribal council and the authorities at Washington became wary of this procedure; in fact by this time applications were coming in from people "all over the United States" who claimed Menomini blood and desired to participate in the profits of the lumbering business. Some actually attempted to force their way on to the roll by taking legal proceedings, and in the minutes of a

[1] *Indian Population in the United States and Alaska*, 1915. During the twenties the number away at any one time varied from 120 to 250; perhaps 50 live permanently off the reservation, these mostly women married to members of other tribes or else to whites.

[2] The census of 1930 showed a total of 1,969, of whom nearly 52 per cent were under twenty years of age; males totalled 1,054 and females 915.

Menomini council in 1921 there is even found a resolution to employ an attorney at Washington to "defend" the tribe against these insistent mixed bloods. The subject continued to loom in all councils until in 1926 a Menomini committee was set up to investigate the genealogies of claimants to discover who really were descended from the 1849 mixed bloods; as a result some 460 applications then before the council were rejected. According to the official record book at Keshena agency, a total of 202 individuals were admitted permanently to the roll between 1902 and 1929.

This recrudescence of the difficult "half-breed" question is a reminder that numbers of Menomini were marrying outsiders during the period of reservation occupancy as in earlier times, whites, and in the case of the Mitawin folk members of the conservative groups of Chippewa, Potawatomi, and other tribes. By 1885 officials calculated that 675 out of 1,308 Menomini were of mixed blood, or 52 per cent. In 1893 it was said that "even now a full-blooded Indian is almost unknown here", while another official wrote ten years later:

> The population . . . is composed mostly of Menominee Indians, mixed with a large percent of white blood, and a sprinkling of Chippewa, Winnebago, and Potawatomi.

The federal census of 1910 reported 716 mixed bloods out of 1,422 Menomini, or 50.4 per cent. From 1906 there are much fuller records concerning miscegenation, and in most years official estimates are given as to whether the individuals are "more than half" or "less than half" Menomini. The following years may be cited:

	1916	1919	1922	1925	1927	1928	1929
Total population	1,736	1,733	1,819	1,890	1,941	1,940	1,939
Full bloods	434	395	380	300	300	477	463
More than ½ Meno.	868	897	900	900	900		
Less than ½ Meno.	434	441	539	690	741	1,463[3]	1,476[3]
% of full bloods	25	22.8	20.9	15.9	15.4	24.6	23.9

[3] In 1928–29 a thorough official inquiry was made concerning intermixture, resulting in a more conservative estimate of the amount of white blood in the tribe, while all mixed bloods were taken together as a unit.

In the federal census of 1930, 496 or 25.2 per cent classed themselves as of full blood. Clearly there is a marked tendency for the full bloods to diminish, and for the total white strain within the tribe to increase.

Such figures, of course, represent the beliefs of living Menomini as to their ancestry. The student of tribal history, however, may well be justified in doubting whether by this time there were any Menomini wholly of Indian descent. The official calculations in no instances went back beyond four generations, and rarely that far, yet the tribe had been mingling with whites for at least eleven generations.[4] When Hrdlička of the Bureau of Ethnology paid a visit to the Menomini in 1908 he wrote that, of the five hundred members of the tribe he met, "not more than two aged individuals had the appearance of pure-blood Indians".

This does not necessarily mean that the Menomini were being absorbed rapidly into the whites. Even should there have been no pure bloods, there were doubtless many with merely the smallest amount of white blood, and generally speaking the Indian strain still strongly predominated. Again, after the passing of the lumbermen and the coming of a more settled white culture into the Menomini region, the mixing of whites with the tribe greatly lessened; while those of fullest Menomini blood married out into the more mixed families, those of strong white blood would often marry back into the predominantly Indian strain. The modern trend is therefore towards stabilization of a mixed type markedly Indian. Since economic benefits if not other linkages hold the people together, and difficulties of adjustment in the larger American milieu tend to keep them on the reservation, it is not to be expected that biological assimilation of the Menomini will take place short of a very long time.

As an introduction to a more detailed survey of Menomini conditions in the recent years some extracts from the report prepared by Hrdlička in 1908 can be given:

[4] In this connection the significant statement is made by Hoffman (p. 48) that: "Neopit and his brothers are perhaps the only full-blood Menomini Indians alive today. Oshkosh himself claimed this distinction for himself nearly fifty years ago." As Neopit married into the mixed blood Carron family, it would appear that none today are of entirely pure blood.

The people are, in general, well advanced in civilization; this is especially true of those in the neighborhood of the agency (Keshena). The majority live in fairly good log or frame houses, built according to the plans of the whites. These dwellings are, as a rule, isolated, and surrounded by good-sized gardens, or by vacant grounds on which grow forest trees. The floors of the houses are, with few exceptions, made of board, lumber being abundant. The log dwellings are warmer than the frame houses . . . As to cleanliness, a majority of the dwellings were found in a fairly good condition . . .

The clothing of the people is quite clean, being similar to that of the whites. There was observed, however, a tendency to wear too much clothing . . .

For food, the Menomini prefer meat, especially salt pork, which is very extensively eaten . . . their meals . . . (are) less regular than among the whites and often poor in every respect . . . Gravies and pastries are much favored; coffee and tea are drunk in large quantities, often at the expense of more nourishing substances; and everyone seems fond of sweets. Beans and other garden produce are liked, but the supply is small. Some of these Indians catch a fair quantity of fish, while others raise a few chickens. Game is scarce. During spring and summer large quantities of berries . . . are gathered . . .

The chief occupations of the Menominees are logging and lumbering, which furnish work to nearly all the able-bodied male Indians for seven or eight months each year. During this "season" there is very little idleness among the men who can work . . . Farming is neglected on account of the work in the woods and sawmills, yet all cultivate a little ground. The women occupy themselves only with household duties and some gardening . . .

Their main failing is drunkenness which, notwithstanding punishments and precautions, continues to prevail. Liquor is obtained surreptitiously from whites . . . The passion for strong drink affects both men and women.
—in Bulletin 42, *Bureau of American Ethnology*, 1909.

The census of 1910 sets out the occupations of Menomini as follows: farm laborers 181, farmers 13, lumbermen 34, laborers in building 18 and planing mills 12, carpenters 7, sailors 6, operators in sawmills 6, teamsters 5, and teachers (female) 5. Yet this is hardly a satisfactory list. The writer came to know Menomini who had done practically all of these things (except the teaching) and many more besides. Perhaps six months before or after the census the occupations would have been very different: the farmer not on his farm but in the lumber mill, the sailor far inland, and the carpenter experimenting with a trading store.

In the official records a number of rather fragmentary statistics show the persistence right into modern times of old forms of exploiting the environment. From forty to fifty people a year are reported engaged in maple sugar manufacture, making up to some 20,000 lbs. of sugar each season, though the amount declined considerably in the later years; some two hundred individuals are enumerated as gathering berries; the products of hunting and fishing were valued at several thousand dollars annually; and from forty to seventy people manufactured about seven thousand dollars worth of bead and basket work. The products of these activities, however, were mainly sold commercially.

It has been seen how from earliest reservation days the officials used every possible means to encourage the Menomini in farming, but, in spite of several spectacular bursts of effort, a variety of factors conspired to keep the great majority to a mere garden patch agriculture. In 1913 a fresh upsurge of farming enthusiasm commenced, the result of a newly instituted system of "reimbursible loans" to individuals from the tribal funds. The status of Menomini farming just before this is revealed in an inquiry conducted by a "United States Joint Commission" on Indian affairs. One of the subjects under investigation was the dismissal of a "scientific farmer" employed for the Menomini tribe, and in this man's elaborate evidence the following statement occurs:

> (An official) informed me that they did not need a scientific farmer there; that the Indians were not far enough advanced to need scientific instruction in farming and the land was not allotted and sometimes the neighbors trespassed upon one another . . . The most of their work in gardens and fields is hand cultivation, as they have few teams or tools to work with.—*Joint Com. Hearings,* Serial 2, 8A, 923–24.

In 1912 the Menomini council had passed a significant resolution urging that provision be made for temporary loans from their tribal funds to "enable deserving Indians to rise". This was put into effect by the Indian Department the following year, matters being so arranged that the buying of stock and equipment as well as the decision as to who were the deserving individuals was placed in the hands of the reservation superintendent.[5]   As a result a number of Menomini, particularly mixed bloods, started into farming on a scale much more ambitious than ever before.   Yet the records show considerable discontent on account of such loans being denied to certain individuals, and of the price and quality of official purchases; there was also increasing dissatisfaction about the lack of autonomy in handling tribal funds and a suspicion of the growing power of officialdom.

In 1914, a "Menomini Indian Fair" was organized, and has been held every year since as a successful annual feature. Special fair grounds were built, and every effort made to stimulate farming through competition in the annual exhibits.   Not long afterwards a series of "farmers' institutes" were organized on the reservation with annual sessions in which the agricultural extension department of the University of Wisconsin cooperated.   New government farms were started in various districts, two farmers were employed to help and instruct Menomini farmers, while farm clubs were started in the agricultural communities at South Branch, West Branch, Crow and Zoar.   A new phase of farming developed, dairying, the centers for this being near the reservation line on the main roads, such areas alone being accessible to factories off the reservation.   By 1921 there were reported to be several Menomini farms more than one hundred acres in extent; however, the owners of these were all mixed bloods predominantly white, so that they are hardly representative of the Menomini farming effort of the time.[6]

After 1921 this new burst of farming in turn declined steadily except among the few whose farms were particularly well situated for dairying.   The annual fair became largely a carnival.   A superintendent writes that "the Indian does not conform easily to routine or to any task

[5] From this time forward the head official on the reservation will be called the "superintendent", though the Indians still use mainly the older name "agent".

[6] From annual reports and statistical summaries, as filed at Keshena agency office.

which makes his presence necessary at home each day".[7]
He comments also upon a practice very difficult to discourage, namely the clearing and cultivation by an Indian family of a small patch of land for a short period, followed by a shift to another patch and an exaction of toll from the next occupant of the vacated "farm". The officials at one stage made every effort to get the Menomini to lease large areas of their open lands for grazing purposes to the surrounding white farmers, but this was steadily opposed by the tribe, who jealously resented any white encroachment. It is interesting to note in the reports that the farming communities in 1917 held secret meetings, following which they refused to participate in the annual "institute" gatherings unless the government granted them certain desired concessions, indicating that the new farm experiments were not working altogether smoothly.

Passing now to the all important experiments in lumbering, the threads of the survey can be picked up by reference to the initiation between 1906 and 1908 of the new system by which the Menomini were to mill their own lumber. A great storm had razed an area of valuable pine forest along the northwest line of the reservation, and the milling of this "blown down" district provided the immediate occasion for the change in policy. By act of Congress in 1908, authority was given for the erection of three mills on the Menomini lands. But it was finally decided to invest instead in one large up to date mill at the Norway dam on the West Wolf, just where the new railroad spanned the river; thus Neopit came into being. By January, 1909, the mill commenced operation; two years later the Commissioner of Indian Affairs said of the project:

(It) has a status all of its own in that the Government in 1908 built a large lumber mill, using funds of the tribe; thus the Menominee Indians have become owners of a large modern mill . . . The Neopit project was established with a twofold object—as a school of industry for the Indians and as a business investment . . .

Neopit is a small lumbering town. An electric power plant furnishes the town and mill with light . . . For the Indian buildings are being constructed with proper regard to light, air, and health.—*R.I.A.*, 1911.

[7] Report, July 27, 1917, Keshena office files.

PLATE VII

THE LUMBERING ENTERPRISE

THE MENOMINI MILL, NEOPIT

MENOMINI LUMBER WORKERS

On the right is Reuben Oshkosh, who, as descendant in the eldest line of the Oshkosh family, would be ''chief'' if the title had not been officially abolished.

PLATE VIII

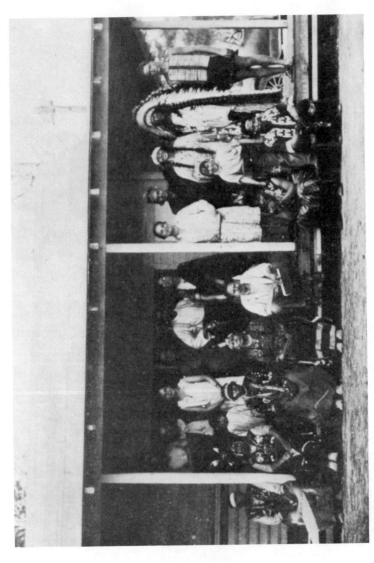

THE MENOMINI TURN MOVIE ACTORS

At a tourist stand owned by the late "Chief" Reginal Oshkosh, a visiting camera-man poses his company. Oshkosh is standing fifth from the left. Note the heterogeneous costumes. Four older women at left (sitting) are in the neo-Indian skirt and waist. The "brave" sitting to the right has beaded epaulettes, mark of the military influence. The feather warbonnet (second from right) was brought in by the director to make the local Indians look more realistic!

During these first years some ten miles of logging railroad were constructed, with modern equipment; an average of 205 Menomini were employed each quarter, "being in excess of 38% of male members of the tribe over 18," in addition to about 56 members of other tribes. In 1912 the reservation superintendent wrote in the Carlisle Indian School Journal, *The Red Man,* a vivid description of the whole Menomini milling operations; of the river work he said:

> In driving the logs on the streams the Indian comes into his own, delighting in danger, skipping from log to log, tossing and tumbling in the turbulent waters as they slip down the stream to the mill.—"The Menominee Indians at Work," in Vol. v, no. 1.

In 1910 an "Indian Forest Service" was created at Washington, and this took over the supervision of lumber operations among tribes having such resources. Under this new management the old Menomini methods of contracting by individuals or groups were practically abolished and regular lumber camps to supply the mill were started under the supervision of the government foresters.

In the first two decades the reservation timber was cut out at an average rate of about twenty million feet a year. Improvements were added in the way of equipment, also in developing the town of Neopit, creating a nursery for reforestation purposes, and organizing fire protection by means of specially trained guards and the use of watchtowers. The railroad replaced the river for the transport of logs. In 1925 the Menomini mill was burnt, but in its place was built a larger and more modern concrete structure. Neopit itself came to have a growing white population mainly of mill officials and employees, and the forest camps became a resort of white lumberjacks. The northwest townships rapidly developed into what might be termed the essential economic center of the tribe, leaving Keshena as the administrative and educational center.

What of the Menomini reaction to all these elaborate developments under enthusiastic white control? Already, perhaps, it has been sensed that supervised lumber camps, an efficient railroad system to transport the lumber, and a mill that worked the year round according to the daily rhythms of the government whistle, involved very different patterns of work from those of the "good old days" of the winter contract system and of the spring river driving. Almost immediately there was trouble. By 1914 agitation had risen to such a pitch that a special commissioner was sent from Washington to investigate. He found the tribe itself divided on the question of how far to trust certain mixed bloods who were leading complaints against the administration, also an "appalling" amount of outside influence from parties interested in getting the mill abolished. The main grievances of the Menomini were: too many high salaried whites occupying all positions of responsibility, a discrimination against Menomini workers in the matter of such positions, on account of which many refused to have anything to do with mill jobs, alleged inefficient methods and waste of "over a million dollars", and failure to produce any profits such as were forthcoming from the earlier lumbering operations. Some extracts from the evidence placed before the commissioner can be given:

Commissioner's question: "271 (Indians) have been employed . . . every day of the year on the average. Don't you think this was a good portion of the 480 ablebodied men in the tribe?"

Answer: "They could have got more. We have had men here who were as good carriage riders as white men, but they could not see any prospect of advancement, and so they quit . . . and went at other work . . . Before this plant was here the Indians had more work—logging."

C.: "But they only logged three or four months a year."

A.: "Yes; but after they would get through they used to work on the farms, but now you have got to work every day and you have nothing to farm with, and if you stop work for a week you are going to starve."

C.: "I am going to recommend that the Government will advance money enough to those who want to farm to build a house and barn and get a team. Won't that help you?"

A.: "(From the leader of the Zoar people) My opinion is that when a man comes here I like to have him go and be my witness to the poor conditions we are placed in up there (Zoar) . . . We have no lumber; some of my people up there have bark for their roofs. We have no money to buy this lumber up there . . . (We) go around and hunt and trap . . . Some of us . . . are old and sick . . . If this plant were a paying proposition would I be poor; would I be hungry? The white people you see here, they are the people who have good things to eat."

(*Remarks by witnesses*): "These are always the same ones who are dissatisfied . . . there seems to be a half-breed at the head of this who is making complaints."

"I think the reason the tribe are dissatisfied is that the annuity is decreasing every year."

"If they have so much money (from profits) . . . why are they starving the Indians?"—from *Ayer Report*, 1914.

There is no need for the purpose of this study to go into the details of the complaints brought before the commissioner; apparently his recommendations were not effective enough or were not put into effect sufficiently to quell the agitation,[8] which continued unabated over the years. The records show that numerous councils were held including many without official sanction, deputations went to Washington, and a never ceasing protest was voiced against the administration, and especially against the lack of opportunity for the Menomini leaders to have any say in the lumbering affairs. A council of November, 1921, may be taken as a fair sample; for the sake of brevity the proceedings as represented in the minutes are given in note form:

A full blood: The Indians have long been dissatisfied; the mill is steadily losing money.

A Mitawin leader: It was said in 1908 that if the Menomini were dissatisfied, the act would be amended.

A mixed blood: The Menomini should be given executive positions so far as they can handle them; "The Menominee Tribe never stood back in times of war," now they should be allowed to come forward and manage.

A full blood: The system is wasteful; unsound and hollow logs are used.

A mixed blood: The Menomini should be given a voice in the operations.

A mixed blood: "The Menominees had to borrow the money to start in logging years ago under the old law; they used unshod Indian ponies; they did not have windows in their camps; they lacked the proper equipment, and were handicapped in several other ways; in spite of the odds against them, they made money . . . not only for themselves, but accumu-

[8] His main recommendations were: an accurate survey of the timber, allotment of land and financial help in farming, library facilities, a tribal store, a bank, and young men to be sent for training in agriculture at Madison.

lated a tribal fund . . . ; under the present law, our logging camps are
fully equipped . . . (with) electric lights, running water, modern machinery and everything in the way of convenience and comfort, and still we are
losing instead of making money."

A committee appointed to suggest amendments to the act of 1908
advanced a proposition for a Menomini "Board of Control" to supervise
the expenditure of the foresters.   Plans were made for a delegation to
present this at Washington.

This outline covers fairly well the gamut of Menomini ideas
and complaints.[9]   Further discussion of the lumbering situation can be held over to the study of the present; here need
be noted only the main official replies as set out frequently
in the documents:

> The mill is run primarily as a school for industry and not to make
> money; the policy of employing Indians means lessened efficiency, but
> Indian welfare is put before the balance sheet; the Menomini worker will
> not stick consistently at his job to learn responsibility; the agitators are
> those least desirous of working.[10]

Such then is something of the position of extreme strain
that quickly arose as the patterns of lumbering changed, dis-
rupting the work effort of the tribe.   It would appear that
the various commissions appointed from time to time to try
and better the situation hardly appreciated the significance
of the modifications involved in this modern phase of the
tribal economy.   Apart from the visible grievances so
charged with accumulated emotion it may be surmised that
the task of making an efficient lumber factory worker out
of a Menomini woodsman may have been comparable in difficulty with that of turning a hunter into an efficient farmer.

In the third decade of the new century still other resources were discovered on the reservation which came to
be very much in demand by whites: the rivers and waterfalls.   Yet two different groups of whites wanted these for

[9] When the mill was burnt in 1925 there was strenuous opposition to the
government plan for a large mill.   Nevertheless this was built, and has provided
added grievance.

[10] Detailed analyses of the Menomini milling operations, together with
official rebuttals of alleged inefficiency etc. are found in two reports issued by
the Office of Indian Affairs: *Survey of Management, Menominee Indian Mills,
Wisconsin,* 1932, and Muck, L., *Report upon the Statement of Hughes, Schurman
& Dwight to the Advisory Board of the Menominee Indians,* 1933.

very different purposes. With the development in 1923 of modern highways and a consequent inevitable relaxing of regulations against the admission of whites, the reservation soon became a resort known for its beauty spots and its fishing. A movement was therefore set afoot within the state of Wisconsin to have the area kept as a scenic reserve. At the same time, however, certain power interests took steps to gain the right of placing dams on the reservation at five waterfalls along the Wolf river. In 1927 permission was given by the Menomini council for a survey of the proposed dam sites; a resolution was passed to the effect that:

We favor a development of the several power sites . . . provided the terms thereof be agreeable to and confirmed by the tribe.

This preliminary move was completed amid protests from those whites who wished in the words of an official, ''to conserve the reservation in its natural state, with a primitive Indian here and there in the background to complete the setting''. The Menomini motive in approving of the scheme seems to have been purely economic, for those leaders in favor of the power permits agreed that if the scenic organizations could find the equivalent in cash to any offer made by the power interests they would willingly drop negotiations with the latter. At one period the power question raised controversy within the tribe rivalling in intensity some of the longer standing mill troubles. The depression of 1929 on, however, put an end to the power schemes, at least temporarily.

The earlier documents of the reservation period contained many requests that the government allot Menomini lands in severalty; a number of outside organizations and individuals interested in Indian welfare also pressed the government hard to allot all remaining tribal lands including those of the Menomini. The annual report of the ''Indian Rights Association'' for 1918 says:

With the exception of the Indians in the State of New York and the Red Lake Chippewas, the Menominee tribe in Wisconsin is the only remaining one in the eastern half of the United States whose reservation lands have not been segregated by allotment . . . This is partially accounted for by

. . . timber. It is believed that an average allotment of forty acres may be made to each member, equalizing them in value in cases where there is standing merchantable timber . . .

There can be only slight improvement in the condition of the Indians until the communal interests are discarded and they assume responsibility under our laws . . . (there is) need of dissolving the tribal relations at as early a time as practicable . . . Long years of subjugation to irksome supervision must bear its share of responsibility for physical and moral retrogression.—from *36th Annual Report.*

The government however made no move in favor of individualization, and indeed there came about a reaction against it among the Menomini themselves. In 1928 a survey made at the request of the Secretary of the Interior by the Institute for Government Research (*The Problem of Indian Administration,* by Merriam and associates) recommended that tribal lands like those of the Menomini should be placed under some corporate form of organization rather than allotted. Recent administrative policies as regards Menomini land tenure have been along these lines.

One special aspect of the land question may be referred to briefly here, namely the dispute of some seventy years standing between the Indian department, representing the Menomini, and the state of Wisconsin, concerning the rights to all sixteenth sections of the reservation townships, claimed by the latter as "school lands", also some 21,049 acres claimed as "swamp lands". This dispute emerged again and again, after apparently being each time settled. Incidentally the state in earlier times sold these school sections to private individuals, and in the 'eighties, when it seemed proved that their title was valid, the Menomini had the rather sorry task of logging off under contract to these owners the timber which under treaty rights they considered to be their own. Apparently the swamp land question has never been settled, though some Menomini believe that the courts ruled in their favor years ago.

On June 2, 1924, all Indians of the United States were given the privileges of American citizenship, here the Menomini now have voting power in both federal and state affairs. Increasingly they have taken an active part in politics, though their positions as ''citizens'' and ''wards'' are not at all points compatible. As regards the internal politics of the tribe, however, records show that the traditional leadership was giving way almost completely before the new forms of social control. In 1912 Neopit died, and his passing, for all practical purposes, wrote finis to the old chiefly authority, except among the Mitawin group. A number of younger men back from Carlisle, Haskell and Hampton, some with graduation dates after their names now became the new ''speakers'' and leaders of public opinion. It was they who spoke at the occasional tribal councils sanctioned by the officials, and who organized the unofficial councils at which Menomini troubles were aired; they too went in delegations to Washington, voiced eloquently the grievances, shaped tribal requests to the officials, and generally moulded thought upon current matters. While several were descendants of the old tribal leaders, practically all had a considerable portion of white blood, and some were even among the new-comers admitted on the roll; their activities, too, were guided in part by whites interested in Menomini matters for personal or philanthropic reasons. Their great cry was for Menomini self-determination and an end to officialdom. A remark by one such leader may be given from the minutes of a council meeting:

The Indian has been trying for 150 years (!) to get out of the clutches of the Indian Bureau. They all call the Bureau rotten. The Indian is just as human as the white man but he hasn't been given his dues.

Some of the most fantastic statements may be found in such documents concerning what has been done to the Indian in the past, and equally fantastic propositions advanced as to what should be done for the Indian in the future.

''We have a Board; that is one step.'' Early in the new century the experiment was tried officially of establishing a tribal ''Business Committee''; but in 1909 this was abolished because of ''crookedness'' among its members. As a result of continued agitation by tribal leaders and sympathisers both on the reservation and in Washington to get a greater say for the Menomini in their business affairs, the Indian

Office in 1924 again allowed an "Advisory Council" to be formed. But as by its constitution the officials controlled a majority and so suppressed the radical element, it soon became ineffective and pased out of existence. In February 1928 it was resuscitated with a new constitution by which its members were wholly elected by the tribe in council. Just how successful such experiments in giving a measure of self-expression to the new leadership and so countering the rather acute political disorganization, especially under the policies of the "New Deal" in Indian affairs, will be an important theme in the study of the present.

The Indian court and police system were retained into the new century, but modifications took place in the direction of transferring the real power to whites and white officials. The Indian judges resigned or were removed with considerable frequency. During the prohibition era a federal officer assumed authority over all Menomini offenses relating to liquor, thus considerably reducing the functions of the Indian court; and as the same officer acted as clerk of the court when other offenses were tried, the influence of his judgment tended to bear on all decisions, instead merely of those relating to the Eighteenth Amendment. A move was made likewise to replace Indians by whites as reservation police. The following relevant quotations may be given:

> The crimes and offenses of a serious nature which are committed by these Indians or against them . . . are principally against morality, and the present method of punishing the offender with a short sentence to the agency jail seems to have little deterrent effect.—*Annual Report* of superintendent, 1917.

> One officer (is placed) in each settlement, and they not only are expected to assist in bringing in the pupils at school time, returning runaways, detaining violators of the liquor and other laws, but they also assist in apportioning and delivering rations to the old and helpless, and keep close watch upon the health conditions in the various parts of the reserve.—*Letter* of superintendent, May 29, 1914.

The crimes and misdemeanors dealt with by the Indian court, as shown by the annual reports, are an interesting index to Menomini behavior; in order of frequency they are: drunkenness and traffic in liquor, family troubles and unlawful cohabitation, disorderly conduct and resisting arrest, perjury, slander, running from school, and rarely, theft. Of fidelity to marriage ties a superintendent wrote:

> Frequent separations occur—both among those united by the church or the state—and where the church regulations forbid remarriage there is almost sure to result trouble through one or other of the contracting parties . . . selecting other companions without observing the usual formalities.—*Report*, 1917.

Further references to the "marked immorality" on the reservation indicate a very considerable disorganization in family and social life. Gambling is referred to as another source of trouble, also Indian dancing, which though discouraged by both officials and missionaries "seems to flourish with little change from year to year", and "laziness", especially among the "mixed-blood non-members". Yet there was another side to the situation; a superintendent writes of the Menomini:

> One marvels at the vigorousness of the tribe today, surrounded on all sides by the lumber-jack, with his noted carelessness and proverbially happy-go-lucky ways . . . The lumber-jack's inclination to strong drink naturally surrounded the Indian with liquor saloons, and their overabundance and marked effect on him would have a natural downward tendency on his physical condition.—in *The Red Man*, 1912, p. 112.

By this time health and welfare services had been extensively developed, using the now ample Menomini funds. The first hospital equipment had soon become inadequate, indicating increased reliance upon the white physician, so that a branch hospital was established at Neopit. In 1929 a large modern hospital was opened at Keshena; two full time doctors were by then at work on the reservation, and the Catholic sisters were replaced by professional nurses. The statistics relating to health show that the most prevalent trouble continued to be tuberculosis, particularly of the respiratory system, from which some ten per cent of the tribe were said to have been suffering.[11] Venereal disease

[11] A special investigation of tuberculosis on Indian reservations indicated that the Menomini had a higher death rate from this disease than any other tribe except one. Where the average death rate for Indian reservations was 6.3 per 1,000, the Menomini in the year taken showed 25.4 per 1,000. See *The Problem of Indian Administration*, pp. 202–03.

was found among something under three per cent. In addition a certain amount of trachoma (an eye trouble) was reported though not nearly so extensively as on many other Indian reservations. Nevertheless the health work seems to have been a prime factor in bringing about the natural increase in tribal numbers spoken of earlier.

From year to year some 40 to 90 Menomini continued to receive government rations, now enlarged to include in addition to flour and pork some tea, coffee, beans, sugar, prunes and soap, indicating the changing standards of living. The number of rationers, however, was in general lessening and in the 'twenties the system was abolished in favor of a plan of giving small cash "loans." In 1923 officials estimated that of the able-bodied male Menomini about 100 were entirely self-supporting, 700 were partially so, and 41 were rationers; in 1929 some 850 were said to be self-supporting, 50 partially so, and 50 entirely dependent. Whether this represents any remarkable advance in the economic capacity of the tribe, or merely different judgments of Menomini worth will have to be seen in the later study. It may be noted, however, that in these modern days the Menomini had their income from personal economic effort supplemented with occasional "per capita" payments from the tribal funds, comprising amounts up to nearly four hundred dollars at a time; especially when controlled by the agency officials such money served to aid in the support of the less competent.

Concerning such per capita payments, the records show two points of view. By the Menomini they were regarded as rightful profits accruing to them as owners of the timber, and all too small and infrequent. The officials, however, write that such payments were producing a real economic and social disruption: that long before each was given out, Menomini workers "quit by the score" and idled around; that once received, the money was wasted immediately on luxuries, gambling and liquor; also that ill-feeling resulted from any attempts of the officials to supervise the way the "incompetent" spent their shares.

One significant aspect of white control remains to be mentioned: the development of schooling. It was seen how boarding schools were established both by the government and by the Catholic authorities to serve Menomini boys and girls and to some extent those of other tribes; also that after the fourth grade numbers of the pupils were sent out to larger Indian schools. Apart from certain adjustments in equipment and curricula, the main innovation in reservation schooling during the first three decades was the founding of a government and a parochial day school at Neopit to serve both Indian and white children. In 1910 a request appears in the records from the people of Zoar asking that a branch school be started by the government for the forty-two children of their settlement, as they were "too timid to go to Keshena Boarding school";[12] but as the government policy of the period was to remove the children out of their Indian environment, the request was not acted upon.

Those children whose parents approved were sent to continue their schooling in outside institutions, and frequently spent years without returning to the reservation. Usually some twelve to fifteen scholars went annually to the famous Carlisle Indian School, until its abolition in 1918. Subsequently as many as twenty-one a year were sent to Haskell. In the 'twenties, however, the official policy of large "concentration schools" for the tribes was somewhat modified, and most of the Menomini children were sent to smaller but nearer Indian schools at Tomah, Flandreau, Wittenburg, Fort Lapwai and Odanah, or more usually were kept on the reservation itself through extension of the number of grades in the local Menomini government and parochial schools to the high school level. In addition a small but increasing number of Menomini families preferred to send their children for both grammar and high school grades to non-Indian schools off the reservation, some to mission, others to public institutions.

12 Minutes of tribal council, 1910. This was apparently a reaction to the law making attendance of Indian children compulsory, rather than any manifestation of a new enthusiasm for schooling.

The keynote of government policies until recently was to remove the children from the "backward" influences of home and reservation, and so to prepare them for assimilation into the larger American setting. The resulting disorganization and personal maladjustment, while not shown in the official records, was considerable. A critique of these school experiments must be held over to the later study, but in general it can be said that the concentration school proved more successful in uprooting the Menomini youth from their traditional setting and values, bringing to an end the old customs, than in providing any new integration of personality, any design for living adjusted to realistic conditions either on the reservation or outside. Since 1933 the government has reversed its historic educational policies as part of the "New Deal" for Indians, and is attempting to provide schooling in the local communities of a kind directly related to Menomini conditions and problems.

One matter intimately connected with schooling is progress in language and literacy. By the 'eighties officials estimated that some 250, or nineteen per cent of the tribe could speak, read and write English, though they do not specify the degree of efficiency in the new accomplishment. The census of 1910 gives sixty-two per cent of the tribe over ten years of age as literate, and that of 1930 lifts this figure to 95.5 per cent. In 1926 it was estimated that the English language was spoken in about half the Indian homes. Evidently, however tenacious the Menomini language was proving in the modern reservation life, the tribesfolk were steadily acquiring the tools of communication with surrounding white society.

In reviewing these decades it seems clear that the Menomini had moved far culturally from the life of pre-reservation and early reservation days. Old ways had passed, become modified or the area of their importance diminished. New ways were adopted, with more or less success in adjustment. Paternalism assumed shape in definite organization from the highest officials in Washington to the most minor official at Keshena, and this control tended to penetrate all aspects of the tribal life. Notably during the last few years the isolation between the Menomini and the general white life has been breaking down.

What has been the reaction of the Indian? The records have shown a considerable disturbance and disorganization, especially as regards the lumbering enterprise. While any full analysis of the Menomini response must be held over until the Indian life of the present day is examined, nevertheless two facts may be cited here as perhaps offering significant illustrations of the modern Menomini attitudes. Whereas at the time of the Civil War one hundred and twenty-five Menomini enlisted for active service with the whites, during the Great War of 1914–18 only sixteen of the tribe, all mixed bloods, volunteered. Again when, after years of pressure, permits were issued to allow whites to fish within the reservation boundaries, there came a steady opposition from many Menomini in spite of the revenue such white penetration produced. In a general council of the tribe in 1927 the question was raised as to whether such permits should be continued; one group fought the measure strenuously with the slogan "the reservation for the Indians", another group, while wishing to increase the license charge, gave their support on the grounds that it "benefits the Indians to associate with the tourists". When a vote was taken the group for the exclusion of whites won by a ballot of seventy-four to fifty-seven. Yet it was symptomatic of the new order that the majority vote of the council was over-ruled by the officials, and whether the Menomini likes it or not the white man can now enter the reservation as he wishes.

XI A REVIEW

Three main threads have emerged in this study of some
three centuries of Menomini-white interaction: first, the progressive modification and in most recent times the disintegration of the old Menomini culture; second, the building up
of a reservation life based on the dependence relation of
wardship; and third, the manifestation of not a little social
and personal disorganization, also of opposition to white
control and penetration.

The Menomini were seen as allies of the whites, then as
subjects, wards and citizens. Their practical life became
dominated by the fur trade, then by land moneys and by
lumbering. From a small group, indeed apparently a mere
remnant, they expanded numerically and territorially, mingling and mixing with other tribes and with frontier whites;
then as white settlement advanced and their lands passed
from them they became confined in a special reservation
area. Here they were subjected to a civilizing process both
by officials and by missionaries. Their culture, more or less
stabilized on the basis of the fur trade after a first revolution, then considerably shaken by its passing and also by the
uncertain conditions of the land treaty period, became reorganized as a reservation life a main mark of which has
been government control. Such reorganization was not a
haphazard affair, but appears to have followed fairly defin-
able processes of cultural dynamics. Under changing conditions the older Indian ways tended to break down and
especially among the Catholic section of the tribe were fairly
completely replaced by new; yet because of isolation and the
peculiar modern circumstances these did not correspond at
all exactly to white ways. What may be termed a special
Menomini reservation culture developed and reached a considerable degree of stability. Finally in most recent times
this in turn appeared to be showing signs of disintegration
as a result of more intense contact with whites and an of-

ficial policy which, at least until the coming of the New Deal, aimed at rapid assimilation. As a result of all these experiences the Menomini have been considerably 'disrupted as a group, torn by conservative and progressive influences, in some cases retreating into exclusiveness, even finding solace in mystical religious movements—these it may be noted initiated by other Indian tribes which have been experiencing like cultural pressure—in others apparently venturing out to try themselves against the whites. Finally there appeared to be some revulsion against the official supervision of their lives especially insofar as it appeared to them to curtail liberties and benefits.

On the biological side the Menomini were seen as neither dying out nor being rapidly amalgamated with the general white population—destinies variously prophesied by earlier observers. Instead they are a vigorous group, increasing in numbers, and tending to stabilize through intramarriage as a mixed type still dominantly of Indian ancestry. Doubtless they will continue as a racial entity for a long time to come. The possession of common tribal resources as well as difficulties of adjustment into the larger setting of white life have kept the great majority of them within the reservation community. Even amid the disorganization referred to above, and in the face of official policies until recently looking towards assimilation, the tribe has shown no signs of breaking up, though it is to be granted that in recent years the binding ties have tended to be increasingly political and geographic, since social and racial bonds have slackened.

In the economic sphere the Menomini have on the whole not found congenial the regular and intensive work rhythms of white society as represented in farm and mill. Many still prefer the irregular cycle of seasonal activities as a means of support, even though these are in a modern commercial setting; picking berries and fern-leaves, making baskets, giving "pow-wows" for tourists in the summer, doing odd jobs off the reservation, and the like. It was noted how the coming of tourists has given a new lease of life to certain of the Indian arts and crafts.[1] Above all, woven tightly into the patterns of what has been called the special "reservation culture" of modern days, are the factors of wardship: the existence of tribal funds, plentiful land, and rich timber resources (the Menomini are intensely conscious that these belong to *them,* even if managed by the authorities); the habits developed during four generations of expecting "per capita payments" and other benefits; and the relation of dependence inevitably built up by government policies of controlling tribal affairs, and of almost always doing things *for* the Indian rather than *with* the Indian. The "Great Father at Washington" has indeed come to occupy a prominent place in the modern cosmogony among the deities from whom economic benefits are derived. Actually, however, the gap between the Menomini and his white fellow-citizen in this respect was far greater in 1929 than it is today.

On the social and political sides the reservation community shows a marked degree of individualism, and not a little anti-social behavior. This may in some measure reflect the ancient personality values. But for the most part it seems a consequence of the passing of customary Indian standards and restraints without adequate substitution of new controls. Important factors in this have been the later official policies of liquidating the tribal leadership (though at first the chiefs and band leaders had been administratively utilized), likewise the government practice of dealing with the tribesmen as individuals, and the emphasis laid in the education of youth upon "making one's own way." Among such groups as the Menomini "rugged individualism" can

[1] While the actual performers in "pow-wows" and the craftsmen making "curios" for sale are usually members of the Mitawin group, the organization and selling has been developed mainly by several enterprising members of the Christian group. As the business has become more sophisticated the tendency has been to discard special tribal trappings in favor of a kind of generalized Indian paraphernalia which never had any real existence in any one locality but which has taken form in the white man's mind as "what Indians look like": fringed buckskin clothes, feather warbonnets, conical tipis, etc. Adapted at first perhaps as a matter of shrewd salesmanship, it is apparently coming to be appreciated by many of the Indians themselves as a kind of idealized "Indian" art and craft. (See p. 207.)

be observed actually operating minus the multitudinous disciplines and controls which the ordinary white American absorbs more or less unconsciously, and the moralist may well consider the result not very pleasant. For the most part, however, cooperative family and kin units have survived, even though the wider forms of organization have, especially among the Christians, so largely broken down. In recent years a new promise of leadership has come into the picture; some of the educated younger people have come to the fore. Under the advisory council system pictured in the last chapter their outlet was mainly limited to verbal criticism, since the government made little attempt to transfer practical responsibilities into their hands. Official policies since 1933, by contrast, have aimed definitely at utilizing such leadership and building up the Menomini tribe as a cooperative entity.

In 1934 the Menomini, by a vote of 596 to 15, accepted the Indian Reorganization Act containing plans for a reorientation of economic, social and educational affairs, in general looking towards Indianization within a modern setting rather than high-pressure assimilation. The reservation has thus become one of a number of laboratories for the testing out of policies in many respects the reverse of those traced in the study. The attempt is being made to get the Indian to work out his modern adjustments in his own way and at his own pace, with due guidance and within the protective setting of the reservation, to foster a positive pride in being an Indian and in the worthwhile elements of the Indian past, and to solve economic and other problems on the basis of cooperation and a greater measure of self-government.

Whatever the difficulties of such a plan, it cannot but appeal to the objective observer as having greater promise for groups like the Menomini than the emphasis on assimilation. In the further study it will be shown how, even when individual Indians have become competent to participate in the general American life, their attempts to establish themselves outside their own community have been thwarted by racial prejudice and discrimination. The Indian in his own setting may be an object of romance, but outside the immediate vicinity of his reservation he is generally taken for a "colored" person and treated accordingly; even when he identifies himself the old slogan about the only good Indian being a dead Indian often still holds. At best he is likely to find a place along the unstable economic and social margins of white society as a kind of American gypsy. Until, therefore, the folk who have occupied his country and turned his feet along the new cultural trail are prepared to receive him with equality, it seems wise to fit him for life in his own group —in the case of the Menomini, the reservation community.

BIBLIOGRAPHY

This bibliography is more in the nature of a summary of the literature than a detailed list of all the reference documents in which Menomini materials are available. This is made possible largely through the labor of historians who have, over a period of years, assembled and published documents relating to the history of the Wisconsin area. In the text itself there are direct references to most of the records available in these collections which are important for the study, and for the rest there are index volumes that may be consulted.

The order of setting out will be: first, anthropological references; second, historical records prior to the reservation period; third, post-reservation references other than those given in the first.

ANTHROPOLOGICAL REFERENCES

HOFFMAN, W. J.
> The Menomini Indians, in 14th Annual Report, Bureau of American Ethnology, 1892–93.

JENKS, A. E.
> The Wild Rice Gatherers of the Upper Lakes, in 19th An. Rep., Bur. Am. Eth., 1900.

HRDLIČKA, A.
> Tuberculosis among Certain Indian Tribes, Bulletin 42, Bur. Am. Eth., 1909.

MOONEY, J., AND THOMAS, C.
> Menominee Tribe, in Handbook of American Indians, Bulletin 30, Bur Am. Eth., 1907.

BARRETT, S. A.
> The Dream Dance of the Chippewa and Menominee Indians, Bulletin, Public Museum, Milwaukee, vol. 1, 1911.

MICHELSON, T.
> Menominee Tales, in American Anthropologist, vol. 13, number 1, 1911.

SKINNER, A.
> War Customs of the Menomini, in Am. Anth., vol. 13, number 2, 1911.
> A Comparative Sketch of the Menomini, in Am. Anth., vol. 13, number 4, 1911.
> Social Life and Ceremonial Bundles of the Menomini Indians, Anth. Papers, American Museum of Natural History, vol. xiii, 1913.

Associations and Ceremonies of the Menomini Indians, *idem,* vol. xiii, 1915.

Medicine Ceremony of the Menomini, etc., Indian Notes and Monographs, Museum of the American Indian, Heye Foundation, 1920.

Material Culture of the Menomini, *idem,* 1921.

Menomini Sketches, in Wisconsin Archeologist, vol. 20, number 2, 1921.

Collecting Among the Menomini, *idem,* vol. 23, number 4, 1924.

Skinner, A., and Satterlee, J. V.

Folklore of the Menomini Indians, in Anth. Papers, Am. Mus. Nat. Hist., xiii, 1915.

Schumacher, J. P., and Glaser, J. H.

Indian Remains in Northeastern Wisconsin, in Wisconsin Archeologist, vol. 11, number 4, 1913.

Fox, G. R., and Younger, H. O.

Marinette County, *idem,* vol. 17, number 2, 1918.

Smith, H. H.

Ethnobotany of the Menomini Indians, *idem,* vol. 4, number 1, 1923.

Bloomfield, L.

The Menomini Language, Proceedings 21st International Congress of Americanists, The Hague, 1924.

Menomini Texts, Publications of the American Ethnological Society, vol. xii, 1929.

Densmore, F.

Menominee Music, Bull. no. 102, Bureau of American Ethnology, 1932.

In addition there are references to the Menomini in general anthropological works such as:

Wissler, C.

The American Indian, New York; 3rd edition, 1938.

Spier, L.

Kinship Systems in North America, Publications, University of Washington, Seattle, 1925.

Olson, R. Le R.

Clan and Moiety in Native America, University of California Press, 1933.

Bureau of American Ethnology

Handbook of American Indians, Bulletin 30, 1907; under various topics.

Brown, C. E. (editor)

Wisconsin Archeologist, Madison.

No attempt will be made here to give a bibliography of the comparative material for other tribes of the region, though it will be noted that a number of works are referred to in the text.

THE PRE-RESERVATION PERIOD, 1634–1852

Hoffman (pp. 12–14) gives a somewhat detailed bibliography and synonymy relating to the tribe. The best published collection of documents relating to the area up to 1830 are the Wisconsin Historical Collections, to which the student should refer under "Menomini" and other headings in the index volumes. Much material is also to be found in the Proceedings of the Wisconsin Historical Society, and the Wisconsin Magazine of History. Other more specific references are:

EARLY VOYAGES

Voyages of Jacques Cartier, edited by BIGGAR, H., in Canadian Archives, vol. ii, Ottawa, 1924.

Voyages of Champlain, ed. by BOURNE, A., vol. ii, New York, 1906.

Voyages of La Salle, ed. by Cox, I. J., New York, 1905.

Voyages of Peter Radisson, ed. by SCULL, G. D., Boston, 1885.

New Discovery of Hennepin, ed. by THWAITES, R., Chicago, 1903.

Lahontan, ed. by THWAITES, R., Chicago, 1905.

JESUIT RELATIONS

Cleveland Reissue, 72 volumes, Refer to index vols.

BLAIR, E.

The Indian Tribes of the Upper Mississippi Valley, Cleveland, 1911–12. This contains English translations of the Memoir of PERROT, and the Histoire of LA POTHERIE.

LA POTHERIE, B. DE

Histoire de l'Amérique Septentrionale, Paris, 1753.

KELLOGG, L.

Early Narratives of the Northwest, 1634–1699, New York, 1917. A compilation of the earliest documents from NICOLET on.

The French Regime in Wisconsin and the Northwest, Madison, 1925.

Also a number of other writings, as in the Wisconsin Archeologist.

THWAITES, R.

Wisconsin, Boston, 1908. Also other published works on the area.

PARKMAN, F.

The Conspiracy of Pontiac, Boston, 1889, and other works.

HENRY, A.

Travels and Adventures, 1760–76, ed. Lakeside Classics, Chicago, 1921.

LONG, J.

Voyages and Travels, ed. Lakeside Classics, Chicago, 1922.

PIKE, Z.

Account of Expeditions to the Sources of the Mississippi, Philadelphia, 1810.

MORSE, J.

Report on Indian Affairs, Washington, 1822.

SCHOOLCRAFT, H.

History, Condition, and Prospect of the Indian Tribes, Philadelphia, 1851–60, and other works.

FEATHERSTONHAUGH, G.
A Canoe Voyage up the Minnay Sotor, London, 1847.
KRAUTBAUER, F.
Sketch of the History of the Menominee Indians, in Amer. Catholic Histor. Researches, 1887.
MCKENNEY, T.
Indian Tribes of North America, Philadelphia, 1837–44.
CATLIN, G.
North American Indians, London, 1841, also other works, including very important illustrations.
A VISIT TO THE MENOMONIES, series of articles in *The Friend,* vol. xxiii, 1849. (Copies of this publication are rare; the writer consulted a set in the Wisconsin Historical Society, Madison.)
COMPILATION OF ALL TREATIES, WASHINGTON, 1873, and other official publications giving details of Indian land treaties; note especially Indian Land Cessions, in 18th An. Rep. B.A.E., 1896–97, ii.
TUTTLE, C.
Illustrated History of Wisconsin, Madison, 1875.
SCHAFER, J.
Agriculture in Wisconsin, in Wisconsin Domesday Book, 1922.

POST-RESERVATION REFERENCES

The main sources for the period must necessarily be the official documents, though it has been seen in the text that the works of ethnologists yield much information. The most important published documents are the annual reports of the Office of Indian Affairs. The serious student can supplement these by examining the vast amount of unpublished materials such as correspondence and reports filed both in Washington and at the reservation agency. In addition there are a number of published reports of special commissions, of Senate hearings, documents presented to Congress, acts passed by Congress, departmental materials dealing with aspects of Indian affairs such as administrative regulations, school reports and schemes of work, health, Indian court, farming and forestry information. These are too numerous to be listed, though many have received special mention in the text. Other materials are:

BOARD OF INDIAN COMMISSIONERS
Annual Reports.
CENSUS BUREAU
Materials from the periodic census, in various publications. Note particularly: Indian Tribes of the United States and Alaska, Washington, 1915 and 1930.
NEWSPAPER FILES
Notably the *Shawano County Journal* and *Shawano Leader-Advocate.* These date back to early reservation days and contain much topical material on Menomini affairs.

Indian Rights Association
    Reports.   Also reports of the Lake Mohonk Conferences.
The Red Man, Carlisle Indian School paper, particularly vol. v, number 1,
    Nicholson, A., The Menominee Indians Working Their Way.
Society of American Indians
    Quarterly Journal, Washington.
Schmeckebier, L.
    The Office of Indian Affairs, Baltimore, 1927.
Merriam and associates
    The Problem of Indian Administration, Baltimore, 1928: also a critique
    of this report by the Board of Indian Commissioners.

In addition there is a growing bibliography on Indian affairs in general,
but this has little specific reference to the Menomini.   Examples are:
Lindquist, G.
    The Red Man in the United States, New York, 1923.
McLeod, W. C.
    The American Indian Frontier, New York, 1928.
Palmer, R. A.
    The North American Indians, New York, 1934.
Wise, J. C.
    The Red Man in the New World Drama, Washington, 1931.

The only other study extant giving any comprehensive picture of the
modern experience of an Indian tribe is:
Mead, M.
    The Changing Life of an American Indian Tribe, New York, 1932.

INDEX